BAR BRERA

W9-CZR-162

Shopping p.181

Nightlife p.173

Festivals p.196

The Guide p.43

Walks p.125

Where to Stay p.153

Entertainment p.173

Eating Out p.161

Sports and Green Spaces p.185

TEATRO ALLA SCALA

LA BOHEME

EL-DIOUF

Contents

Introducing

Introduction 1
The Neighbourhoods 2
Days Out in Milan 9
Roots of the City 19
Art and Architecture 35

The Guide

01
Travel 43

Getting There 44
Tour Operators 48
Entry Formalities 49
Arrival 49
Getting Around 50

02
Practical A–Z 53

Climate 54
Crime and the Police 54
Disabled Travellers 55
Duty-free Shopping 56
Electricity, Weights and
  Measures 56
Embassies and Consulates 56
Etiquette 56
Health, Emergencies and
  Insurance 57
Internet 58
Laundrettes 59
Lost Property 59
Media 59
Money, Banks and
  Taxes 59
Opening Hours and
  Public Holidays 61
Packing 62
Photography 62
Post and Fax 62
Smoking 63

Strikes 63
Students and Seniors 63
Telephones 63
Time 64
Tipping 64
Toilets 64
Tourist Offices 64
Women Travellers 65
Working and
  Long Stays 65

03
The Centre 67

Piazza del Duomo
  and Around 70
Duomo 70
Palazzo Reale and
  Museo del Duomo 73
Galleria Vittorio
  Emanuele II 73
Palazzo della Ragione 74
Corso Vittorio Emanuele II 74
Piazza della Scala
  and Around 75
La Scala 75
San Fedele 76
Casa del Manzoni 77
San Giuseppe 77
The Financial District 78
The Ambrosiana 78
San Satiro 79

04
Brera and the
  Northeast 81

Brera 84
Pinacoteca di Brera 84
Palazzo Cusani 86
Santa Maria del Carmine 87
San Marco 87
Corso Garibaldi
  and Around 88
Via Manzoni 88

Museo Poldi-Pezzoli 88
Archi di Porta Nuova 90
Quadrilatero d'Oro 90
Palazzo Bolognini and
  Museo di Milano 91
Museo Bagatti Valsecchi 91
Giardini Pubblici
  and Around 91
Villa Reale and
  Galleria d'Arte Moderna 91
Esposizione Permanente
  delle Belle Arti 92
Corso Venezia and
  Around 92
Stazione Centrale 94
Pirellone 94

05
University and the
  Southeast 95

Ca' Grande and Around 98
Ca' Grande 98
Corso di Porta Romana 98
Torre Velasca 99
Santo Stefano and San
  Bernardino alle Ossa 99
Palazzo Sormani
  Andreani 100
Palazzo di Giustizia
  and Around 100
Palazzo di Giustizia 100
Rotonda della Besana 101
San Pietro in Gessate 101
Santa Maria della
  Passione 101
Conservatorio di
  Musica Giuseppe Verdi 102
Palazzo Isimbardi 102
Corso Italia and Around 102
Sant'Alessandro 102
Santa Maria dei Miracoli/
  San Celso 103
Abbazia di Chiaravalle 103

06
Ticinese and Navigli 105

Ticinese District 108
San Lorenzo Maggiore
  (alle Colonne) 108
Parco delle Basiliche 108
Sant'Eustorgio 109
San Vincenzo in Prato 109
Navigli 110
Vicolo Lavandai 110

07
The West End 111

Castello Sforzesco
  and Around 114
Castello Sforzesco and
  Civici Musei d'Arte e
  Pinacoteca del Castello 114
Parco Sempione 115
Corso Magenta
  and Around 116
Santa Maria delle Grazie 116
The *Last Supper* 117
Museo Teatrale alla Scala 119
Palazzo Litta 119
San Maurizio 119
Sant'Ambrogio and
  Around 119
Sant'Ambrogio 119
San Vittore al Corpo 121
Leonardo da Vinci
  Museo Nazionale della
  Scienza e Tecnica 122
San Bernardino alle
  Monache 122
Fiera di Milano 123
Cimitero Monumentale 123
Meazza Stadium
  (San Siro) 124
Certosa di Garegnano 124

08
Walks 125

A Walk Through the
  Navigli 126
A Shopping Trip 130

09
Day Trips 135

Monza 136
Lake Maggiore 138
Lake Como 139
Bergamo 141
Cities of the
  Lombard Plain 144
Pavia 145
Cremona 147
Mantua (Mantova) 150

Listings

Where to Stay 153
Eating Out 161
Nightlife and
  Entertainment 173
Shopping 181
Sports and
  Green Spaces 185
Children's and
  Teenagers' Milan 189
Gay and Lesbian
  Milan 193
Festivals 196

Reference

Language 199
Index 204

Maps

Unmissable Milan *inside front cover*
The Neighbourhoods 2–3
The Centre 68–9
Brera and the Northeast
  82–3
University and the
  Southeast 96–7
Ticinese and Navigli 106–7
The West End 112–13
A Walk Through the
  Navigli 126–7
A Shopping Trip 130–1
Around Milan 136–7
Bergamo 142–3
Cremona 148–9
East Milan Hotels 156–7
West Milan Hotels 158–9
North Milan Restaurants
  and *Caffès* 166–7
Central and South Milan
  Restaurants and *Caffès*
  170–1
Colour Street Maps *end of guide*
Metro and Tram *final page*
Off the Beaten Track *inside back cover*

Introduction

The phrase 'fashion capital' inevitably appears straight off the bat in introductions to Milan, which is a little like reducing Cannes to its annual film festival. Nevertheless, when you touch down and emerge into the foggy haze of Milan's Linate airport, the first thing that greets you is the huge neon insignia of Emporio Armani, leaving little doubt of the city's preferred image.

Where once the aristocratic, art-patronizing Viscontis, Sforzas and Borromeos set the local tone with castles and luxurious *palazzi*, it is now the upper crust of fashion, the Armanis and the Pradas, with their exaggerated sensitivity to style and beauty, who shape not only Milan's, but the world's modern-day image of deadpan cool. Yet fashion here is just skin deep. In reality, Milan's role as the national purveyor of style was only recently annexed from Florence, and the extreme fashion shows that periodically parade into the city are hardly accessible to the average Milanese. Indeed, for most residents, fashion means safe, conformist 'V-neck and brogues', which reflects the more conservative heart of a city sometimes termed the most southern state of Germany.

Milan, after all, has been the financial and industrial capital of Italy since the 19th century, home to its stock market, and regional capital to Lombardy's rich, well-educated and opera-loving residents. Media mogul and Italian Prime Minister Silvio Berlusconi runs his international empire from Milan, leading many to believe that the city could soon become the country's administrative capital. As a further clue to its global aspirations, Milan has a strongly Americanized business and social language; even the city's taxis were once a deliberate New York yellow.

For all its ambitions, Milan is often misunderstood. Never a first choice of culture travellers, it nevertheless has the famous La Scala opera house and one of the top art hoards in Italy, including Leonardo da Vinci's *Last Supper*. Badly bombed in the Second World War and littered with ill-judged and speedy rebuilding projects, it represents a firmer aesthetic challenge than most Italian cities. But visitors willing to explore the backstage of its catwalk high streets will be amply rewarded with a glimpse of a vibrant city, keen to shrug off its dour image for a slice of *la dolce vita*, learning to drink *aperitivos* and dawdle lazily over brunch, Roman-style. Nowhere is this more apparent than in the buzzing Navigli district, home to artists, designers and quirky shops, all atmospherically set amidst the city's medieval canals, Roman ruins and historic churches. Milan's fresh new attitude and growing international appeal mean that there has never been a more exciting time to visit.

The Neighbourhoods

4 La Scala, p.75

10 Antiques-shop in the Brera, p.184

3 Castello Sforzesco, p.114

The West End

1 Leonardo da Vinci's *Last Supper*, p.117

Ticinese and Navigli

6 The Ambrosiana, p.78

9 Late-night bars on the Naviglio Grande, p.176

5 Pinacoteca di Brera, p.84

8 *Bella Figura* in the Quadrilatero d'Oro, p.90

Brera and the Northeast

7 Galleria Vittorio Emanuele II, p.73

Centre

University and the Southeast

2 Duomo, p.70

In this guide, the city is divided into the five neighbourhoods outlined on the map above, each with its own sightseeing chapter. This map also shows our suggestions for the Top Ten activities and places to visit in Milan. The following colour pages introduce the neighbourhoods in more detail, explaining the distinctive character and highlights of each.

The Centre

Milan's vortex for the past 600 years or so has been its magic mountain of a cathedral, the Duomo, which still exerts its magnetic pull on locals and visitors alike. Created in the 19th century in homage to Paris, its home, Piazza del Duomo, plays the part of the Étoile, with radiating streets – Vias Mazzini, Manzoni, Torino, Orefici and Mercanti – dividing the city like a pie. Grand buildings such as La Scala opera house to the north, the Palazzo Reale and the Galleria Vittorio Emanuele II chime in with the cathedral's paean to Milan's outsize ambition. To the west is another magnet, this one for high rollers – Milan's financial district, with Italy's stock exchange, the Borsa, as a centrepiece.

From top: Duomo, Galleria Vittorio Emanuele II, La Scala memorabilia.

The Centre
The Centre chapter p.67
Hotels p.154 Restaurants p.164 Bars p.174

Brera and the Northeast

Bisected by elegant Via Manzoni, Milan's northeast quarter reveals stately *case nobili*, neoclassical *palazzi* and the Holy Grail for the world's fashion victims, the Quadrilatero d'Oro. It has another mood as well, in the cosier medieval streets of the Brera district, where artists between jobs and latter-day Italian Baudelaires pose in cafés, waiting to be discovered. At the core of the district lies the magnificent art collection of the Pinacoteca di Brera, rich enough in masterpieces to rival the Uffizi in Florence. Further out lie the relaxing Giardini Pubblici and Milan's talismanic Stazione Centrale. By night, the city's nocturnal heart thumps around Corso Como and Garibaldi station.

Clockwise from top: Pinacoteca di Brera, Brera nightlife, Quadrilatero d'Oro, Palazzo Bolognini and Museo di Milano.

Brera and the Northeast
Brera and the Northeast chapter p.81
Hotels p.155 Restaurants p.164 Bars p.174

University and the Southeast

Business and fashion may rule Milan, but here the vast university campus of the Ca' Grande, originally built in the Renaissance as the city's hospital, sets a more relaxed tone, with bustling cafés and bookshops, as well as Milan's oldest public park. The adjacent Sormani library is full of treasures, and amidst the faculties you'll find lovely churches such as Santa Maria della Passione and San Pietro in Gessate. Further north is the city's prestigious music conservatory (which famously did not admit the young Giuseppe Verdi). Beyond the Porta Romana, many of Milan's finest Liberty-style buildings sit prettily alongside some the city's trendiest lounges and nightclubs.

Clockwise from top left: nightlife, park life, café culture.

University and the Southeast
University and the Southeast chapter p.95
Hotels p.160 Restaurants p.168 Bars p.175

Ticinese and Navigli

Amsterdam or Venice it is not, but Milan's surviving *navigli* (canals) – the Darsena lock, Naviglio Grande and Naviglio Pavese – are vestiges of a system that once permeated the whole city, and nowadays provide an atmospheric backdrop for the city's most genuinely urban neighbourhood. Here, long-standing jazz venues and antiques and flea markets rub shoulders with the numerous lofts, clubs and bars rapidly filling the old canal warehouses and factories. The pulse of the city's newfound *aperitivo* culture beats under the Roman columns of San Lorenzo church, while shops along Corso di Porta Ticinese offer a lighter, more frivolous sense of design than the elegant conservatism and studied coolness that preside over Milan's more famous emporiums.

Clockwise from top left: Naviglio Grande, street life, San Lorenzo Maggiore, Navigli by night.

Ticinese and Navigli
Ticinese and Navigli chapter p.105
Hotels p.160 Restaurants p.169 Bars p.176

The West End

The West End has a monumental air to it, not least because for centuries it was Milan's centre of power, beginning in 379 AD when its fiesty bishop-prince St Ambrose founded the basilica of Sant'Ambrogio. In the Middle Ages, the bishops were succeeded by the Visconti and Sforza dukes, who lorded over Lombardy and much of northern Italy from the Castello Sforzesco, their glittering court now replaced by an array of fine museums. In the nearby refectory of Santa Maria delle Grazie, the city's most famous employee, Leonardo da Vinci, graced Milan with his masterful *Last Supper*; his innovations continue to inspire the exhibits in the nearby science museum. Even today, the area hosts Milan's ruling passions – the Triennale architecture and design show in the Palazzo dell'Arte, football in the outlying San Siro stadium, and industrial innovation at the Fiera di Milano complex.

From top: Santa Maria delle Grazie, Castello Sforzesco.

The West End
The West End chapter p.111
Hotels p.160 Restaurants p.172 Bars p.176

Days Out in Milan

Art City p.10

Architectural Milan p.12

Bella Figura p.14

Foodie Milan p.18

Trendy Milan p.16

ART CITY

Milan has never been on the Grand Tour of travellers seeking the art that oozes from the very pores of Rome, Venice and Tuscany. They may have got off the train to see the most famous dinner party ever painted, Leonardo da Vinci's *Last Supper*, and the celebrated Pinacoteca di Brera, with its dazzling collection of medieval art and its northern Italian paintings by Raphael and company, but *basta*: before evening they were back on the train to Florence.

What did they miss? A score of churches housing 5th-century mosaics, medieval sculpture and Baroque frescoes; the Grand Masters in the Ambrosiana and the Museo Poldi-Pezzoli; the unique collection of mummies, Renaissance pieces and musical instruments held in Castello Sforzesco; and, of course, the unforgettable La Scala opera house, the ultimate expression of the Lombard love of art and artifice.

As for modern art, Milan's museums feature big names such as Cezanne and Picasso, as well as the glories of the Italian 20th century, the Futurists and Metaphysicists, and sculptures by Marino Marini. Add to this the huge sums Milan splashes out on major art exhibitions and the international exhibits it attracts, and you can thank yourself for missing that train back to Florence.

One

Start: Metro Moscova.

Breakfast: Get in the mood with a brioche and cappuccino at the **Art & Soul Cafe**.

Morning: Visit the **Pinacoteca di Brera** (*photo opposite, top*) and view masterpieces from the 13th century to the avant-garde.

Lunch: Head north towards Porta Garibaldi to enjoy the traditional atmosphere of the 19th-century **Antica Trattoria della Pesa**.

Afternoon: Wander through the fascinating collections in the **Castello Sforzesco** (*photo opposite, bottom*), then digest it all with a stroll through the surrounding **Parco Sempione**. Walk southwest to **Santa Maria delle Grazie** and feast your eyes on Leonardo's famous *Cenacolo* (*Last Supper*) in the flesh.

Dinner: Head southeast to dine in the luxuriant artistry of **Il Giardino dei Segreti**'s hanging gardens.

Evening: Immerse yourself in sensuous operatic style at a **La Scala** production (*photo above*).

Food and Drinks

Antica Trattoria della Pesa, p.172
Art & Soul Café, p.167
Il Giardino dei Segreti, p.168

Sights and Activities

Castello Sforzesco, p.114
La Scala, p.75
Last Supper, p.117
Parco Sempione, p.115
Pinacoteca di Brera, p.84

ARCHITECTURAL MILAN

Milan does not conform to many visitors' image of a typical Italian city. Its medieval cohesiveness was ravaged by 19th-century ambitions to imitate Haussmann's Paris, when much was razed to create would-be boulevards. To make matters worse, the Allies in the Second World War took unerring aim when they bombed Milan, reducing much of its core to rubble, and making it ripe for dubious planning ideas of the 1950s and 60s. The bombers did, however, leave a taste of old Milan in the winding streets of the old Brera district, and the grandiose *palazzi* around Via Manzoni reek of *fin-de-siècle* self-satisfaction. Though the city is best known for a handful of singularly colossal buildings, such as the Duomo, Castello Sforzesca, Stazione Centrale and the stark, totalitarian Palazzo di Giustizia, it is worth seeking out some of Milan's less swaggering gems: Bramante's *tour de force* in the churches of San Satiro and Santa Maria delle Grazie; the Cappella Portinari in Sant'Eustorgio; the charming Liberty-style villas on the city's east side; and the graceful Pirellone, or Pirelli Tower, in the north.

Two

Start: Metro Duomo, for a morning cappuccino in the locals' favourite, **Panino del Conte**.

Morning: Visit Milan's medieval core – the **Duomo** and its forest-like interior (*photo above*), the **Palazzo della Ragione** and Bramante's **San Satiro**, then walk through the 19th-century **Galleria Vittorio Emanuele II** (*photo opposite, left*), to see the *palazzi* along **Via Manzoni**. Catch the metro or tram to visit the monolithic **Stazione Centrale** and adjacent **Pirellone**, Gio Ponti's beautiful skyscraper.

Lunch: Choose from a range of dishes and a lunchtime glass at New York-styled **Vini e Cucina**, or go for more traditional fare in the family-run inn of **Latteria San Marco**.

Afternoon: Take the metro or tram to **Sant'Ambrogio**, the first Lombard Romanesque church, then head south to visit the basilicas of **Sant'Eustorgio** and **San Lorenzo Maggiore**, ending up at adjacent **Piazza della Vetra** in time for an *aperitivo* by San Lorenzo's **Roman columns** (*photo above*).

Dinner: Dine amidst Milan's watery past near the Darsena, at **Al Porto**, once a 19th-century toll house.

Evening: Stroll around the Navigli to see Milan's former dockyard and canals, then take in some jazz at **Grilloparlante**, entered through an old Navigli house.

Food and Drinks

Al Porto, p.169
Latteria San Marco, p.165
Panino del Conte, p.164
Vini e Cucina, p.165

Sights and Activities

A Walk Through the Navigli, p.126
Duomo, p.70
Galleria Vittorio Emanuele II, p.73
Palazzo della Ragione, p.74

Piazza della Vetra, p.108
Pirellone, p.94
San Lorenzo Maggiore, p.108
San Satiro, p.79
Sant'Ambrogio, p.119
Sant'Eustorgio, p.109
Stazione Centrale, p.94
Via Manzoni, p.88

Nightlife

Grilloparlante, p.178

BELLA FIGURA

According to Orson Welles, 'Italy is full of actors, 50 million of them in fact, and they are almost all good. There are only a few bad ones and they are on the stage and in films.'

Acting is innate to Italians, and their appearance, like a costume, is an essential part of the roles they act out from day to day. *Fare bella figura*, meaning both 'to look good' and 'to make a good impression', is essential to social and business life in Milan.

And yet, far from signalling flair and individual style, this need underlines the profoundly conservative nature of a population religiously conformist in its adherence to V-neck jumpers, slate-grey or navy-blue suits and brown brogues. That is not to say that Milan does not deserve its fame as an engine of *haute couture*; as one says in Rome, faith is made here and believed elsewhere.

If you feel like mortgaging your house, or perhaps have too many houses, a trip to the Quadrilatero d'Oro, the golden fashion grid between Via Montenapoleone and Via della Spiga, should be to your taste. Here, you will find an

Morning: Head straight for the **Quadrilatero d'Oro**, to either shop 'til you drop, or at least mingle with Milanesi watching you watching them faking it.

Lunch: Drop in and say 'hi' to Giorgio in the **Armani Caffè** for a fashionably late lunch.

Afternoon: See what *bella figura* was like in the old days, in the Renaissance paintings in the **Museo Poldi-Pezzoli**, then travel west across town to see what all Italians secretly wish they could swan around in every day – the opera costumes in the **Museo Teatrale della Scala**.

Dinner: Return to Giorgio's store, this time for a meal at **Nobu**, the most reassuringly stylish and expensive meal in town.

Evening: Head to **Hollywood** nightclub – glitzy haunt of fashion models, open until the wee hours.

unparalleled concentration of emporia – retail theatres in themselves – stocking minimalist collections of clothes, designs and labels rare in Paris, London or New York, and where you almost have to be wearing the right clothes to be served at all.

Three

Start: Metro Moscova.
Breakfast: Steel your fashion nerves with a cappuccino at **Radetsky**.

Food and Drinks
Armani Caffè, p.165
Nobu, p.164
Radetsky, p.168
Sights and Activities
A Shopping Trip, p.130

Museo Poldi-Pezzoli, p.88
Museo Teatrale alla Scala, p.119
Quadrilatero d'Oro, p.90
Nightlife
Hollywood, p.177

TRENDY MILAN

Until a few years ago, Milan was considered to be a fundamentally boring city, where people went to work, and when the day was over, went home to get a good night's sleep. There was none of the café life, sparkle and general feel of humanity and vibrancy so palpable elsewhere in Italy – and the smog, rush-hour traffic and grids of suburban architecture didn't exactly lend themselves to lighthearted conviviality. Then suddenly, the Milanese woke up to fun – to the art of the *aperitivo* and hanging around doing nothing but looking cool. Underneath its suave Armani exterior, Milan is finally showing a more hedonistic approach to life, with trendy bars and weekend brunch spots sprinkled throughout the city, and fusion and late lounges livening up the Porta Garibaldi and Porta Genova areas.

Four

Start: Tram 3 or bus 94 to Corso di Porta Ticinese.

Breakfast: Make a fresh start at **Ecologica**, Milan's first eco-organic café.

Morning: Check out the off-beat shops and loft-cafés down **Corso di Porta Ticinese**, then along the banks of the **Naviglio Grande**.

Lunch: Take the metro north to Porta Garibaldi, for artwork and a sushi and fusion lunch at nearby **10 Corso Como Caffè**.

Afternoon: Soak up a bit of cutting-edge culture at an exhibition at the **Palazzo Reale**, then meet 'under the Colonne', at the Roman columns in

front of the basilica of **San Lorenzo** (*photo above*), for *aperitivos* from one of the square's bars, such as **L'Exploit**.

Dinner: Detour northeast to the **Diana Garden** for pre-dinner cocktails, where you can lounge *al fresco* in a luminous Liberty-style setting. Don't forget your sunglasses, to be worn after dark, on the eyes, or else in varying positions on your neck or above your eyebrows. Return south to the Navigli and immerse yourself in the ultimate contemporary fusion food experience of **Quattrocento**.

Evening: Travel via metro or tram to the West End and relax in the eclectic chic surroundings of **Roialto** for an early evening drink, then move on to **Gattopardo** for dancing, or to **Light**, where you can sip cocktails through the night.

Food and Drinks
10 Corso Como Caffè, p.167
Diana Garden, p.174
Ecologica, p.172
L'Exploit, p.176
Quattrocento, p.169
Sights and Activities
A Shopping Trip, p.130
A Walk Through the Navigli, p.126

Corso di Porta Ticinese, p.108
Naviglio Grande, p.110
Palazzo Reale, p.73
San Lorenzo Maggiore's Roman Columns, p.108
Nightlife
Gattopardo, p.177
Light, p.176
Roialto, p.177

FOODIE MILAN

There is no doubt that Milan takes its food as seriously as its appearance, with a wide range of well-turned-out restaurants, delis and cafés. From centuries-old *trattorias* serving hearty stews and meat *alla Milanese* (battered in breadcrumbs), to the latest trend of fusion food lounges doubling as art galleries and bars, Milan will impress the food lover who bothers to sniff out its more surprising gastronomic secrets. To devote your day to this most ephemeral art:

Five

Start: Metro Duomo.

Breakfast: Begin the day at **Caffè Sant'Ambroeus**, one of Milan's oldest cafés.

Morning: Make the foodie rounds near the Duomo. Visit **Peck**, long the *ne plus ultra* in Milanese gastronomy – which has now incorporated the historic **Casa del Formaggio** – then hunt amongst the remarkable array of kitchen gear in **La Rinascente**.

Lunch: Enjoy Milanese specialities at **L'Altra Pharmacia** in the West End.

Afternoon: Work up another appetite studying the still lifes at the **Ambrosiana**, then indulge in a *gelato* at **Antica Gelateria del Corso**, or walk to the Quadrilatero d'Oro to sample the deli offerings from well-stocked **Il Salumaio**. Then head west via the metro to the covered **market at Piazza Wagner**, with its mouthwatering array of cheeses, fish and sausages.

Dinner: Travel to **Aimo e Nadia**, near San Siro stadium, for the best in Lombard cuisine.

Evening: Listen to jazz while snacking at the bohemian **Le Trottoir**.

Food and Drinks

Aimo e Nadia, p.169
Antica Gelateria del Corso, p.164
Caffè Sant'Ambroeus, p.164
L'Altra Pharmacia, p.172
Le Trottoir, p.179

Sights and Activities

Ambrosiana, p.78
Casa del Formaggio, p.183
Il Salumaio, p.183
La Rinascente, p.183
Mercato di Piazza Wagner, p.184
Peck, p.183

Roots of the City

100 BC–AD 493: THE HEIGHTS AND DEPTHS OF EMPIRE 20

493–753: GOOD GOTHS AND NASTY LOMBARDS 21

750–1000: THE THRESHOLD OF THE MIDDLE AGES 22

1000–1220: THE RISE OF THE *COMUNE* 23

1200–1450: GUELPHS, GHIBELLINES AND DUKES 24

1451–1508: LODOVICO IL MORO 26

1508–1796: HARDSHIPS OF FOREIGN RULE 27

1796–1919: FROM NAPOLEON TO ITALIAN UNIFICATION 29

1919–45: MUSSOLINI AND THE WAR 30

POST-WAR MILAN 31

Milan was born cosmopolitan. Although it lacks a navigable river and sits in the midst of the fertile but vulnerable Lombard plain, it occupies the natural junction of trade routes through the Alpine passes, from the Tyrrhenian and Adriatic ports and from the River Po. This commercially strategic position has also put Milan square in the path of every invader tramping through Italy.

100 BC–AD 493: The Heights and Depths of Empire

Milan's earliest history is obscure – in the Bronze Age, at any rate, people preferred to live by lakes. However, once the Romans beat everyone and annexed most of Italy by 283 BC, the spotlight came to shine on **Mediolanum**, Milan's Celtic name for its first millennium or so. After a failed attempt to rebel at Hannibal's side, Mediolanum, by the 1st century BC, had soon settled into its role as a Roman city.

Being less developed, Mediolanum and its surrounding area, Cisalpine Gaul, suffered less from Roman misrule than other parts of Italy. There was little wealth to tax, and little for rapacious Roman governors to steal. The region managed to avoid most of the endless civil wars, famines and oppression that accompanied the death throes of the Roman Republic elsewhere. It did endure a last surprise raid by two Celtic tribes, the Cimbri and Teutones, who crossed over the Riviera and the Alps in a two-pronged attack in 102 BC. Gaius Marius, a capable though illiterate Roman general, defeated them decisively, using his popularity to seize power in Rome soon after.

In the Pax Romana of Augustus and his successors, the northern regions evolved from wild border territories to settled, prosperous provinces full of thriving new towns. Of these the most important was Mediolanum, not least because the nearby lakes had become a favourite holiday destination for Rome's elite. But after over

two centuries at the noonday of its history, in the 3rd century AD, the Roman empire began to have troubles from without as well as within: a severe long-term economic decline coinciding with a shift in military balance to thwart the Barbarians on the frontiers. **Diocletian** (284–305) completely revamped the structure of the state, converting it into a vast bureaucratic machine geared solely to meeting the needs of its army; he also initiated the division of the empire into western and eastern halves, out of military and administrative necessity. And because of its location as a convenient place to keep an eye on both the Rhine and Danube, in 286 Mediolanum was made capital of the West.

It was then, in the twilight of Rome, that Milan first truly sashayed onto the world stage. It was the headquarters of the Mobile Army and the seat of the court and government of the West, the *de facto* capital of the empire while Rome itself decayed into a marble-veneered backwater. Diocletian's successors spent much of their time here.

Times were hard all over the West and, although northern Italy was relatively less hard-hit than other regions, cities decayed and trade disappeared, while debt and an inability to meet high taxes pushed thousands into serfdom or slavery. The confused politics of the time were dominated by **Constantine the Great** (306–37), who ruled both halves of the empire, and adroitly moved to increase his political support by the Edict of Milan (313), which decreed toleration for Christianity, setting it on its path to become the empire's religion. Later in the century, Milan became an important centre of the new faith under its great bishop **St Ambrose** (*see* p.120), who considered Milan the equal to Rome. To this day, true Milanese are called *Ambrosiani*.

The inevitable disasters began in 406, when the Visigoths, Franks, Vandals, Alans and Suevi overran Gaul and Spain. Italy's turn came in 408, when Western Emperor Honorius had his brilliant general Stilicho (who was himself a Vandal)

100 BC–AD 753

Amfiteatro Romano, for the remains of the Mediolanum's theatre, p.108

Museo Archeologico, for displays on the city's growth and early history, p.119

Pavia, northern Italy's Gothic capital, p.145

San Lorenzo Maggiore (alle Colonne), for its imported Roman columns and 5th-century mosaics, p.108

Sant'Ambrogio, founded in the 4th century by Milan's most revered bishop, p.120

Santa Maria della Vittoria, for Roman and Lombard archaeological finds, p.108

Treasury of Queen Theodolinda, Monza, for 5th-century treasures, p.136

murdered. A Visigothic invasion followed; Alaric sacked Rome in 410; and in Milan, St Augustine wrote that the end of the world was near. Italy should have been so lucky; judgement was postponed long enough for Attila the Hun to pass through in 451.

So completely had things changed, it was scarcely possible to tell the Romans from the Barbarians. By the 470s the real ruler in Italy was a Gothic general named **Odoacer**, who led a half-Romanized Germanic army and probably thought of himself as the genuine heir of the Caesars. In 476 he decided to dispense with the lingering charade of the Western Empire. The last emperor, **Romulus Augustulus**, was retired to Naples, and Odoacer had himself crowned king at Italy's new Gothic capital, Pavia.

493–753: Good Goths and Nasty Lombards

At the beginning, the new Gothic-Latin state showed some promise; certainly the average man was no worse off than he had been under the last emperors. In 493, Odoacer was replaced (and murdered) by a rival Ostrogoth, **Theodoric**, nominally working on behalf of the Eastern Emperor at Constantinople. Theodoric proved a strong and able, though somewhat paranoid, ruler; his court witnessed a minor rebirth of Latin

letters, while trade revived and cities were repaired. A disaster as serious as those of the 5th century began in 536 with the invasion of Italy by the Eastern Empire, part of the relentlessly expansionist policy of Emperor **Justinian**. The historical irony was profound: in the birthplace of the Roman Empire, Roman troops now came not as liberators, but as foreign, largely Greek-speaking conquerors. Justinian's brilliant generals Belisarius and Narses ultimately prevailed over the Goths in a series of terrible wars that lasted until 563, but the damage to an already stricken society was incalculable.

Italy's total exhaustion was exposed only five years later with the invasion of the **Lombards**, a Germanic people who worked hard to maintain the title of Barbarian. While other, more courageous tribes moved in to take what they could of the empire, the Lombards had ranged on the frontiers like mean stray curs. Most writers, ancient and modern, mistakenly attribute the Lombards' name to their long beards; in fact, these redoubtable nomads scared the daylights out of the Italians not with beards but with their long *bardi*, or poleaxes.

Narses himself first invited the Lombards in, as mercenaries to help him overcome the Goths. Quickly understanding their opportunity, they returned with the entire horde in 568. By 571, they were across the Apennines; Pavia, one of the old Gothic capitals and the key to northern Italy, fell after a long siege in 572. The horde's progress provided history with unedifying spectacles from the very start: King Alboin, who unified the Lombard tribes and made the invasion possible, met his bloody end at the hands of his queen, Rosmunda – whom he drove to murder by forcing her to drink from her father's skull.

The Lombards certainly hadn't come to do the Italians any favours, and considered the entire population their slaves; in practice, they were usually content to sit back and collect exorbitant tributes. Themselves Arian Christians, they enjoyed oppressing both the orthodox and pagans. Throughout the 6th century their conquest continued apace. The popes, occasionally allied with the Lombards against Byzantium, became a force during this period, especially after the papacy of the clever, determined **Gregory the Great** (590–604), who in 603 managed to convert the Lombard queen **Theodolinda** and her people to orthodox Christianity. By then the situation had stabilized. Northern Italy was the Lombard kingdom proper, centred at Pavia and Monza (both more defensible than vulnerable Milan) while semi-independent Lombard duchies controlled much of the peninsula. One of the few things we know of during the period is that Mediolanum's name was shortened to Mailand, the prized 'Land of May', for so it seemed to the frost-bitten Goths and Lombards.

In Pavia, a long succession of Lombard kings left little account of themselves until Byzantine weakness made the doughty king **Liutprand** (712–44) exert himself to try to unify Italy. Liutprand won most of his battles but gained little territory. A greater threat was his ruthless successor **Aistulf**, who by 753 conquered almost all Byzantine lands, including their capital, Ravenna. If the Lombards' final solution was to be averted, the popes had to find help from outside. The logical people to ask were the Franks.

753–1000: The Threshold of the Middle Ages

At the time, the popes had something to offer in return. The powerful **Mayors of the Palace of the Frankish Kingdom** longed to supplant the Merovingian dynasty and assume the throne for themselves, but needed the appearance of legitimacy that only the mystic pageantry of the papacy could provide. At the beginning of Aistulf's campaigns, Pope Zacharias had foreseen the danger, and gave his blessing to the change of dynasties in 750. To complete the deal, the new king Pepin sent his army over the Alps in 753 and 756 to foil Aistulf's designs.

By 773, the conflict remained the same, though with a different cast of characters. The Lombard king was Desiderius, the Frankish king his cordially hostile son-in-law **Charlemagne**, who also invaded Italy twice, in 775 and 776. Unlike his father, though, Charlemagne meant to settle Italy once and for all. His army captured Pavia, and after deposing his father-in-law he took the Iron Crown of Italy for himself.

The new partnership between pope and king failed to bring the stability both parties had hoped for. With Charlemagne busy elsewhere, local lordlings across the peninsula scrapped continually for slight advantage. Charlemagne returned in 799 to sort them out, and in return got what must be the most momentous Christmas present in history. On Christmas Eve, while he was praying in St Peter's, Pope Leo III crept up behind him and deftly set an imperial crown on the surprised king's head. The revival of the dream of a united Christian empire changed the political face of Italy, beginning the contorted *pas de deux* of pope and emperor that was to be the mainspring of Italian history throughout the Middle Ages.

Charlemagne's empire quickly disintegrated after his death, divided among squabbling descendants, and Italy reverted to anarchy and the endless wars of petty nobles and battling bishops. To north Italians, the post-Carolingian era is the age of the *reucci*, the 'little kings', a profusion of puny rulers angling to advance their own interests. After 888, when the Carolingian line became extinct, ten little Frankish kings of Italy succeeded to the throne at Pavia, each with less power than the last, constantly at war with the Lombard **Dukes of Spoleto** and the occasional foreign interloper. Worse trouble for everyone came with the arrival of the barbarian **Magyars**, who overran the north and sacked Pavia in 924.

The 10th century proved somewhat better. Even in the worst times, Italy's cities never entirely disappeared; even inland cities like Milan were developing a new economic importance. From the 900s, many were looking to their own resources, defending their interests against the Church and nobles alike. A big break for the cities came in 961 when **Adelheid**, the beautiful widow of one of the *reucci*, Lothar, refused to wed his successor, Berengar II, Marquis of Ivrea. Berengar had hoped to bring some discipline to Italy, and began by imprisoning the recalcitrant Adelheid in a tower by Lake Como. With the aid of a monk she made a daring escape to Canossa and the protection of the Count of Tuscany, who called in reinforcements from the King of Germany, **Otto the Great**. Otto came over the Alps, got the girl, deposed Berengar and was crowned Holy Roman Emperor in Rome the following year. Not that any of the Italians were happy to see him, but the strong government of Otto and his successors beat down the great nobles, divided their lands and allowed the cities to expand their power and influence.

1000–1220: The Rise of the *Comune*

On the eve of the new millennium, business was very good in the towns, and the political prospects even brighter. The first mention of a truly independent *comune* (a free city-state; the best translation might be 'commonwealth') was in Milan under the leadership of another great bishop Heribert, who in 1024 organized the first popular assembly (*parlamento*) of citizens and a citizen militia to decide which side the city would take in the imperial wars. And when that was done Heribert invited the German Frankish King Conrad to be crowned in Milan, founding a new line of Italian kings.

The new *comune*, in defiance of imperial pretensions, at once began subjugating the surrounding country and especially its rivals Pavia, Lodi and Como. To inspire the militia, Heribert also invented that unique Italian war totem the *carroccio*, a huge ox-drawn cart that bore the city's banner, altar and bells into battle, to remind the soldiers of the city and church they fought for.

753–1220
Archi di Porta Nuova, for a bit of Milan's remaining 12th-century medieval Spanish walls, p.90
Museo della Criminologia, for medieval torture instruments and weapons, p.121
Palazzo della Ragione, Milan's medieval Halls of Justice, p.74
Piazza Mercanti, the centre of life under the *comune*, p.74

During this period the papacy had declined greatly, a political football kicked between the emperors and the Roman nobles. In the 1050s a monk named **Hildebrand** (later Gregory VII) worked to reassert Church power, beginning a conflict with the emperors over investiture – whether the church or secular powers would name church officials. The result was a big revival for the papacy, but more importantly Milan used the opportunity to increase its influence, and in some cases achieve outright independence, razing the nobles' castles and forcing them to move inside the town.

While all this was happening, the **First Crusade** (1097–1130) occupied the headlines, partially a result of the new papal militancy begun by Gregory VII. For Italy the affair meant nothing but profit. Trade was booming everywhere, and the accumulation of money helped the Italians to create modern Europe's first banking system. It also financed the continued independence of the *comuni*, who began to discover there simply wasn't enough Italy to hold them all. Milan, the biggest bully of them all, took on Pavia, Cremona, Como and Lodi with one hand tied behind its back.

By the 12th century, far in advance of most of Europe, Italy enjoyed prosperity unknown since Roman times. The classical past had never been forgotten: free *comuni* in the north called their elected leaders 'consuls', and artists and architects turned ancient Roman styles into the Romanesque. Milan's proudest monument of the period is **Palazzo della Ragione**, the seat of its self-rule.

Meanwhile, emperors and popes were still embroiled in the north. **Frederick I – Barbarossa** – of the Hohenstaufen or Swabian dynasty, was strong enough back home in Germany, and he made it his special interest to reassert imperial power in Italy. And the *comune* he chose to crush *pour encourager les autres* was Milan, the oldest and boldest of the lot.

It was Lodi's complaint about Milanese aggression that gave old Red Beard his excuse to come to Italy for the first of five times in 1154. The *Ambrosiani* promised to behave but attacked his German garrison and punished the cities that had supported him as soon as the emperor was back safely over the Alps. Back came Frederick in 1158; he set up Imperial governors (*podestà*) in each *comune* and for two years laid waste to the countryside around Milan, then grimly besieged the defiant city. When it surrendered in 1161 he was merciless, demanding the surrender of the *carroccio*, forcing the citizens to kiss his feet with ropes around their necks, and inviting Milan's bitterest enemies, Lodi and Como, to raze the city to the ground, sparing only the churches of Sant'Ambrogio and San Lorenzo. And back over the Alps Frederick went once more, confident that he had taught Milan and Lombardy a lesson.

What he had instead taught northern Italians by the humiliation of Milan, was that the liberties of their *comuni* were in grave danger. Galvanized, they formed a united opposition, called the **Lombard League**, which by 1167 included every major city between Venice and Asti and Bologna (except Pavia, which hated Milan too much to join), with spiritual backing in the person of Frederick's enemy Pope Alexander III, whom the emperor had exiled from Rome in order to set up another pope more malleable to his schemes.

Twice the Lombard League beat the furious emperor back over the mountains, and when Frederick crossed the Alps for the fifth time, while his forces were in Legnano preparing to attack Milan, the Milanese militia surprised and decimated his army, forcing Frederick to flee alone to Venice (1176). Now the tables had turned and the empire itself was in danger of total revolt. To preserve it, Barbarossa had to do a little foot-kissing himself in Venice, the privileged toe in this case belonging to Pope Alexander III. To placate the Lombard *comuni*, the **Treaty of Constance** was signed after a six-year truce in 1183. It might as well have been called the Peace of Pigheads: all that the *comuni* asked was the right to look after their own interests and fight each other whenever they pleased. The more magnanimous idea of a united Italy was still centuries away.

1220–1450: Guelphs, Ghibellines and Dukes

Frederick's grandson **Frederick II** was not only emperor but also King of Sicily, thus giving him a strong power base in Italy itself. The second Frederick's career dominated Italian politics for 30 years (1220–50). With his brilliant court, his half-Muslim army, his dancing girls, eunuchs and elephants, he provided Europe with a spectacle the like of which it had never seen. The popes excommunicated him at least twice. Now the battle had become serious. Italy divided into factions: the **Guelphs**, under the popes' leadership, supported religious orthodoxy, the liberty of the *comuni* and the interests of their emerging wealthy merchant class. The **Ghibellines** stood for the emperor, statist economic control and (sometimes) religious and intellectual tolerance. Frederick's campaigns and diplomacy in the north met with very limited success, and his death in 1250 left the outcome much in doubt.

His son Manfred, not emperor but merely King of Sicily, took up the battle with better luck. In 1261, however, Pope Urban IV set an ultimately disastrous precedent by inviting in Charles of Anjou, the ambitious brother of the King of France. As champion of the Guelphs, Charles defeated Manfred (1266), murdered the last of the Hohenstaufens, Conradin (1268), and held unchallenged sway

1220–1450

Certosa di Pavia, commissioned by Gian Galeazzo Visconti in the 14th century, p.147

Duomo, also begun by Gian Galeazzo Visconti, p.70

Naviglio Grande, expanded by the Visconti to bring in the Duomo's building materials, p.110

Parco Sempione, once a hunting reserve for the Visconti dukes, p.115

San Bernardino alle Ossa, covered in the bones of the city's 14th-century plague victims, p.99

over Italy until 1282. By now, however, the terms 'Guelph' and 'Ghibelline' had ceased to have much meaning; men and cities changed sides as they found expedient, and the old parties began to seem like the black and white squares on a chessboard.

Some real changes did occur out of all this sound and fury. Everywhere the liberties of the *comuni* were in jeopardy; after so much useless strife the temptation to submit to a strong military leader often proved overwhelming. If Milan was precocious in becoming a *comune*, it was also one of the first cities to give it up.

Local economic factors contributed to the change. Unlike their counterparts in Florence, Milan's manufacturers had widely varying trades (although textiles and armour predominated) and limited themselves to small workshops, failing to form the companies of politically powerful merchants and trade associations that were the power base of a medieval Italian republic. Instead, medieval Milan became the most successful and dazzling signorial government in Italy. The first family to fill the vacuum at the top were the Torriani (or *della Torre*), feudal lords who became the city's bosses in 1247, only to lose their position to the Visconti in 1277.

The Visconti were leading figures in the paradoxical Italy that continued through the 15th century, where a golden age of culture and an opulent economy existed side by side with continuous war. With no

threats over the border, the myriad Italian states menaced each other joyfully without outside interference. War became a sort of game, conducted on behalf of cities by *condottieri*, leading paid mercenaries who were never allowed to enter the cities themselves. The arrangement suited everyone well. The soldiers had lovely horses and armour, and no real desire to do each other serious harm. The cities were making too much money to really want to wreck the system anyway.

By far the biggest event of the 14th century was the **Black Death** of 1347–8, in which Milan, like the rest of Italy, lost one-third of its population. The shock brought a rude halt to what had been 400 years of almost continuous growth and prosperity, though its effects did not prove a permanent setback. In fact, the plague's grim joke was that it actually made life better for most of the survivors; working people in the city, no longer overcrowded, found their rents lower and their labour worth more.

In the meantime, the Visconti made Milan the strongest state in Italy, basing their success on the manufactures of the city, improved communications through canals, and the bountiful, progressively managed agriculture of southern Lombardy. The Visconti court functioned on a kingly scale, and marriages into the French and English royal houses brought the family into European affairs (they fêted a certain Geoffrey Chaucer, in town to find a princess for a Plantagenet). Most ambitious and successful of all the Visconti was **Gian Galeazzo** (1351–1402), who bought the title of Duke off the emperor, then married his daughter Valentina off to the King of France (later to become the fateful base for French claims in Lombardy).

For his second marriage, Gian Galeazzo chose the daughter of his powerful and malevolent uncle Bernabò, whom he then packed off to prison before conquering northern Italy, the Veneto, Romagna and Umbria. His army was ready to march on Florence, the gateway to the rest of the peninsula, when he suddenly died of plague. In his cruelty, ruthlessness and superstitious dependence on astrology, and in his love of art and letters (he founded the Certosa of Pavia, began the Duomo, and supported the University of Pavia), Gian Galeazzo was the first archetypal Renaissance prince.

The Florentines and the Venetians took advantage of his sudden demise to carry off tasty bits on the fringes of his empire and, while his sons, the obscene Giovanni Maria (who delighted in feeding his enemies to the dogs) and the gruesome, paranoid Filippo Maria, did what they could to regain their father's conquests, Milan's influence was eventually reduced to Lombardy, which its dukes ran as a centralized city-state.

Filippo Maria left no male heirs, but a wise and lovely daughter named Bianca, whom he betrothed to his best *condottiere*, **Francesco Sforza** (1401–66). After Filippo Maria's death, the Milanese declared the **Aurea Repubblica Ambrosiana** (Golden Ambrosian Republic), but after three troubled years, having neither a republican tradition nor support from an elite torn between wanting to hold on to the Visconti domains and their own rivalries. the republic's leaders called in Francesco Sforza to be their *condottiere*, and then duke. One of Milan's best rulers, he continued the scientific development of Lombard agriculture and navigable canals and hydraulic schemes (notably the Martesana canal that linked Milan with the river Adda) and kept the peace through a friendly alliance with the Medici. His son, Galeazzo Maria, was assassinated, but not before fathering Caterina Sforza, the famous virago, and an infant son, Gian Galeazzo II, whose mother Bona of Savoy claimed Milan.

And what of the Renaissance? No word has ever caused more mischief for the understanding of history and culture – as if Italy had been Sleeping Beauty, waiting for some Prince Charming to come and awaken it from a 1000-year nap. On the contrary, Italy even in the 1200s was richer, more technologically advanced and far more artistically creative than it had ever been in the days of the Caesars. The new art and scholarship that began in Florence and spread across the nation grew from a solid foundation of medieval accomplishment. The gilded Italy of the 15th century felt complacently secure in its cultural and economic pre-eminence. The long spell of freedom from outside interference lulled the country into believing that its political disunity could continue safely forever; except perhaps for the sanguinely realistic Florentine Nicolò Macchiavelli, no one realized that Italy was in fact a plum waiting to be picked.

1451–1508: Lodovico il Moro

The rightful heir, the infant Gian Galeazzo II and his mother Bona of Savoy had no chance against Francesco Sforza's second son, **Lodovico il Moro** (1451–1508), who took power and went on to became Milan's most cultivated ruler, taking the title of Duke of Milan in 1494 after the death of Gian Galeazzo. His nickname 'the Moor' either came from his dark colouring or from his middle name Mauro. He was helped by his wife, the delightful Beatrice d'Este, who ran one of Italy's most sparkling courts until her early death in childbirth.

Lodovico was a generous and knowledge-able patron of the arts, commissioning from **Leonardo da Vinci** the *Last Supper*, as well as engineering schemes and magnificent theatrical pageants – and

1451–1508

Castello Sforzesco, lived in by Lodovico il Moro after his father's death, p.114

Last Supper, commissioned by Lodovico il Moro, p.117

Leonardo da Vinci Museo Nazionale della Scienza e Tecnica, for Leonardo's more scientific exploits, p.122

Museo del Duomo, for a chronology of the cathedral's progress under its successive dukes, p.73

Leonardo was only one of the many artists, historians, poets and engineers in his court, which he ran with the aid of professional administrators and an inner counsel, the *deputati del denaro*. Italy scholar Burckhardt called him 'the perfect type of despot.'

But Lodovico also bears the blame for one of the greatest political blunders in Italian history, when his quarrel with Naples (where Bona of Savoy had influence) grew so touchy that he invited **Charles VIII** of France to come and claim the Kingdom of Naples for himself. Charles took him up on it and marched unhindered down the peninsula. Lodovico soon realized his mistake, and joined the last-minute league of Italian states that united to trap and destroy the French at Fornovo. They succeeded, partially, but the damage was done: the French invasion had shown the Italian states, beautiful, rich, in full flower of the Renaissance, to be disunited and vulnerable. Charles VIII's son, **Louis XII**, took advantage of the Orléanist claim on Milan through his Visconti grandmother Valentina and captured the

city, and Lodovico with it. The Duke of Milan died a prisoner in Louches, in a Loire château, an unhappy Prospero, covering the walls of his dungeon with bizarre graffiti that perplexes visitors to this day.

1508–1796: Hardships of Foreign Rule

The inconclusive Battle of Fornovo showed just how helpless Italy was at the hands of new nation-states like France. When the Spaniards saw how easy it was, they too marched in, and restored Naples to its Spanish king the following year. Before long the German emperor and even the Swiss, who briefly took control of Milan, entered this new market for Italian real estate. The popes did as much as anyone to keep the pot boiling. Alexander VI and his son **Cesare Borgia** carried the war across central Italy in an attempt to found a new state for the Borgia family, and Julius II's madcap policy led him to egg on the Swiss,

The *Caffè* of Italian Enlightenment

Java had little to do with it, but *Il Caffè* had the same effect as an espresso on sleepy 18th-century Lombardy – a quick jolt of wakeful energy. *Il Caffè* was in fact the name of Italy's first real newspaper. It was published for only two years in the 1760s, by brothers Pietro and Alessandro Verri and a small circle of young Milanese aristocrats who called themselves the *Accademia dei Pugni*, 'the Academy of Fists'.

The opinions published in *Il Caffè* derived from England and the philosophers and Encyclopedists of France. They wrote of the need for economic, humanitarian and judicial reforms, not once challenging the authority of the absolute monarchy of the Austrian Habsburgs in Lombardy, or even suggesting anything as radical as Italian unity. But at a time when Italy was still languishing in ignorance enforced by the

Church and foreign rulers, this newspaper, such as it was, was revolutionary for merely encouraging people to think.

When *Il Caffè* was published, only a few thousand lay Italians were literate enough to read it. But they were the elite, and it was their opinions that the Verri brothers hoped to influence in their editorials. Also, conditions in Milan, if nowhere else, were ripe for change. While the rest of Italy (with the exception of Venice) festered under papal and Spanish Bourbon rule, Lombardy's sovereign, Maria Theresa of Austria, not only overhauled the economy but was prepared to tolerate a certain amount of local autonomy and opinion. Thanks to her, Milan was on the verge of its great capitalist destiny.

The most important fruit of the Fists' endeavours came from the youngest member of the Academy, a plump stay-at-home mamma's boy named Cesare Beccaria. Pietro Verri saw potential in this muffin that

French and Spaniards in turn, before crying, 'Out with the barbarians!' when it was already too late.

By 1516, with the French ruling Milan and the Spanish in control of the south, it seemed as if a settlement would be possible. The worst possible luck for Italy, however, came with the accession of the insatiable megalomaniac **Charles V** to the throne of Spain; in 1519 he emptied the Spanish treasury to buy himself the crown of the Holy Roman Empire, making him the most powerful ruler in Europe since Charlemagne.

Charles wanted Milan as a base for communications between his Spanish, German and Flemish possessions, and the wars began anew, bloodier than anything Italy had seen for centuries, climaxing with the defeat of the French at Pavia in 1525, a devastating siege of Milan, and the sack of Rome by an out-of-control Imperial army in 1527. The French invaded once more in 1529, and were defeated, this time at Naples, by the treachery of their Genoese allies. All Italy, save only Venice, was now at the mercy of Charles and the Spaniards.

The final peace negotiated at Château-Cambrésis left Spanish viceroys in Milan and Naples, and pliant dukes and counts toeing the Spanish line almost everywhere else. The broader context of the time was the bitter struggles of the Reformation and Counter-Reformation. In Italy, the Spaniards found a perfect ally in the papacy; together they put an end to the last surviving liberties of the cities, while snuffing out the intellectual life of the Renaissance with the help of the Inquisition and the Jesuits.

Nearly the only place where anything creative came out of this new order was Lombardy. In Milan, that incorruptible Galahad of the Counter-Reformation, **Archbishop Charles Borromeo** (1538–84), came out of the Council of Trent determined to make his diocese a working model of Tridentine reforms. One of the most influential characters in Italian religious history, he relentlessly went about creating an actively pastoral, zealous clergy, giving

---

no one else could fathom and assigned him the task of writing a pamphlet on the group's opinions on justice. This was at a time when torture was the most common way of extracting a confession and in Milan alone someone was executed nearly every day. There was even a strict hierarchy of death: nobles got a quick decapitation with a sharp axe and cardinals had the right to be strangled with a gold and purple cord, while the lower classes could expect a host of nasty preliminaries – their tongues and ears chopped off, their eyes put out and their flesh burned with hot irons.

Even Pietro Verri was astonished when Beccaria roused himself to produce the brilliant, succinct *Dei Delitti e delle Pene* (Of Crimes and Punishments), published in 1764 in Livorno, out of the reach of local censors. Although the Church hastily consigned the work to the Index of prohibited books, it can be fairly said that no other work on jurisprudence had such an immediate effect on the day-to-day lives of everyday men and women. Beccaria's eloquent logic against torture and the death penalty, his insistence on equality before the law and for justice to be both accountable and public, moved Voltaire to write that Beccaria had eliminated 'the last remnants of barbarism'. The absolute monarchs of the day (with the notable exception of Louis XVI) moved at once to follow Beccaria's precepts, at least in part: Maria Theresa in Austria, Charles III in Spain, Catherine the Great in Russia, Frederick the Great of Prussia, Ferdinand I in Naples, and most of all, Duke Peter Leopold of Tuscany, who went the furthest by completely abolishing torture and capital punishment. Beccaria wrote of the 'greatest happiness shared by the greatest number', a phrase adopted by Jeremy Bentham and Thomas Jefferson, who used Beccaria's ideas of equal justice for all as a starting point in framing the American constitution.

1508–1796

Ambrosiana, legacy of the 16th-century Borromei family, p.78

Ca' Grande, Francesco Sforzesca's consolidation of the city's hospitals, p.98

La Scala, for the beginnings of Verdi and Toscanini, p.75

Museo di Milano, for paintings of old Milan, p.91

Museo Teatrale alla Scala, for a history of the opera house's sumptuous costumes, p.119

the most prominent teaching jobs to Jesuits and cleansing Lombardy of heresy and corruption. By re-establishing the cult of Milan's patron, St Ambrose, he developed a sense of Lombard regional feeling; with his nephew and successor **Federico Borromeo** he promoted sorely-needed cultural and welfare institutions, instilling in the Lombard elite an industrious Catholic paternalism still present in the region today.

Despite political oppression, the 16th century had generally been a prosperous period for most of Italy, embellished with an afterglow of late-Renaissance architecture and art. After 1600, though, nearly everything started to go wrong for the Italians. The textiles and banking of the north, long the engines of prosperity, both withered in the face of foreign competition. The old mercantile economies built in the Middle Ages were failing, and the wealthy began to invest in land instead of business or finance. Milan suffered the **Great Famine of 1627–8**, followed in 1630 by a deadly outbreak of plague that took years to recover from. The city lost its momentum; as Spain slouched into decadence, Lombardy snoozed.

In 1713, after the War of the Spanish Succession, the Habsburgs of Austria came into control of the Duchy and improved conditions somewhat. Especially during the reigns of **Maria Theresa** (1740–80) and her son **Joseph II** (1780–92), two of the most likeable Enlightenment despots, Lombardy underwent serious, intelligent economic reforms. The Habsburgs did much to improve agriculture (especially the production of rice and silk), rationalize taxes and increase education. They also oversaw the building of La Scala, the creation of the Brera Academy and most of central neoclassical Milan, giving the city a head start over the rest of Italy that has directly contributed to its prominence today.

1796–1919: From Napoleon to Italian Unification

After centuries of Baroque hibernation, the *Ambrosiani* were stirring again, and when **Napoleon**, that greatest of Italian generals, arrived in 1796, sweeping away the Austrians on behalf of the French Revolutionary Directorate, the city welcomed him fervently. With a huge festival, Milan became the capital of Napoleon's 'Cisalpine Republic'.

In 1799, however, while Napoleon was off in Egypt, the advance through Italy by an Austro-Russian army, aided by Nelson's fleet, restored the status quo. In 1800 Napoleon returned in a campaign that saw the great victory at Marengo, giving him the opportunity to reorganize Italian affairs once more, and to crown himself King of Italy in Milan's Duomo. Napoleonic rule lasted only until 1814, but in that time, important public works were begun (including the Simplon Highway, linking Milan to Paris) and laws, education and everything else reformed after the French model; Church properties were expropriated and medieval relics everywhere put to rest. The French, however, soon wore out their welcome through high taxes, oppression and the systematic looting of Italy's art. When the Austrians chased them out in 1814, no one was sad to see them go.

Though the post-war **Congress of Vienna** put the clock back to 1796, the Napoleonic experience had given Italians a taste of the opportunities offered by the modern world, as well as a sense of national feeling that had been suppressed for centuries. Although in the eyes of Austrian prime minister Metternich, Italy was 'a mere geographic expression' agitators and secret societies all over the country were determined to prove him wrong. The movement for Italian Unification and liberal reform was greatest in the north, and in the decades of the national revival, the **Risorgimento**, Milan remained an important centre of nationalist sentiment.

In March 1848, a revolution in Vienna gave Italians their chance to act. Milan's famous **Cinque Giornate** revolt began with a boycott of the Austrian tobacco monopoly. Some troops, conspicuously smoking cigars in public, caused fighting to break out in the streets. In five incredible days, the populace of Milan rose up and chased out the Austrian garrison (led by Marshal Radetzky, he of the famous march tune). Events began to move rapidly. On 22 March, revolution spread to Venice, and soon afterwards Piedmont's King Carlo Alberto declared war on Austria and his army crossed the Ticino into Lombardy. But under his timid leadership, the army failed to take the initiative, and the Austrians were back in control by the end of July. Perhaps Milan's most lasting contribution during this period, however, was the novelist **Alessandro Manzoni**, whose masterpiece *I Promessi Sposi* caused a nationwide sensation and sense of unity in a peninsula that had been politically divided since the fall of Rome.

Despite failure on a grand scale in 1848, the Italians knew they would get another chance. Unification was inevitable, and at the time it was most likely under the House of

Savoy that ruled Piedmont. In 1859, with the support of Napoleon III and France, the Piedmontese tried again and would have been successful had the French not double-crossed them and signed an armistice with Austria in the middle of the war; as a result, though, Piedmont gained Lombardy and Tuscany. That left the climactic event of Unification to be performed by the revolutionary adventurer **Giuseppe Garibaldi**. When Garibaldi sailed to Sicily with a thousand volunteers in May 1860, nearly half his men were from Lombardy. Their unexpected success in toppling the Kingdom of Naples launched the Piedmontese on an invasion from the north, and Italian unity was achieved.

While life under the corrupt and bumbling governments of the new Italian kingdom wasn't perfect, it was a major improvement over the Austrians. The integration of the northern industrial towns into a unified Italian economy gave trade a big boost. Milan in particular saw its industry expand dramatically, and the face of the city change, as banks and insurance companies took over the centre, and smart residential districts grew up on the fringes. As the country's economic dynamo, Milan attracted thousands of workers from the poorer sections of Italy. Many of these joined the first Italian Socialist Party, the **Partito Operaio Italiano**, when it was founded in Milan in 1882. Strikes and riots were common in the depression of the 1890s; over a hundred people were killed in police cannon-fire in one clash in 1896. Yet for the luckier Milanese, the time just before the First World War was one of bourgeois happiness, sweet Puccini operas, the first motor cars, and blooming 'Liberty'-style architecture.

1919–45: Mussolini and the War

The war changed everything. In 1919, Milan saw the birth of another movement, Fascism. **Mussolini** founded his newspaper, the *Popolo d'Italia*, and organized bands of *squadre*,

1796–1919

Casa del Manzoni, museum and home of 18th-century writer Alessandro Manzoni, p.77
Corso Sempione, commissioned by Napoleon as part of the Simplon Pass, p.115
Galleria Vittorio Emanuele II, built in 1878, once the world's largest glass arcade, p.73
Museo del Risorgimento, dedicated to the history of Italian Unification, p.87
Villa Reale, once Napoleon's residence, p.91

toughs who terrorized unions and leftist parties. The upper classes got on well enough with the Fascists, especially during the boom of the 1920s, when big Milanese firms like Montecatini-Edison and Pirelli came into prominence. A vast urban redevelopment scheme in the 1930s left much of old Milan a memory and buried its canals to create streets for cars. Massive projects such as the train station and law courts exuded the power of the corporate state; but this was also the time when Milan hosted its first Triennale exhibition (1933) dedicated to its new core interests in indus-trial production, craftsmanship and design.

In the **Second World War**, as an industrial city, Milan suffered heavily from Allied bomb-ings after the capture of Sicily in July 1943. After Italy signed an armistice with the Allies in September 1943, the German army moved in massively to take control of northern Italy. They established a puppet government at Salò on Lake Garda, and re-installed Mussolini as its figurehead. As the war dragged on for another year and a half, Italy finally gave itself something to be proud of: a determined, resourceful **Resistance** that established free zones in many areas of Lombardy and other regions, and harassed the Germans with sabotage and strikes. The *partigiani* caught Mussolini in April 1945, while he was trying to escape to Switzerland; after shooting him and his mistress, they hanged both upside down from the roof of a petrol station in the Piazzale Loreto in Milan, where the Germans had shot a number of civilians a week before.

Post-war Milan

With a heavy dose of Marshall Plan aid and some intelligent government planning, Milan helped lead the way for the 'economic miracle' of the 1950s, drawing in still more thousands of migrants from the south. Meaningful politics almost ceased to exist, as the nation was run in a constantly renegotiated deal between the Christian Democrats and smaller parties, but Lombard

1919–the Present
Civico Museo di Storia Contemporanea, for Italian history between 1914 and 1945, p.91
Palazzo di Giustizia, Fascist-era courts of justice, which also held the trials for Milan's 'Clean Hands' investigation, p.100
Pirellone, Gio Ponti-designed skyscraper, now headquarters for Lombardy's regional government, p.94
Quadrilatero d'Oro, the grid of streets which is the jewel of post-war Milan's claim as fashion capital of Italy, p.90
Stazione Centrale, another symbol of Mussolini's Fascist visions of grandeur, p.94
Tempio della Vittoria, First World War memorial, p.121

industry surged ahead, creating around Milan a remarkably diverse economy of over 60,000 concerns, from multinational giants like Olivetti to the small, creative, often family-run firms that are the model of what has been called 'Italian capitalism'. Milan's most glamorous industry, fashion, began to move to the city from Florence around 1968, owing to the lack of a good airport in the latter. The climax of the boom came in 1987, when it was announced that Italy had surpassed Britain to become the world's fifth largest economy; 'Il Sorpasso', as Italians called it, was a great source of national pride – even though it was later discovered that government economists fiddled the figures.

Yet with some 8,500,000 people, Milan's region Lombardy is still the richest and most populous region of Italy; it produces a quarter of the gross national product and a third of Italy's exports. The average income is twice that of the south, and higher than any region of Britain or France. On Milan's frantic stock market, the number of shares traded in a day occasionally exceeds New York's. Along with prosperity has come a number of serious worries: a big increase in corruption and crime, unchained suburban sprawl and pollution, in the air and in Europe's filthiest river, the Po. Some 250,000 immigrants from southern Italy and Sicily have moved to Milan since the war, and the inability of

Timeline

222 BC	Celtic *Mediolanum* (Milan) comes under Roman rule.
AD 284	Diocletian divides Roman Empire in two; Milan becomes most important city in West, pop. 100,000.
313	Edict of Milan: Constantine makes Christianity the religion of the empire.
374–97	St Ambrose, Bishop of Milan.
539	Goths slaughter most of male Milanese.
572	Lombards overrun most of Italy, and make Pavia their capital.
603	Pope Gregory the Great converts Queen Theodolinda and the Lombards to orthodox Christianity.
799	Charlemagne defeats Lombard King Desiderius. Repudiates wife (Desiderius' daughter), and is crowned King of Italy at Pavia.
1024	Bishop Heribert founds Italy's first *comune* in Milan.
1127	Como destroyed by Milanese, rebuilt by Barbarossa.
1154	Milan sacked by Barbarossa.
1158–61	Barbarossa does it again.
1158	Milan obliterates rival Lodi; Lodi rebuilt by Barbarossa.
1183	Treaty of Constance recognizes independence of Lombard cities.
1252	Inquisitor St Peter Martyr axed in the head.
1277	The Visconti overthrow the Torriani to become *signori* of Milan.
1335	Como becomes fief of Milan.
1347–8	The Black Death wipes out a third of all Italians.
1386	Gian Galeazzo Visconti begins Milan's Duomo.
1402	Gian Galeazzo Visconti dies of plague.
1441	Bianca Visconti weds Francesco Sforza; Cremona is her dowry.
1447–50	Ambrosian republic – Milan's brief attempt at democracy.
1450	Francesco Sforza made Duke of Milan.
1494	Wars of Italy begin with French invasion led by Charles VIII.
1495	Battle of Fornovo; Leonardo begins the *Last Supper*.
1500	Duke of Milan, Lodovico il Moro, captured by French at Novara.
1525	Battle of Pavia; Spaniards capture French King Francis I.
1527–93	Milan's Giuseppe Arcimboldo, the first Surrealist.
1538–84	St Charles Borromeo, Archbishop of Milan.
1559	Château-Cambrésis Treaty confirms Spanish control of Italy.

many of them to adapt and get ahead, largely thanks to the bigotry of the Lombards, fuels a host of social problems.

The Milanese believe their city is the real capital of Italy – because it pays the bills. But, following its old traditions, the city has remained traditionally indifferent to politics and stolidly unproductive in the arts. Milan can offer fashion and industrial design – both of course highly profitable; it is the nation's publishing centre, and probably its art centre, with more galleries than anywhere else. Endlessly creative in business, it has so far had little else to offer the world.

In politics, at least, the indifference may be gone forever. The lid blew off Italy's cosily rotten political system and its Byzantine web of bribery and kickback in 1992 in Milan.

It will make a good film some day – no doubt somebody's already working on the screenplay. **Antonio di Pietro** was a poor boy from the most obscure region of Italy, the Molise. He worked in electronics while studying law at night in Milan, and became a judge in the early 1980s. The electronics background gave him a thorough knowledge of computers, and he used them skilfully to pile up and collate evidence and connections between cases. He first made a name for

1630	Plague in Milan (described by Manzoni in *I Promessi Sposi*).	1925	Mussolini makes Italy a Fascist dictatorship.
1700–13	War of the Spanish Succession.	1940	Italy enters Second World War.
1713	Austrians pick up Milan.	1943	Mussolini deposed; rescued
1745	Alessandro Volta, the physicist, born in Como.		by Germans to found puppet government of Salò; Milan burns
1778	La Scala inaugurated.		for days in air raids.
1785	Alessandro Manzoni, author of *I Promessi Sposi*, born in Lecco.	1945	Mussolini tries to flee to Switzerland but is executed by
1796	Napoleon enters Italy, defeats Austrians at Lodi, makes Milan capital of his Cisalpine Republic.	1946	*partigiani* at Lake Como. National referendum makes Italy a republic; Umberto II
1805	Napoleon crowns himself with Iron Crown of Italy in Duomo.	1956	exiled in Portugal. Italy becomes a charter member
1814	Overthrow of French rule.		in the Common Market.
1848	Revolutions across Italy; Austrians defeat Piedmont at war.	1978	Prime Minister Aldo Moro is kidnapped and killed by the Brigate Rosse.
1849	Restoration of autocratic rule.	1990	Emergence of Umberto Bossi's
1859–60	Piedmont, with the help of Napoleon III, annexes Lombardy at battle of Solferino.	1992	separatist Lombard League. The arrest of Mario Chiesa starts the 'Clean Hands' investigation.
1870	Italian troops enter Rome; unification completed and Rome becomes capital.	1994	Berlusconi's Forza Italia party wins the elections; he is prime minister for seven months.
1871	Mont Cenis (Fréjus) railway tunnel opened between France and Italy.	2000	Italy is flooded with pilgrims for the Jubilee year. Craxi dies in exile in Tunisia.
1900	King Umberto I assassinated by anarchist.	2001	Back comes Berlusconi.
1901	Verdi dies in Milan.	2002	Berlusconi faces trial on charges
1902–7	Period of industrial strikes.		of corruption; ex-Prime Minister
1915	Italy enters First World War.		Giulio Andreotti found guilty of the murder of a journalist.

himself in 1987, breaking open bribe scandals in the vehicle licence bureau and city bus company. In 1992 a divorced woman wrote him a letter complaining of how her ex-husband, an official in a city old age hospice, was driving around in a new Alfa and wearing silk suits while claiming he couldn't afford her alimony. That man was the now famous Mario Chiesa, a hapless grafter and Socialist party hack who had been skimming off 100,000 *lire* from undertakers for every corpse they took out of the place. He was caught, and he squealed, revealing a wealth of interesting information about similar shady deals all over Milan.

One thing led to another – to put it mildly. Even di Pietro was amazed at how information on one racket tied in inevitably with others, each one bigger than the last in what became known as **Tangentopoli**, or 'Bribe City', as hundreds of leading politicians and business magnates were convicted in the subsequent *Mani Pulite* ('Clean Hands') investigation. One of the country's most respected business leaders, Raul Gardini, committed suicide in his cell. The Christian Democrat and Socialist parties were utterly annihilated and the face of Italy's politics changed forever.

There are other spoons busily stirring the pot as well. Even before *Tangentopoli*, a new Lombard League, or Lega Lombarda, led by the noisy yet enigmatic **Umberto Bossi** (the only Italian political figure to dress badly since the time of King Aistulf), made its breakthrough in the 1990 elections, and became the leading party of the region in 1992. On most issues the Lega's position can change by the hour, but its basic tenet of federalism, to cut out the voracious politicians and bureaucrats in Rome and allow the wealthy north to keep more of its profits for itself, has understandably struck a deep chord in the Lombard soul; other 'leagues' emerged in other northern regions, uniting in 1994 as the Lega Nord. In September 1996, Bossi attracted a lot of media attention by declaring the north (as far south as Umbria and the Marches) the independent Republic of Padania, accompanied by a three-day rally and march down the Po to Venice. The whole affair turned into a badly staged comedy – arguments about crowd counts, tiffs with journalists (Bossi and the media hate each other's guts), rumblings about just what might happen if Bossi's promised Padania militia turned out to be more than hot air. These days the Lega concentrates mainly on plain old xenophobia.

That leaves Milan's other gift to Italian politics, **Silvio Berlusconi**, in some ways the essence of Milan distilled into a single individual, the self-made man (self-made as a property speculator and developer of the suburb Milano 2, with the help of his connections, notably to the late, disgraced Socialist kingpin Bettino Craxi). A cruise ship singer in the 1960s, Berlusconi's empire now includes half of Italy's television stations, the AC Milano football club (and several other sports teams), the Mediolanum bank, Italy's largest publishing house Mondadori (and a few others), the leading daily newspaper *Il Giornale* and the best-selling news magazine *Panorama*, a department-store chain and a political party, **Forza Italia**, created in 1994.

Thanks to the political vacuum on the right, Forza Italia exploded on the scene by winning the elections in 1994, only to rule in an uncomfortable and ultimately untenable coalition with the Lega and the neo-Fascist Alianza Nazionale. Berlusconi put on a not entirely convincing and occasionally shrill show as prime minister for a season.

His party was succeeded by a centre-left coalition, which, before collapsing, managed to squeak Italy into Euroland in 1999. Two further coalitions took power before the May 2001 elections, which fell resoundingly to Berlusconi's Forza Italia, with 30 per cent of the vote, to become Italy's dominant political party, in a coalition Berlusconi calls the **Case della Libertà** (Houses of Freedom). In reality, it is a triumvirate with post-Facist Fini and xenophobe Bossi. Without any meaningful opposition in parliament or in the media, Berlusconi seems on track to create what Nobel-prize winner Dario Fo has called a 'new Fascism'.

Only a few years ago, no journalist or author ever dared to mention some of the things about Italy that everyone knew – say, the close alliance between the Christian Democrats and the Mafia. Nowadays, however, the country's justice system is looking very closely into how Berlusconi and his allies came by all these prizes, and is in the process of putting the prime minister himself on trial for corruption.

Yet Berlusconi continues on despite the scrutiny, even in the face of political ally and former Italian premier **Giulio Andreotti**'s recent 24-year sentence for conspiracy to commit murder. And in true megalomaniac-style, Berlusconi has begun to wage war on what he calls Italy's 'Jacobin' magistrates, whom he claims are out to ruin his political career. In his coalition's 17 months in power, false accounting has been decriminalized (a charge that Berlusconi faced on three counts), and a law was passed enabling defendants to freeze trials while claims of a judge's bias were examined. Whether this blatant ploy to escape justice works remains to be seen.

Art and Architecture

EARLY YEARS: PRE-1000 36

ROMANESQUE AND GOTHIC 36

RENAISSANCE 37

BAROQUE 39

NEOCLASSICISM 41

20TH CENTURY 41

Although it is not usually the first stop for those seeking Italy's more artistic treasures, wealthy Milan brims with art and architecture. Because of this wealth, however, there is no one dominant 'golden age' comparable to the Renaissance in Tuscany or the Baroque in Rome. On the other hand, you'll find examples of art from all periods, and from nearly every school – for what the Milanese didn't make, they had the money and taste to buy.

Early Years: Pre-1000

Most of the little that remains of Celtic-Roman Mediolanum is safely housed in the **Museo Archeologico**, which has an interesting model of what the city looked like back then. The early Christian period (when Milan was still the capital of the Western Empire) has left some rare works; all of these are worth seeking out – especially the beautiful 5th-century mosaics in the chapels in Sant'Ambrogio and **San Lorenzo Maggiore**, which were probably the work of itinerant Greek-trained artists.

The population in Lombard times was certainly not without talent; see the superb 8th-century gold and silver altarpiece in Sant'Ambrogio, by one of the earliest Lombard artists to leave his name behind, Master Wolvinus; and the treasury of 6th-century Lombard Queen Theodolinda in Monza is not to be missed. The key work of this age is Milan's **Sant'Ambrogio**, founded by the saint in the 4th century and rebuilt in its final form, more or less, in the 880s, in a design that would become the prototype of the Lombard Romanesque, 'the first Romanesque' in Europe.

The chief ingredients – some borrowed from Byzantine Ravenna (the main artistic inspiration in the north at this time) are all there: the broad, triangular façade, the decorative rows of blind arches, known as 'Lombard arcading', the rich decoration of the apse, the passages under exterior porticoes; and a rib-vaulted interior, with the presbytery raised over the crypt, and aisles delimited by arches (in some churches supporting internal galleries).

Whatever their lack of social graces early on, the Lombard kings and dukes respected and protected builders, and granted them many privileges. As early as 643, king Rotharis is recorded favouring the *magistri comacini* – the soon-to-be-famous master builders, presumably headquartered around Lake Como, who, in spite of all the invasions, had remembered Roman techniques of building in stone and brick.

Yet their building styles were quite distinct from the Romans. The latter built in long flat bricks or square stones to reinforce walls made of rubble infill covered with concrete: the Lombard masons built more simply, with higher-quality Byzantine brick, and cut stone without the rubble. When their thin walls became too high, they devised a variety of buttresses to keep them standing.

Romanesque and Gothic (11th–14th Centuries)

In many ways, the Romanesque was the most vigorous phase in Italian art history, when the power of the artist was almost that of a magician. Lombardy shone in particular, with its roving schools of builders and sculptors (the Maestri Comaschi and Maestri Campionesi) from Lakes Como and Lugano.

Prime examples of Lombard Romanesque, based on Sant'Ambrogio, are the cathedrals of Cremona and Monza, Sant'Abbondio in Como, and San Michele Maggiore and San Pietro in Ciel d'Oro in Pavia. Gabled porches supported by crusty lions (usually having a human for lunch) or hunchbacked telamones were a common fixture, even into the 14th century. Milan also has a classic brick Romanesque town hall in its **Palazzo della Ragione** (1233), with an arcade on the ground floor, where the militia could be rallied if necessary, supporting the meeting hall of the leaders of the medieval *comune*.

The Lombard Romanesque style ultimately derived from the 5th-century Palace of Theodoric in Ravenna; Como's Broletto is another beautifully preserved example.

Early Lombard sculpture is vivid and lively, and the best place to find it is in **Pavia**, the old capital of the Lombards. The frieze on the façade of San Michele Maggiore is worn, but its eroded figures still hint of an almost barbaric energy. Pavia also has three surviving tower houses – the 'skyscrapers' that characterized medieval Italian cities, built by the nobles when the *comunes* compelled them to live within the walls of the densely packed cities. Unfortunately, Milan's tower houses have all vanished without a trace. In fact, Milan also had an early school of painting, but thanks to Frederick Barbarossa's thorough razing of the city in 1160, nothing of this has survived.

Medieval Lombard sculpture remained solid and conservative – the tomb of Ottone Visconti (d. 1295) is a prime example – until the rather elusive Tuscan Giovanni de Balduccio and his workshop arrived in Milan to sculpt the *Arca di San Pietro Martire* (1339) in the church of **Sant'Eustorgio**. It was a revolution in its day, and inspired the *Arca di Sant'Agostino* in Pavia's San Pietro in Ciel d'Oro, although the result is somewhat busier and less elegant. Giovanni de Balduccio's most important Lombard follower was Bonino da Campione, author of the *Monument to Bernabò Visconti*, now in the Castello Sforzesco – he later went on to sculpt similar equestrian monuments for the Scaligers in Verona.

The last two decades of the century were the high water mark of medieval Milan's power, wealth and influence under its great proto-Renaissance *signore*, Gian Galeazzo Visconti, whose empire stretched into the Veneto and the borders of Tuscany. The buildings he commissioned show the scale of his ambition, including the enormous Castello Viconteo (1360) in Pavia and extraordinary, spire-forested Duomo of Milan, begun in 1386.

The Lombards, like other Italians, had such a strong local building tradition that Gothic ideas imported from France never made much of an impression, and caught on only briefly – but just long enough to reach a singular climax and size in this cathedral. To crown it all off, Gian Galeazzo began the magnificent Certosa di Pavia in 1396 to be his dynasty's Pantheon, but left the Renaissance to complete it (*see* below). Other Gothic works arround Milan are rare, but the transition from pointy, vertical Gothic to the more rounded, classical proportions of the Renaissance reads like a textbook in the Duomo in Como, built half in one style, and half in the other.

The last years of the 14th century saw Lombardy go to the top of the class in a lesser known field – the illumination of manuscripts, what the French called the *ouvraige de Lombardie*; again the patrons were the Visconti. It's a courtly art anticipating the **International Gothic**, especially in the works of the wonderful Giovanni dei Grassi, an acute observor of animals (bits survive in the Bibilioteca Trivulziani, but most of his manuscripts have gone to Paris or Florence). He also worked inside the Duomo, designing decorative schemes (that were later compromised) for the French and German sculptors who left it as one of Italy's greatest hordes of Gothic sculpture, although little of it is exceptional. The last word in **Lombard Gothic** is to be found in the delicately worked *Voghera Monstrance* (1406), now in the Castello Sforzesco.

Renaissance (15th–16th Centuries)

The fresh perspectives, technical advances and discovery of the individual that epitomize the Renaissance were born in *quattrocento* Florence and spread to the rest of Italy at varying speeds. The Sforza dukes, who had close ties with the Medici, played a major role in bringing these new ideas relatively early to Milan.

Finding Milan's Art

Pre-1000

Duomo, in Monza, for the 6th-century Treasure of Queen Theodolinda, p.136

San Lorenzo Maggiore (alle Colonne), for 5th-century mosaics in the chapel, p.108

Sant'Ambrogio, for 8th-century gold and silver altarpiece by Master Wolvinus, and 5th-century mosaics in the chapel, p.119

Romanesque and Gothic

Castello Sforzesco for the *Monument to Bernabò Visconti*, by Bonino da Campione, p.114

San Michele Maggiore, in Pavia, for Early Lombard sculpture on the façade, p.146

San Pietro in Ciel d'Oro, in Pavia, for the *Arca di Sant'Agostino* by the Tuscan Giovanni de Balduccio, p.146

Sant'Eustorgio, for the *Arca di San Pietro Martire* by the Balduccio and his workshop, p.109

Renaissance and Baroque

Ambrosiana, for works by Milanese painter, Michelangelo Merisi da Caravaggio, p.78

Casa degli Omenoni, home of Tuscan Mannerist sculptor Leone Leoni, p.77

Castello Sforzesco, for the Lombard Gothic illuminated manuscript *Voghera Monstrance*,

and one masterpiece by Giuseppe Arcimboldo, p.114

Colleoni Chapel, in Bergamo, designed by Giovanni Antonio Amadeo of Pavia, p.144

Duomo, for Leone Leoni's tomb of Il Medeghino, p.70

Pinacoteca di Brera, for its unusual 'three masters' painting of *SS. Rufina and Seconda*, by Crespi (called Cerano), Mazzucchelli (called Morazzone) and Procaccini, and for more works by Caravaggio and Bernardino Luini, p.84

San Maurizio, for the paintings of Bernardino Luini, p.119

Santa Maria delle Grazie, for Leonardo da Vinci's *Last Supper*, p.117

Sant'Eustorgio, for paintings by Vincenzo Foppa, p.109

Neoclassicism and the 20th Century

Pinacoteca di Brera, for works by the Milanese Futurists: Boccioni, Carrà, Rossolo and Severini, p.84

Villa Reale and the **Galleria d'Arte Moderna**, for Mariano Marini's bronzes, works by the romantic-era Lombard artists nicknamed the *Scapigliati* ('Wild-haired ones'), and post-Futurist work and exhibitions, p.91

In 1451, Francesco Sforza hired the Florentine architect **Filarete** to design the city's Ospedale Maggiore, modelled on Brunelleschi's elegant Ospedale degli Innocenti in Florence – only in ducal Milan, he had the money to build on a scale that had been impossible in republican Florence. While in Milan, Filarete wrote his famous illustrated *Trattato d'architettura* condemning Lombard Gothic lavishness as a 'barbarous modern style', but few hospitals were as ornate as this one in Milan – local traditions would not be denied.

The average Milanese did have a chance to see the **Tuscan** in its purest form in Sant'Eustorgio's Cappella Portinari (built for

an agent of the Medici bank), but they didn't care to repeat the experience, making it the only example of this style in Milan.

Francesco's son Lodovico il Moro also spent lavishly on building, finishing the unique Romanesque-Gothic-Renaissance Certosa di Pavia, and inviting architect and painter **Donato Bramante** of Urbino (d. 1514) to Milan, where he designed the amazing, illusionistic 1m-deep apse of Santa Maria presso San Satiro, the cloisters of Sant'Ambrogio, and much of Santa Maria delle Grazie before going on to Rome after Lodovico was overthrown.

In painting, Gothic traditions lingered in the north well after the Tuscan revolution. **Vincenzo Foppa** (d. 1515), a pupil of Pisanello, was the first big name of the Milanese Renaissance school, marked from the beginning by subdued colours and a sombre tonality, which sometimes bordered on the monochrome. Foppa was especially known for his monumental style, as seen in Sant'Eustorgio. Bramante also left Milan most of his few extant paintings: his style of painting and architecture were followed so closely by Milanese local Bartolomeo Suardi (1465–1530), that Suardi became known as little Bramante, or *Bramantino*.

Lodovico also sponsored the Milanese sojourns of Leonardo da Vinci, Castiglione and a host of other artists and writers. Leonardo's *Last Supper* in the refectory of Santa Maria delle Grazie, and the smoky shading (*sfumato*) he used so adroitly to express psychological depth, so dazzled the local painters that the next generation lay heavily under his spell, often with heavy-handed results.

The most talented of his many followers (who included Boltraffio, Giampietrino, Giovanni Ambrogio de Predis, Cesare da Sesto, Andrea Solario, Salaino and Marco d'Oggiono) was **Bernardino Luini** (d. 1532), who was successful probably because he never really attempted to imitate anything more than Leonardo's famous half smiles; some of his greatest works are in the church of San Maurizio and in the Brera Gallery. Even sculptors were inspired by Leonardo, among them **Cristoforo Solari** (1439–1525), whose tombs of Lodovico and Beatrice d'Este are among the many treasures at the Certosa di Pavia.

Lombardy's traditional art of sculpture reached its florid epitome in the Renaissance in the person of Giovanni Antonio Amadeo of Pavia (d. 1522), best known for the extraordinary ornate façade of the Certosa di Pavia and for the design of the Colleoni Chapel in Bergamo. Even more prolific than Amadeo was his follower **Bergognone** (d. 1530s), sculptor and painter, whose calm, undramatic style is often enhanced by lovely landscape backgrounds (especially in the *Incoronata* in Lodi).

Despite the upheaval, art carried on even after Milan lost its independence to France and then Spain. A leading figure in the city was the Tuscan Mannerist sculptor Leone Leoni, who spent much of his career in the employ of Emperor Charles V and left Milan his curious house, the **Casa degli Omenoni**, and the fine tomb of Il Medeghino in the Duomo. Lombardy also produced two extraordinary native geniuses: Arcimboldo and Caravaggio.

Giuseppe Arcimboldo (d. 1593) of Milan painted portraits made up entirely of seafood, vegetables or flowers, which anticipate the Surrealists and the collages of *objets trouvés*. Arcimboldo became the court painter to the Habsburgs in Prague but left one of his masterpieces in Milan, in the Castello Sforzesco.

More immediately influential, not only in Italy but throughout 17th-century Europe, was **Michelangelo Merisi da Caravaggio** (1573–1610) who, despite a headlong trajectory through life (perhaps the first true Bohemian – anarchic, rebellious and homosexual, he murdered a man over a tennis game, was thrown out of Malta by the Knights, and was almost killed in Naples before dying on a Tuscan beach), left behind paintings of unique dramatic power.

His use of light, of foreshortening, and of simple country people as models in major religious subjects were often copied but never equalled. Although most of his paintings are in Rome, where he moved in 1590, some of his best known works are in Milan (in the Ambrosiana and the Pinacoteca di Brera).

Baroque (17th–18th Centuries)

In Milan, these two centuries were in general more austere than in Rome or Turin, in part thanks to its archbishop Charles Borromeo, who wrote a book of guidelines

Finding Milan's Architecture

Pre-1000

Museo Archeologico, for a model of Roman Mediolanum, p.119

Sant'Ambrogio, the prototype of the Lombard Romanesque, p.119

Romanesque and Gothic

Broletto, in Como, for an example of Lombard Romanesque, p.140

Castello Viconteo, in Pavia, a Visconti commission, p.146

Duomo, in Pavia, another Visconti commission, p.145

Palazzo della Ragione, Milan's classic brick Romanesque town hall, p.74

Tower houses, in Pavia, for Lombardy's remaining medieval high-rises, p.145

Renaissance and Baroque

Ambrosiana, the façade designed by Fabio Mangone, p.78

Ca' Grande, designed by Filarete, p.98

Duomo, in Como, for an example of Gothic-Renaissance, p.140

San Guiseppe, for its two centralized domes, designed by Francesco Maria Ricchino, p.77

Sant'Alessandro, designed by Lorenzo Binago, p.102

Sant'Ambrogio, the cloisters designed by Donato Bramante, p.119

Sant'Eustorgio, for its Tuscan-style Cappella Portinari, p.109

Santa Maria delle Grazie, much of it designed by Donato Bramante, p.116

Santa Maria presso San Satiro, the apse designed by Donato Bramante, p.79

Seminario Arcivescovile, for its concave palace façades, p.93

Neoclassicism and the 20th Century

Acquario Civico, for an example of Art Nouveau, p.115

Casa Terragni, in Como, an example of post-war architecture, p.140

Galleria Vittorio Emanuele II, a 19th-century feat of engineering, p.73

La Scala, designed by Giuseppe Piermarini, p.75

Palazzo della Giustizia, post-war Fascist design, p.100

Pirelli Tower, or Pirellone, designed by Gio Ponti, p.94

Stazione Centrale, for an example of pre-war Fascist design, p.94

Torre Velasca, for its debatable post-war aesthetics, p.99

Triennale, by Giovanni Muzio, p.115

---

for Counter-Reformation architects. **Fabio Mangone** (d. 1629) epitomized this new austerity (the façade of the Ambrosiana, Santa Maria Podone); the more interesting Lorenzo Binago (d. 1629) designed Sant'Alessandro, with its innovative combination of two centralized domed areas, creating new scope for imaginative longitudinal designs.

The most important Baroque architect in Milan was **Francesco Maria Ricchino** (d. 1658), who in his San Giuseppe created a style of crossings and domes that enjoyed tremendous success all across Italy. Other works include the Palazzo di Brera (now the Pinacoteca di Brera), and the Collegio Elvetico (now the Archivo di Stato), with Ricchino's then-revolutionary concave palace façade.

Milan's best painters of the age all worked in the early 17th century – the excellent but short-lived Daniele Crespi (d. 1630), the mystic and somewhat cloying Giovanni Battista Crespi, called *Cerano* (d. 1632) and the fresco master of Lombardy's sanctuaries, Pier Francesco Mazzucchelli, called *Morazzone* (d. 1626). The latter two, along with the more workmanlike Giulio Cesare Procaccini, teamed up to paint the Pinacoteca di Brera's unusual 'three masters' painting of *SS. Rufina and Seconda*.

After 1630, when Milan and its artists were devastated by plague, the torch of Lombard painting was taken up in the provinces, particularly in Bergamo and Brescia.

Neoclassicism (Late 18th–19th Centuries)

Baroque proved to be a hard act to follow. The French, in the mid-18th century, were the first to react against its excesses, and when it came time to rebuild the centre of Milan under the Austrians, Milan got not only its Public Gardens but a neoclassical core, much of it built by the capable **Giuseppe Piermarini**; his La Scala opera house soon became the yardstick by which all others were measured.

The period also sprinkled the shores of the lakes with superb private **villas**: one, the Villa Carlotta, on the banks of Lake Como, is a triumph of the style, with statues by the master of the age, Antonio Canova, and his meticulous follower Thorvaldsen. Napoleon, too, left his mark in the Parisian-style urban planning of Milan's West End, and in the pastiche of the Duomo façade.

The next century in Milan brought 19th-century triumph of engineering **Galleria Vittorio Emanuele II** in Milan, as well as a group of romantic-era Lombard artists, nicknamed the *Scapigliati* ('Wild-haired ones'), whose paintings enliven the walls of Milan's Galleria d'Arte Moderna.

20th Century

Lo Stilo Liberty is the Italian name for **Art Nouveau**, the short-lived artistic and architectural movement that flourished in many European countries around the turn of the century. It refers, curiously, to Liberty's, the London shop whose William Morris-influenced, flower-patterned fabrics and ceramics were some of the first articles in the style imported into Italy, and which became enormously popular at the time. It was never as important in Italy as its equivalents became in France, Austria or Catalunya – nor was it usually as extravagant but it was in vogue for a time among the newly wealthy Milanese middle classes,

especially in their hotels and villas around the lakes, and in their residences along Corso Venezia. One of the most important Liberty architects was Giuseppe Sommaruga (1867–1917), whose achievements include the **Palazzo Castiglione** on Corso Venezia, characterized by richly ornamental lines and an uninhibited use of space.

But Liberty's pretty, bourgeoise charm and the whole patrimony of Italian art only infuriated the young **Futurists**, beginning with Umberto Boccioni, whose *Brawl in the Milan Galleria* (1909), which showed furious movement, signalled a big break with the past. By the next year, Boccioni, along with Carlo Carrà, Luigi Rossolo and Gino Severini were propogating the first *Futurist Manifesto*, and doing all they could to speed Italy into the modern age. They first used the Neo-Impressionist mode, then adapted the more formal prismatic breakdown of Cubism (*see* Pinacoteca di Brera, p.84).

This same urge to race out of the past also created modern Italy's most coherent and consistent sense of design, under the **Fascists**, at a time when the rest of Europe was suffering a bad case of architectural doldrums. The Fascists took the lead in promoting local craftsmanship and industrial design, first in 1923, with the International Exposition of Decorative Arts at Monza's Villa Reale, and eventually with the Triennale in Milan, one of the city's better buildings from the era, by Giovanni Muzio.

The period left Milan with a mixed bag, however, including two ripe examples of big and bombastic (the Stazione Centrale – although it was designed before the war – and the post-war Palazzo della Giustizia). Remarkable exceptions to the 'big is better' rule are the visionary works of Giuseppe Terragni (Casa Terragni, in Como), and Gio Ponti's Montecatini building and Domus houses in Milan.

However uneven the Fascist contribution, modern Italian architects have yet to match it, few ever rising above saleable and boring modernism (Milan's 1959 **Pirelli Building** by

Gio Ponti and Pier Luigi Nervi is the great exception, *see* p.94), and the technically daring if not as aesthetically satisfying Torre Velasca (1958) by Enrico Peressutti and Ernesto Nathan Rogers.

The forementioned museums in Milan have fairly extensive and changing collections of contemporary art. Of these, the bronzes of **Mariano Marini** in the Galleria d'Arte Moderna in Milan deserves special mention.

Most artistic talent these days is sublimated into film, or the *shibboleth* of Italian design – clothes, sports cars, furniture – and even these consumer beauties are often more packaging than content. As if to emphasize this point, Milan's smaller modern art galleries, though growing in number, tend to walk hand-in-hand with the city's ever-present fashion industry, often providing little more than an extension of the fashion catwalk.

Travel

GETTING THERE 44
By Air 44
By Train 46
By Coach 47
By Car 47

TOUR OPERATORS 48

ENTRY FORMALITIES 49

ARRIVAL 49

GETTING AROUND 50
By Metro 50
By Bus and Tram 50
By Car 51
By Bicycle 51
By Taxi 51
By Train 52
By Coach 52
Guided Tours 52

GETTING THERE

By Air

Inter-continental flights use Malpensa Airport, about 50km northwest of the city; domestic and European flights use Linate Airport about 7km east, or Orio al Serio Airport, Bergamo, 50km northeast. In winter, flights are frequently diverted to Malpensa due to fog. Between late October and early March, try to book a flight that will arrive between 10am and 3pm; this is the window of time when the fog lifts, reducing the chances of diversion.

Children travel for greatly reduced fares (10% for under-twos on an adult's lap; 33% discount for children aged 2–11). Students with suitable ID also receive handsome discounts. Special fares booked in advance, however (APEX and so on), may save you as much as 50% of the cost. The real challenge is not so much finding a flight, but finding a bargain, especially in the high season (mid-May to mid-September); the trick is to start hunting well in advance, or, if you're a gambler, at the last moment. A flight is often cheaper if you can organize to stay over a Saturday night.

From the UK

Scheduled Flights

The advantage of shelling out for a full scheduled fare is that few restrictions are imposed on when you travel or how long you stay. To sweeten the deal, promotional perks like car rental, discounts on domestic flights and accommodation, tours, etc. may also be included. Besides London, you can also fly from Birmingham or Manchester. Typical fares to Milan on British Airways or Alitalia are currently around £150–300 return in high seas on. Booking restrictions apply: for special fares, you may have to stay a Saturday night abroad (although British Airways recently lifted this restriction), and ticket changes may involve high penalties. Direct scheduled flights to Milan are operated by:

Flights on the Internet

The best place to start looking for flights is the web – just about everyone has a site where you can compare prices (*see also* the airlines listed in the main text), and booking online usually confers a 10–20% discount.

In the UK and Ireland

w *www.airtickets.co.uk*
w *www.cheapflights.com*
w *www.flightcentre.co.uk*
w *www.lastminute.com*
w *www.skydeals.co.uk*
w *www.sky-tours.co.uk*
w *www.thomascook.co.uk*
w *www.trailfinders.com*
w *www.travelocity.com*
w *www.travelselect.com*

In the USA

w *www.air-fare.com*
w *www.airhitch.org*
w *www.expedia.com*
w *www.flights.com*
w *www.orbitz.com*
w *www.priceline.com*
w *www.travellersweb.ws*
w *www.travelocity.com*
w *www.smarterliving.com*

In Canada

w *www.flightcentre.ca*
w *www.lastminuteclub.com*
w *www.newfrontiers.com*

Alitalia, t 0870 544 8259, w *www.alitalia.co.uk*.
British Airways, t 0845 773 3377, w *www.britishairways.com*.

Low-cost Airlines

The cheap, no-frills, low-cost carriers such as easyJet and Ryanair can offer astonishingly low prices to airports in and near Milan if you book well in advance (usually 2 month in peak travel times). You can book directly over the Internet and a discount is usually offered if you do so. Prices go up the closer you get to your leaving date; fares booked last minute are, in fact, often not much cheaper than those of the major carriers. Each ticket has various conditions attached, for example whether you can get a refund or whether the date of the flight can be changed. All services may be less frequent in the winter. Prices quoted are usually for one-way fares, and may not include airport tax, handling fee for flights booked by credit card and an extra charge for flights not booked over the Internet.

bmibaby *(British Midland offshoot)*, **t** *0870 264 2229,* **w** *www.flybmi.co.uk.* Flies once daily from the East Midlands to Bergamo from £80 return.

easyJet, t *08706 000 000,* **w** *www.easyjet. com.* One flight a day from London Stansted to Linate, from about £65 return.

Ryanair, t *08701 569 569,* **w** *www. ryanair.com.* Special offers on the Internet can be incredibly cheap, as low as £9.99 one-way, inclusive of taxes. Ryanair flies to Bergamo, five times daily from London Stansted, and twice daily from Luton (a recently opened route).

Virgin Express, t *(020) 7744 0004,* **w** *www.virgin-express.com.* Flies from Brussels to Linate from €95 return.

Travel Agencies

EBookers.com, *25 Farringdon Street, London, EC4A 4AB,* **t** *0870 010 7000,* **w** *www.ebookers.com.*

Flight Centre, *13 The Broadway, Wimbledon SW19 1RL,* **t** *08708 908 099,* **w** *www. flightcentre.co.uk.*

Trailfinders, *194 Kensington High St, London W8 6BD,* **t** *(020) 7937 1234,* **w** *www. trailfinders.com.*

Student and Youth Travel

The following travel agencies cater for students, offering special deals if you have valid ID. See also deals advertised in London's *TNT* magazine, available near Underground stations:

CTS Travel, t *(020) 7290 0620,* **w** *www. tstravel.co.uk.*

Europe Student Travel, *6 Campden St, London W8,* **t** *(020) 7727 7647.*

STA Travel, t *08701 600599,* **w** *www. statravel.co.uk.* Agents for STA travel are based at many university campuses.

> ## Airline Offices in Milan
> **Air Canada: t** *02 585 81238*
> **Aer Lingus: t** *02 760 00080*
> **Alitalia: t** *02 249 92500*
> **British Airways:** *Malpensa Airport,* **t** *02 748 666 03; Linate Airport,* **t** *02 728 2028*
> **Delta: t** *800 477 999*
> **United Airlines: t** *02 696 33707*

From Ireland
Scheduled and Low-cost Airlines

Direct flights from Ireland are from Dublin to Milan:

Aer Lingus, t *0818 365 000,* **w** *www.aer lingus.ie.* With daily connections from Dublin to Linate, from €44 one way. Also flies direct to Heathrow from Dublin from €16 one way.

Alitalia, t *(01) 677 5171.* Flies twice daily, less often out of season.

You can also fly from Dublin via London:

British Airways, *see* opposite page. Flies direct from Belfast to Heathrow.

British Midland, t *(020) 8745 7321.* For flights to Heathrow from Dublin and Belfast.

Ryanair, t *(0541) 569 569,* **w** *www.ryanair.ie.* No direct flights from Ireland to Milan, but Ryanair often has the cheapest Dublin–London fares, landing at Stansted or Luton, for onward connections to Milan.

Student and Youth Travel

If you're a student, substantial discounts may be available:

USIT, *19–21 Aston Quay, O'Connell Bridge, Dublin 2,* **t** *(01) 602 1600,* **w** *www.usitnow.ie.*

From the USA and Canada
Scheduled Flights

Summer round-trip fares from New York to Italy cost around US$1,300, from Montreal or Toronto about C$1,200–1,600. Apex or SuperApex deals are better value than scheduled fares, though you may prefer to pay extra for security, flexibility and convenience on such a long journey (9–15 hours' flying time). Beware the restrictions imposed on special fares, and plan well in advance. Obviously, low-season flights (between November and March) tend to be a great deal cheaper than peak-season ones, and mid-week fares are generally lower than at weekends. As in Britain, a host of cheap deals are advertised in the travel sections of major newspapers such as *The New York Times*, *LA Times* or Canada's *Globe & Mail*.

The following offer direct flights to Milan from a number of cities:

Air Canada, *USA and Canada*, *t 888 247 2262*, *w www. aircanada.ca*.

Alitalia, *t 800 223 5730*, *w www. alitaliausa.com*. Has the most options.

Delta, *t 800 241 4141*, *w www.delta.com*.

United Airlines, *t 800 241 6522*, *w www.united.com*.

Alternatively, take a flight to London or some other European city and change there, a far more economical option. The following fly to London (as do those listed above):

American Airlines, *t 800 433 7300*, *w www.aa.com*.

British Airways, *t 800 247 9297*, *w www.britishairways.com*.

Continental Airlines, *t 800 231 0856*, *w www.continentalairlines.com*.

Virgin Atlantic, *t 800 862 8621*, *w www.virgin.com*.

Charter, Budget and Discount Flights

For discounted flights, try the small ads in newspaper travel pages (*see* above). Travel clubs and agencies also specialize in discount fares, but may require a membership fee.

Air Brokers International: *t 800 883 3273 or t (415) 397 1383*, *w www.airbrokers.com*.

Council Travel, *205 East 42nd St, New York, NY 10017*, *t 800 2COUNCIL*, *w www. counciltravel.com*.

TFI, *34 West 32nd St, New York, NY 10001*, *t 800 745 8000 or t (212) 736 1140*.

Courier Flights

Global Courier Travel, *w www. couriertravel.org*. A search engine that finds courier flights departing from New York.

Now Voyager, *74 Varick St, Suite 307, New York, NY 10013*, *t (212) 431 1616*, *w www. nowvoyagertravel.com*.

It is also possible for North Americans to take advantage of the explosion of cheap inter-European flights, by taking a charter flight to London, and booking a London–Italy budget flight on the airline's website. This will need careful planning: you're looking at an 8hr flight followed by a 3hr journey across London and another 1½–2hr hop to Italy; it can be done, and you may be able to sleep on a night flight, but you may prefer to spend a night or two in London.

Travel Agencies

Flight Centre, *t 888 967 5331*, *w www. flightcentre.ca*. Centres throughout Canada.

Flight Center, *t 877 96753 47*, *w www. flightcenter.com*. Centres throughout the USA.

Last Minute Travel Club, *132 Brookline Av, Boston, MA 02215*, *t 800 527 8646*, *w www.lastminuteclub.com*.

New Frontiers USA *t 800 677 0720*, *w www.newfrontiers.com*.

Student and Youth Travel

Council Travel, *t 800 2COUNCIL*, *w www. counciltravel.com*.

CTS Travel, *t 877 287 6665*, *w www. ctstravelusa.com*.

STA Travel, *t 800 781 4040*, *w www. statravel.com*.

Travel Cuts, *t 866 246 9762*, *w www. travelcuts.com*.

By Train

Milan is easily accessible by rail from the UK. The journey is usually accomplished in two stages, with a change at Paris. First take the Eurostar from London Waterloo to Paris Gare du Nord (3hrs). From Paris you can either travel by day to Milan on a fast TGV (7hrs), which leaves from the Gare de Lyon; or you can travel overnight (with a couchette) on a slower train (10½hrs) from the Gare de Bercy. Allow one hour to cross Paris (by métro). High season tickets from London to Milan start at about £180 return on the TGV route, and £195 return for the overnight route; in other words, travelling by train from the UK is scarcely cheaper than flying, unless you are able to take advantage of student or youth fares (about £150 for those under 26).

Rail Europe UK, *179 Piccadilly, London W1V 0BA, t 0870 584 8848, w www.raileurope.co.uk.*

Rail Europe USA, *226 Westchester Ave, White Plains, NY 10064, t 800 438 7245, w www.raileurope.com.*

By Coach

Eurolines is the main international bus operator in Europe, with representatives in Italy and many other countries Regular services run to Milan, where they will generally arrive at the Piazza Castello. Needless to say, the journey is long (20–23 hours) and the relatively small saving in price (a return ticket from London to Milan costs about £122 or £99 for under-26s or senior citizens) makes it a masochistic choice in comparison with a discounted air fare, or even rail travel. However, if it isn't pitch-dark, you'll catch a fleeting glimpse of Mont Blanc and Turin on the way.

Eurolines/National Express, *52 Grosvenor Gardens, London SW1, t 0990 808080, w www.gobycoach.com.*

By Car

Italians are famously anarchic behind the wheel, though perhaps a smidgeon less so in the Lombardy region. Warnings, signals and general rules of the road are frequently simply ignored; a two-lane carriageway becomes an impromptu three-lane road at a moment's notice. The only way to beat the locals is to join them. All drivers, from boy racers to elderly nuns, tempt providence by overtaking at the most dangerous of bends, and no matter how fast you are hammering along the *autostrada*, plenty of other drivers, headlights a-flashing, will fly past at supersonic rates. Those used to leisurely speed limits and gentler road

manners may find the Italian interpretation of the highway code especially stressful. Note that tolls are payable on all Italian motorways.

If you are undeterred by these caveats, you may actually enjoy driving in Italy, at least away from the congested tourist centres. Signposting is generally good and roads are usually well maintained. In fact, some of the roads are feats of engineering the Romans themselves would have admired – bravura projects suspended on cliffs, crossing valleys on vast stilts, and winding up hairpins. Milan is a major motorway junction, but take care on the A4 (Milan–Turin); it is very busy and is an accident blackspot.

To bring a GB-registered car into Italy, you need a vehicle registration document, full driving licence and insurance papers. Non-EU citizens should preferably have an international driving licence which has an Italian translation incorporated. Your vehicle should display a nationality plate indicating its country of registration.

From the UK, it's the best part of 24 hours' driving time even if you stick to fast toll roads.

Eurotunnel trains (*t 0870 535 3535, w www.eurotunnel.com*) shuttle cars and their passengers through the Channel Tunnel from Folkestone to Calais on a simple drive-on-drive-off system (journey time 35mins). In off-peak months it may be possible to turn up without a reservation and take the next available service. Eurotunnel runs 24 hours a day, year round, with a service at least once an hour through the night. Standard return fares range from £170 to £350, but special offers can bring them as low as £99.

There are several options if you take your car over by sea (*see* below). Prices range from £51 return for a foot passenger to £450 and upwards return for a vehicle with two passengers in high season, but cheaper APEX fares are available if you book in advance.

Brittany Ferries, *t 0870 536 0360, w www.brittany-ferries.co.uk.* Sail from Poole to Cherbourg, Portsmouth to Caen and St-Malo, and Plymouth to Roscoff.

Hoverspeed Fast Ferries, t *0870 524 0241,* **w** *www.hoverspeed.com.* Super Seacats go from Newhaven to Dieppe (2hrs) and Dover to Calais (1hr).

P&O, t *0870 600 0600,* **w** *www.poferries. com.* Sail from Dover to Calais, and Portsmouth to Le Havre and Cherbourg.

Once on the Continent, the most scenic and hassle-free route is via the Alps, avoiding crowded Riviera roads in summer, but if you take a route through Switzerland expect to pay for the privilege (£14 or SF30 for motorway use). In winter, the passes may be closed and you will have to stick to those expensive tunnels (one-way tolls range from about €16 for a small car). You can avoid some of the driving by putting your car on a train and travelling with it overnight on a sleeper, but only as far as Nice. The service starts from Calais in the summer, and from Paris in the winter. Prices start at £250 one way, so this is scarcely a cheap option.

French Motorail, t *08702 415 415,* **w** *www.frenchmotorail.com.*

Fog and snow can make Milan a hazardous winter destination. Foreign-plated cars are currently entitled to free breakdown assistance from the ACI (Automobile Club Italiano).

Other automobile clubs offer road assistance in Italy:

AA, t *0990 500600,* in the UK.

RAC, t *0800 550055 (50p per minute),* in the UK.

AAA, t *(407) 444 4000,* in the USA.

CAA, t *(416) 221 4300,* in Canada (Toronto).

TOUR OPERATORS

In the UK

Abercrombie & Kent, *Sloane Square House, Holbein Place, London SW1W 8NS,* **t** *(020) 7730 9376.* Milan in all seasons; gardens of Lombardy.

Brompton Travel, *Brompton House, 64 Richmond Road, Kingston-upon-Thames, Surrey KT2 5EH,* **t** *(020) 8549 3334,* **f** *(020)*

8547 1236, **w** *www.bromptontravel.co.uk.* Tailor-made and opera tours.

Italian Expressions, *104 Belsize Lane, London NW3 5BB,* **t** *(020) 7435 2525,* **f** *(020) 7431 4221,* **w** *www.expressionsholidays.co.uk.* City breaks, in elegant and characterful hotels.

Italian Journeys, *216 Earls Court Road, London SW5 9QB,* **t** *(020) 7370 6002.* Specialists in package/tailored holidays to Italy, upmarket and stylish accommodations.

Italiatour, *9 Whyteleafe Business Village, Whyteleafe Hill, Surrey, CR3 0AT,* **t** *(01883) 623363,* **w** *www.italiatour.co.uk.* Milan opera and football, package tours.

JMB, *Rushwick, Worcester WR2 5SN,* **t** *(01905) 425 628,* **f** *(01905) 420219,* **w** *www. jmb-travel.co.uk.* Opera tours.

Kirker, *3 New Concordia Wharf, Mill St, London SE1 2BB,* **t** *(020) 7231 3333,* **f** *(020) 7231 4771,* **w** *www.kirkerholidays.com.* Milan breaks

Magic of Italy, *King's Place, 12–42 Wood Street, Kingston-upon-Thames, KT1 1JF,* **t** *0870 0270500,* **w** *www.magicofitaly.co.uk.* City breaks, flights with accommodation.

Martin Randall Travel, *10 Barley Mow Passage, Chiswick, London W4 4PH,* **t** *(020) 8742 3355,* **f** *(020) 8742 7766,* **w** *www. martinrandall.com.* Duchy of Milan and opera tours (guest lecturers).

Prospect Music & Art, *36 Manchester St, London W1M 5PE,* **t** *(020) 7486 5704,* **f** *(020) 7486 5863.* Opera, villas and gardens.

Travel for the Arts, *12–15 Hanger Green,* **t** *(020) 7483 4466,* **f** *(020) 8998 7965,* **w** *www. travelforthearts.com.* Custom-made Milan opera holidays.

In the USA and Canada

Abercrombie & Kent, *1520 Kensington Rd, Oak Brook, IL 60523-2141,* **t** *(630) 954 2944* or **t** *800 323 7308,* **w** *www.abercrombiekent. com.* City breaks.

CIT Tours, *15 West 44th St, New York, NY 10173,* **t** *800 CIT-TOUR,* **w** *www. cit-tours.com; (Canada) 80 Tiverton Ct, Suite 401, Markham, Ontario L3R 0GA,* **t** *800 387 0711,* **w** *www.cit-tours.com.* City breaks.

Dailey-Thorp Travel, *330 West 58th Street, New York, NY 10019, t (212) 307 1555.* Milan opera.

Italiatour, *666 5th Ave, New York, NY 10103, USA, t (800) 845 3365, in Canada, t 888 515 5245, w www.italiatour.com.* Sightseeing tours organized by Alitalia.

Travel Concepts, *307 Princeton, MA 01541, t (978) 464 0411.* Wine and food.

ENTRY FORMALITIES

Passports and Visas

EU nationals with a valid passport can enter and stay in Italy as long as they like. Citizens of the USA, Canada, Australia and New Zealand need only a valid passport to stay up to three months in Italy; this can be extended by obtaining a special visa in advance from an Italian embassy or consulate (*see* p.56). By law you should register with the police within eight days of your arrival in Italy. In practice this is done automatically for most visitors when they check in at their first hotel. Don't be alarmed if the owner of your self-catering property proposes to 'denounce' you to the police when you arrive – it's just a formality.

Customs

Since July 1999, duty-free goods have been unavailable on journeys within the European Union but this does not necessarily mean that prices have gone up, as shops at airports do not always choose to pass on the cost of the duty. It does mean that if you are travelling within the EU there is virtually no limit on how much you can buy, as long as it is for your own use. Guidelines are issued and, if they are exceeded, you may be asked to prove that you are going to consume it all. Non-EU citizens visiting the EU can buy duty free on their way home, but face restrictions on how much they can take back.

If they have been away for more than 48 hours, Americans over the age of 21 can take 1 litre of alcohol, 200 cigarettes and 100 cigars home with them. They can take $400 worth of goods duty-free, and pay 10% tax on the next $1,000 worth of goods. After that, the tax is worked out on an item-by-item basis.

For more detailed information, look at the website below or call the office and request the free booklet *Know Before You Go*.

US Customs: *PO Box 7407, Washington, DC 20044, t (202) 927 6724, w www.customs. ustreas.gov.*

ARRIVAL

The Airports

Milan has two main airports, Linate (7km from the centre) and the larger Malpensa (50km to the west), both of which receive national and international flights. As a rule, intercontinental flights use Malpensa while Linate handles most of the European and domestic traffic – but check. Charter flights may use a third airport, Orio al Serio, near Bergamo (**t** 035 326 323).

Flight information, *t 02 7485 2200, or visit w www.sea-aeroportimilano.it.*

Travel from Linate

STAM buses run between Linate and Stazione Centrale (every 30mins 5.40am–9pm; approx 20mins; €2.60). City bus no.73 also runs to Linate from Piazza San Babila (every 10mins 5.30am–2am; €0.77).

Travel from Malpensa

Malpensa's second terminal, *ovest* (west), opened in 1998, has increased the airport's capacity by half. The quickest way to reach the city centre from Malpensa is by rail shuttle to Cadorna North railway station:

Malpensa Express, *t 02 27763, every 30mins 5am–11pm; approx 40mins; €7.75, or free for Alitalia and KLM passengers.*

Air Pullman bus shuttles link Malpensa to the Stazione Centrale (t 02 5858 3185; every 20mins 4.15am–midnight; one hour; €6.70). Every hour, a bus service stops at the Trade Fair (Fiera di Milano) upon request.

There is a direct Air Pullman connection from Linate to Malpensa (hourly 6am–8pm; approx 75mins; €8.90). Beware that taxis from Malpensa to Milan cost a fortune.

Travel from Orio al Serio (Bergamo)

STAM buses link it with Milan's Stazione Centrale (t 035 318 472; departure corresponds to the timetable of regular flights; €6.70).

Arriving by Train

Milan's splendiferous main Stazione Centrale (metro lines 2 or 3), designed in the 1930s with the travelling Fascist satrap in mind, dominates the Piazza Duca d'Aosta northeast of the centre (switchboard t 147 888 08; open 7am–11pm). It handles nearly all international trains arriving in Milan.

Useful trams and buses from Centrale include tram no.1 to Piazza Scala and Nord Station, and no.33 to Stazione Garibaldi and the Cimitero Monumentale; bus no.60 goes to Piazza del Duomo and bus no.65 runs down Corso Buenos Aires, Corso Venezia and through the centre to Corso Italia. Stazione Garibaldi (metro 2) is the terminus for car-train services.

Other helpful numbers are:

Left Luggage, *t 02 6371 2212*. *Open 4am–1.30am*.

Lost and Found, *t 02 6371 2667*.

Arriving by Coach

Inter-city coaches arrive in the Piazza Castello (metro Cairoli), where several companies have their offices.

GETTING AROUND

Even though Milan looks like a bloated amoeba on the map, the city marks its age in rings, like a tree, and most of its sights are in the highly walkable innermost ring, the Cerchia dei Navigli. Milan is not a difficult place to find your way around – unless you've brought a car; the one-way system, no traffic zones in the centre and expensive parking make driving distinctly unfun.

By Metro

The Metropolitana Milanese (metro), begun in the 1960s, is sleek and well run, and a boon for the bewildered tourist. There are three lines, the Red (metro 1), Green (metro 2), and Yellow (metro 3), the last of which was completed in 1990. The metro is open from 6am to midnight daily, and tickets are the same as those used for the buses or trams. (*See* metro map opposite inside back cover.)

By Bus and Tram

The buses and dashing Art Deco trams and trolleys are run by the Milan transport authority (ATM). They are convenient and their routes well marked. Most bus routes

Tickets and Transport Maps

Purchase tickets (€0.77, or carnets of 10 tickets €7.20) in advance at tobacco shops, newsstands, metro stations or in the coin-gobbling machines at the main bus stops, and stamp them in the machines on board buses and trams; a ticket is valid for 75 minutes' travel anywhere on the network above ground, regardless of how many transfers you make. Tickets cannot be used twice on the metro. If you plan to ride around, buy a one-day pass (€2.60) or two-day pass (€4.40), valid for buses, trams and the metro. The ATM also publishes a useful map with all the bus routes and metro stops, the *Guida Rete dei Trasporti Pubblici*, available at the tourist office and the Stazione Centrale.

run from about 6am to midnight, after which time special night bus routes operate with reasonable frequency. Remember to stamp your ticket once on board a bus or tram. Modern trams, ridiculously streamlined for the speed they go, have now replaced the cheerful old caboose-like trams, many of which have been sold to San Francisco.

ATM, *freephone from Italy t 800 016857,* **w** *www.atm-mi.it.*

By Car

Driving in Milan requires chutzpah, luck and good navigation skills. One-way streets are the rule, signs are confusing, parking impossible, and bringing a vehicle into the city centre between 8am and 8pm is not only foolhardy but illegal unless you have a foreign number plate.

If you must bring a car into the centre, look for ATM car parks on the outskirts, or dump your car in one of the large parking lots at the termini of the metro lines. Parking is permitted in the areas marked by a blue line, provided you display a '*Sostamilano*' scratch card on the dashboard. You can buy the card at tobacconists, bars or news kiosks. Yellow lines are for residents only, with a special parking permit. The *Sostamilano* card (€1.40 per hour until 8pm) allows you to park in the blue areas for up to 2 consecutive hours. Cost is €7.60 cumulatively for 8pm–12pm.

A car is certainly the best and most convenient way to get to the more remote parts of Lombardy, but quite unnecessary in Milan, where public transport is extremely efficient and parking is hell on wheels. Other large towns, like Bergamo, can also be a headache.

Petrol (*benzina* – unleaded is *benzina senza piombo*, and diesel is *gasolio*) is expensive, about €1.20 a litre. Many petrol stations close for lunch in the afternoon, and few stay open late at night, though you may find a 'self-service' where you feed a machine nice smooth €5 notes, although some have not been updated from *lire*. Speed limits (generally ignored) are 130kph on motorways (110kph or cars under 1100cc or motorcycles), 110kph

on main highways, 90kph on secondary roads and 50kph in built-up areas. Speeding fines may be as much as €250, or €50 for jumping a red light (a popular Italian sport).

Hiring a Car

Hiring a car (basically rent-a-Fiat) is simple but not particularly cheap. There are both large international firms through which you can reserve a car in advance, and local agencies, which often have lower prices. Most companies will require a deposit amounting to the estimated cost of the hire. VAT of 19% is applied, so make sure you take this into account when checking prices. Most companies have a minimum age limit of 21 (23 in some cases). A credit card makes life easier, and you will need to produce your licence and a passport. Current rates are around €120 per day for a medium-sized car with unlimited mileage and collision damage waiver, including tax (hire for three days or longer is somewhat less). Most major rental companies have offices at Milan's airports or the Stazione Centrale.

Avis, Hertz and Europcar have offices at Linate airport (Europcar is also at Malpensa):

Avis, *Piazza Diaz, t 02 89016 0645.*

Europcar, *Via Galbani 12, t 02 6671 0491.*

By Bicycle

Some of the more hardy and fatalistic locals choose to travel the city streets by bicycle, but this is very much a city where the car is king, with little room for cyclists amid the weaving traffic. For rental, however:

AWS Bicimotor, *Via Gallavato 33,* **t** *02 308 2430.*

By Taxi

Milanese taxis are white and their drivers generally honest and reliable. It is not possible to flag down a taxi. You must call to book or go to a stand. They can also be found waiting at ranks in the Piazza del Duomo, by the Stazione Centrale, and in several other central piazzas (to book, call **t** 02 8383/6767/ 5251). On entering the taxi you pay a charge of €1.80. Note that taxi drivers may charge extra for suitcases if you allow them to put them in the boot. They also have an aversion to being paid in coins, believing them to be worth less than bills.

By Train

For most day trips, you'll probably have to travel by train. Stazione Centrale (**t** 147 888 088; open 7am–11pm) handles most domestic routes. Stazione Garibaldi is the terminus for trains for Pavia, Monza, Como and Bergamo. Stazione Lambrate, on the east side of the city, has connections to Genoa, Bergamo and towards the Simplon Pass. Stazione Cadorna is the main station of Lombardy's regional Milan Nord railway (**t** 02 20222; open 24hrs), with connections to Como, Varese, Saronno, Erba and Laveno (Lake Maggiore).

Italy's national railway, recently rebranded as Trenitalia, the most serendipitous national line in Europe, is well run, inexpensive and often a pleasure to ride. (Note that Lombardy also has several private rail lines, which, unlike Trenitalia, won't accept Interail or Eurail passes). Possible unpleasantnesses you may encounter, besides a strike, are delays, crowding (especially at weekends and in the summer), and crime on overnight trains, where someone rifles your bags while you sleep. The crowding, at least, becomes much less of a problem if you reserve a seat in advance at the *prenotazione* counter. Do check when you purchase your ticket in advance that the date is correct; tickets are valid for two months from the day of purchase, unless specified otherwise. Tickets need to be punched before getting on the train (in yellow machines on the platforms and in the station halls). Return tickets must be punched before each journey. Be sure you ask which platform (*binario*) your train departs from; the big boards posted in the stations are not always correct. If you get on a train without a ticket you can buy one from the conductor, with an added 20% penalty.

There is a fairly straightforward hierarchy of trains. At the bottom of the pyramid is the humble *locale* (euphemistically known sometimes as an *accelerato*) which often stops even where there's no station in sight; it can be excruciatingly slow. When you're checking the schedules, beware of what may look like the first train to your destination – if it's a *locale*, it will be the last to arrive. A *diretto* stops far less, an *expresso* just at the main towns. Inter-city trains whoosh between the big cities and rarely deign to stop. Eurocity trains link Italian cities with major European centres. Both of these services require you to pay a supplement, some 30% more than a regular fare.

The real lords of the rails are the ETR 450 Pendolino trains that will speed you to your destination as fast as trains can go (in Italy). For these there is a more costly supplement and, on some, only first-class luxury cars. For further information and schedules:

FS Informa, t *(1478) 88088,* **w** *www. fs-on-line.com.* **Open** *7am–9pm.*

By Coach

Coaches for day trips outside Milan depart from the Piazza Castello (metro Cairoli), where several companies have their offices. Contact the tourist office (*see* p.64) for information on destinations, schedules and prices. Inter-city coach travel is sometimes quicker than train travel, but a bit more expensive. You will find regular coach connections only where there is no train to offer competition, and tickets usually need to be purchased from inside the coach station before you get on.

Guided Tours

Contact the tourist office for full listings:

Autostradale Milan, t *02 7252 4301. €30 per person – cost includes entry fees.* Offers 3hr tours of the city centre.

Hello Milano, t *02 2952 0570. €50.* Tailor-made, one-on-one tours.

Tourist Tram, t *02 7200 2584,* **w** *www. airpullman.com/ciao/ciaoe.htm.* City tours (some in English), on a 1920s tram.

Practical A–Z

Climate 54
Crime and the Police 54
Disabled Travellers 55
Duty-free Shopping 56
Electricity, Weights and Measures 56
Embassies and Consulates 56
Etiquette 56
Health, Emergencies and Insurance 57
Internet 58
Laundrettes 59
Lost Property 59
Media 59
Money, Banks and Taxes 59
Opening Hours and Public Holidays 61
Packing 62
Photography 62
Post and Fax 62
Smoking 63
Strikes 63
Students and Seniors 63
Telephones 63
Time 64
Tipping 64
Toilets 64
Tourist Offices 64
Women Travellers 65
Working and Long Stays 65

Climate

Because it is situated on a plain at the edge of a swamp, Milan's climate differs from the surrounding Lombardy Plain. Instead, the climate of the Alps meets the Mediterranean head on, creating the infamous Milanese fog which, due to the mountains, is rarely dispersed by wind.

In winter, the fog can become so dense as to close Linate airport completely, while in summer the motionless haze can be unrelenting and suffocating. On the bright side, the mountains shield the city from the worst of the winter; this creates a microclimate at pre-alpine altitudes, where beautiful gardens, abundant with olives and lemons, can be cultivated. Winter is best for seeing Milan at its liveliest, when you can meet more natives and find the sights blissfully uncrowded (if sometimes closed). The Lakes themselves, however, may well be shrouded in mist for weeks on end.

Spring brings warmer temperatures, blossoming trees and flowers, and few crowds apart from Easter; a few days of intermittent rain is about the worst that can happen. During the summer, the Lakes are very crowded, and Milan is abandoned to tourists in August and early September. It rarely rains (though isolated, dramatic thunderstorms may occur), and the temperatures can be remarkably pleasant.

Early autumn, especially September, is perhaps the ideal time to go for the blue, balmy days (though rain may intrude during October and November).

Average daily temperatures in °C (°F)

Jan	April	July	Oct
1.9 (35)	13.2 (55)	24.8 (76)	13.5 (56)

Crime and the Police

Police: t 113, or t 62261
Carabinieri: t 112

Milan, Italy's second city, is an angel with very dirty hands and a pocketful of bribes, and in the last few years has even outscandalled Rome. This won't affect you, but a fair amount of petty crime might, such as: purse-snatchings, pickpocketing, minor thievery of the white-collar kind (always check your change) and car break-ins and theft. However, violent crime is rare.

Purse-snatchers can be discouraged if you stay on the inside of the pavement and keep a firm hold on your property (sling your bag-strap across your body, don't dangle it from one shoulder). Be aware that pickpockets strike in crowded buses and gatherings; don't carry too much cash, and split it so you won't lose the lot at once.

At the Stazione Centrale and popular tourist sights, beware of groups of scruffy-looking women or children with placards, apparently begging for money. They use distraction techniques to perfection, and in general the smallest and most innocent-looking child is the most skilful pickpocket.

If targeted, grab sharply hold of any vulnerable possessions or pockets and shout furiously – Italian passers-by or plain-clothes police will often come to your assistance if they realize what is happening.

Be extra careful in train stations, don't leave valuables in hotel rooms, and always park your car in guarded lots or on well-lit streets, with temptations well out of sight.

Purchasing small quantities of soft drugs for personal consumption is technically legal in Italy, though what constitutes a small quantity is unspecified and, if the police don't like you to begin with, it will probably be enough to get you into big trouble.

Political terrorism, once the scourge of Italy, has declined in recent years, mainly thanks to special quasi-military squads of black-uniformed national police, the *Carabinieri*. Local matters are usually in the hands of the *Polizia Urbana*; the nattily dressed *Vigili Urbani* concern themselves with directing traffic and handing out parking fines.

Disabled Travellers

Italy has been relatively slow off the mark in its provision for disabled visitors. Uneven or non-existent pavements, the appalling traffic conditions, crowded public transport and endless flights of steps in many public places are all disincentives. Progress is gradually being made.

The Italian national tourist office or CIT (travel agency) can also advise on hotels, museums with ramps, etc. If you book your rail travel through CIT, you can request assistance if you are wheelchair-bound. If you need help while in Milan or around the Lakes, the local tourist offices can be very helpful and have even been known to find wheelchair-pushers on the spot.

Specialist Organizations
In Italy

Accessible Italy, *Promotur-Mondo Possibile, La Viaggeria, Via Lemonia 161, Rome, t 06 7158 2945, f 06 7158 3433, w www.accessible italy.com.* A travel agency that provides valuable, detailed information on access in Italy.

Centro Studi Consulenza Invalidi, *Via Gozzadini 7, Milan, t 02 657 0425.* Publishes an annual guide, *Vacanze per Disabili*, with details of suitable accommodation in Italy.

CO.IN (Consorzio Cooperative Integrate), *Via Enrico Giglioli 54a, 00169 Rome, t 06 232 67504, t 06 7128 9676 (bookings) and COINtel, t 06 2326 7695 (24-hour information line in English). Open Mon–Fri 9–5.* Can assist with bookings for guided tours with suitable transport, and also provide a 24-hour telephone helpline. Their tourist information centre offers advice and information on accessibility.

In the UK

Assistance Travel Service, *1 Tank Lane, Purfleet, Essex RM19 1TA, t (01708) 863198, f (01708) 860514, w www.assistedholidays. com.* Organizes tailor-made trips, for people with any disability.

Holiday Care Service, *t (01293) 774 535, f (01293) 784 647, Minicom t (01293) 776 943, w www.holidaycare.org.uk.* Information sheets on travel.

RADAR (Royal Association for Disability & Rehabilitation), *t (020) 7250 4119, w www.radar.org.uk.* This association offers information and books on travelling abroad.

Tripscope, *t 0845 758 5641, f (020) 8580 7022, w www.tripscope.org.uk* Practical advice on travel and transport for elderly and disabled travellers. Information can be provided by letter or audio tape.

In the USA and Canada

Alternative Leisure Co, *t (718) 275 0023, w www.alctrips.com.* Organizes vacations abroad for disabled people.

Mobility International, *t (541) 343 1284, f (541) 343 6812, w www.miusa.org.* Advice, information and tours; US$35 annual fee.

MossRehab ResourceNet, *w www. mossresourcenet.org/travel.htm.* Good resource for all aspects of accessible travel.

SATH (Society for Accessible Travel and Hospitality), *t (212) 557 0027, w www.sath.org.* Advice on all aspects of travel for the disabled, for a US$3 charge, or unlimited to members (US$45; concessions US$25).

The U.S. Department of Transportation (DOT), *400 7th Street, SW, 4107, Washington, DC, 20590, t 1 800 778 4838 (voice) or t 1 800 455 9880 (TTY), w http://airconsumer. ost.dot.gov/publications/disabled.htm. Open daily 7am–11 pm.* Assistance and information to travellers with disabilities.

Other Useful Contacts

Access Ability, *w www.access-ability.co.uk.* Information on travel agencies.

Australian Council for Rehabilitation of the Disabled *(ACROD), PO Box 60, Curtin, ACT 2605, Australia, t/TTY (02) 6682 4333, w www.acrod.org.au.* Information and contact numbers for specialist travel agents.

Disabled Persons Assembly, *PO Box 27-524, Wellington 6035, New Zealand, t (04) 801 9100, w www.dpa.org.nz.* All-round source for travel information.

Emerging Horizons, *e horizons@emerging horizons.com*, *w www.emerginghorizons. com*. International on-line travel newsletter for people with disabilities.

Duty-free Shopping

For further information on bringing goods in and out of the country, *see* 'Travel', p.49. For information on VAT refunds, *see* 'Money, Banks and Taxes', p.59.

Electricity, Weights and Measures

The current is 225AC or 220V, the same as in most of Europe. Americans will need converters, and the British will need two-pin adapters for the different plugs. Take one with you, as they are hard to find in the city. Italy uses the **metric** system.

1 centimetre = 0.394 inches
1 metre = 3.094 feet
1 kilometre = 0.621 miles
1 kilogramme (1,000g) = 2.2 pounds
1 litre = 0.264 gallons (1.76 pints)
1 inch = 2.54 centimetres

1 foot = 0.305 metres
1 mile = 1.6 kilometres
1 pound = 0.454 kilogrammes
1 ounce = 25 grammes
1 liquid pint = 0.473 litres
1 gallon = 3.785 litres

Clothing sizes are tailored for slim Italian builds. Shoes, in particular, tend to be narrower than in other Western countries.

Embassies and Consulates

Foreign Consulates in Milan

Australia: *Via Borgogna 2, t 02 777 0421.*
Canada: *Via Vittorio Pisani 19, t 02 67581.*
Ireland: *Piazza San Pietro in Gessate 2, t 02 5518 7569.*
UK: *Via San Paolo 7, t 02 723 001.*
USA: *Via Principe Amedeo 2/10, t 02 2903 51.*

Italian Representation Abroad

Canada: *275 Slater St, Ottawa, Ontario K1P 5HG, t (613) 232 2401, f (613) 233 1484, e ambital@italyincanada.com, w www. italyincanada.com.* Consulates in Toronto, Montreal and Vancouver.

Ireland: *63/65 Northumberland Road, Dublin 4, t (01) 660 1744, f (01) 668 2759, e italianembassy@eircom.net.* Consulate in Dublin.

UK: *14 Three Kings Yard, London W1Y 4EH, t (020) 7312 2200, f (020) 7312 2230, e emblondon@embitaly.org.uk, w www. embitaly.org.uk.* Consulates in Edinburgh, Manchester and Bedford.

USA: *3000 Whitehaven St, NW Washington DC 20008, t (202) 612 4400, f (202) 518 2154, e stampa@itwash.org, w www.italyemb.org.* Consulates in most major cities.

Etiquette

Italians are an infuriating paradox when it comes to manners, often surprisingly abrupt and dismissive no matter what the age, but reverting to a convenient catholic sense of propriety when it suits them. Both attitudes are usually for show. Italians are not known

Clothing Sizes

Women's Shirts/Dresses

UK	10	12	14	16	18
USA	8	10	12	14	16
Italy	40	42	44	46	48

Sweaters

UK	10	12	14	16
USA	8	10	12	14
Italy	46	48	50	52

Women's Shoes

UK	3	4	5	6	7	8
USA	4	5	6	7	8	9
Italy	36	37	38	39	40	41

Men's Shirts

UK/USA	14	14.5	15	15.5	16	16.5	17
Italy	36	37	38	39	40	41	42

Men's Suits

UK/USA	36	38	40	42	44	46
Italy	46	48	50	52	54	56

Men's Shoes

UK	5	6	7	8	9	10	11	12
USA	7.5	8	9	10	10.5	11	12	13
Italy	38	39	40	41	42	43	44	45

for their desire to observe a queue, or, despite the myth of Latin chivalry, to let others go first. So, as with driving in Italy (see p.47), it is advisable not to hesitate but to go for it, lest you be left behind. Having said that, underneath it all, Italy is a formal and conservative nation that respects good manners, particularly where the family and elder generations are concerned; this notion is very in tune with their sense of formal elegance in the way they dress. Generally speaking, however, visitors would not need to alter their etiquette, as it is almost identical to that of most Western countries. If you do have some knowledge of Italian, always try to use the 'Lei' formal form of verbs for adults who you are meeting for the first time. If you are planning to visit a church it is respectful for ladies to cover any revealing tops or short skirts.

Health, Emergencies and Insurance

Fire: t 115
Ambulance: t 113

Non-emergencies can be treated at a *pronto soccorso* (casualty/first aid department), at any hospital clinic (*ambulatorio*), or at a local health unit (*unita sanitaria locale* – USL). Airports and main railway stations also have first-aid posts. Most Italian doctors speak at least rudimentary English, but if you can't find one who does, contact your consulate. Standards of health care in Milan and Lombardy in general are high. If you have to pay for any treatment, make sure you get a receipt to claim for reimbursement later.

Dispensing chemists (*farmacia*) are generally open 8.30am–1pm and 4–8pm. Pharmacists are trained to give advice for minor ills (or ring **t** 0661 14431 for medical information). Any large city will have a *farmacia* that stays open 24 hours (in Milan it's at the Stazione Centrale); others take turns to stay open (the address rota is posted in the window). Prescriptions can be hard to match; bring any drugs you need regularly.

Insurance
EEA Nationals and Australians

The European Economic Area consists of the 15 member states of the European community plus Iceland, Liechtenstein and Norway. Citizens of EU countries and Australia are entitled to reciprocal health care in Italy's National Health Service and a 90% discount on prescriptions. If you are travelling within the EEA, then make sure you fill out an E111 form before you go as this entitles you to free or reduced-cost emergency treatment on the same terms as nationals of the country you are visiting.

If you do have to pay, you can usually claim a full or partial refund back from the country where you were treated. Each country has different rules regarding how you go about this, so check that you follow the correct procedure (listed in the E111 form). An E111 can be obtained from a post office and is free. One E111 can be used to cover an individual, their spouse and children under 16 or under 19 and still in full-time education. If you are travelling outside the EEA, it is best to carry medical insurance, and if travelling to the USA, take a very high level of cover.

There are a few countries outside of the EEA that have reciprocal health care agreements with the UK, which entitles you to some level of emergency treatment only. Again, it is best to carry medical insurance as there may be charges for this treatment and you cannot claim a refund. Check policies before you go, as there can be many exclusions, and you will probably need to pay extra if you are taking part in activities like high-risk sports. Many of the larger credit card companies will offer some degree of travel insurance for health when they are used to book a package holiday or airplane/train tickets.

Further information on health when travelling can be obtained from the **Health Literature Hotline** (**t** 0800 555 777) or you can look at the Department of Health's website, (**w** *www.doh.gov.uk/traveladvice*).

Other Non-EU Visitors

There are no reciprocal agreements between Italy and New Zealand, Canada or the USA. If you have private health insurance, check what medical coverage it provides overseas as policies do vary. If it does provide overseas coverage, make sure you take your insurance policy identity card and a claim form with you.

The American social security medicare programme does not provide any coverage for medical care outside the States. Canadian provincial health plans often provide a degree of overseas medical coverage, but are unlikely to pay the full cost of any treatment. You can insure yourself for almost any possible mishap – cancelled flights, stolen or lost baggage and health problems. Check your current policies to see if they cover you while abroad, and under what circumstances, and judge whether you need a special traveller's insurance policy (check student cards and credit cards to see if they entitle you to some medical cover abroad). Travel agencies as well as insurance companies sell traveller's insurance, but they are not cheap.

Internet

It can be fun and often very useful to have a look at the Internet before you start your trip. The Italians are no slouches in cyberspace; in fact, the Italian slice of the web can be as gaudy as Italian television these days.

Among the directories, Lycos and MSN are probably the best places to look, with an index of sites in a few score of Italian towns; Yahoo and Infoseek (under 'Travel: Destinations') are also helpful. Several sites in these listings offer tips on accommodation, and hotel reservations in Milan and elsewhere. Milan is especially well covered on the web (*see* box, opposite).

When trying to say 'www' in Italian, do not attempt to say the word *doppia-vu* three times! The Italians simply say *vu-vu-vu-punto*.

Useful Italian Websites

w *www.cilea.it/www-map/cities/milano. html*. Provides a list of several websites about Milan.

w *www.cityvox.com*. Highly recommended website for Milan listings.

w *www.milandaily.com*. Excellent English-language site for headlines, sports and entertainment news on Milan.

w *www.citylightsnews.com*. For a Milan street finder and transport map, as well as tourist sights and hotel information.

w *http://www.rcs.it/mimu/english/musei/ musei.htm*. English-language site detailing Milan's museums, with city map, highlighted attractions and children's itineraries.

w *www.smokefreeworld.com/milan. shtml*. For a listing of smoke-free environments in Milan.

w *http://welmilano.itcons.com*. The city of Milan's helpful English-language website, with information on sights, entertainment and working/studying in Milan.

w *www.teatroallascala.it*. La Scala's website (includes ticket sales).

w *http://users.libero.it/kiwi.milano/ mi_engli.htm*. An excellent English language site covering Milan – a virtual offspring of the *Key to Milan* guide.

w *www.inlombardia.it*. The region's general tourism site.

w *www.itwg.com/rg_lomba.asp*. The Italian tourist web guide, with a database on hotels and the possibility of booking online.

Internet Cafés

Most hotels have an Internet facility, as do a large number of the bars and cafés in the Brera and Ticinese districts, although it is often busy. Head for the following centres if neither of these options is available:

Computer Training Center, *Via Lazzaretto 2*, **t** *02 205 21 21*; **metro** *Porta Venezia* or *Repubblica*. Internet facilities and computer courses.

Kipunet, *Via Eustachi 48*; **metro** *Lima*.

Mailboxes etc., *Corso Sempione 38; tram 1.* Post office and Internet point.

Mr. Clean, *Via Gaffurio 3, metro Caiazzo; Largo Giambellino; tram 14.* Coin-operated laundrette and Internet point.

Nashuatec, *Via Larga 9, t 02 583 15546; metro Missori.*

Rizzoli, *Piazza Duomo; metro Duomo.* Free Internet surfing.

Telecom Italia, *Galleria Vittorio Emanuele II, Piazza Duomo; metro Duomo.*

Laundrettes

Laundrettes are spread quite plentifully around Milan although not particularly in the centre. Try the side-streets and look out for the word 'Lavandaio' or 'Lavanderie'. The same places will usually have 'pressing' (dry-cleaning) facilities. If you can't find one, try the coin-operated laundrette and Internet point, **Mr. Clean** (Via Gaffurio, metro Caiazzo; or Largo Giambellino, tram 14. Open 9am–8pm year-round).

Lost Property

The Milan council runs a lost and found office called **Ufficio Oggetti Rivenuti** (Via Fiuli 30, t 02 546 8118; bus 62, 90 or 92, tram 4; open Mon–Fri 8.30–4). If you have lost something near the station or on a train it might turn up at the **Ferrovie dello Stato lost property office** (Via Sammartini 108, behind the Stazione Centrale, t 02 6371 2667; metro Centrale, bus 53, tram 2; open from 7–1 and and 2–8).

Media

Radio

RAI, the state-owned broadcaster, has three channels, predictably called **RAI1** (FM89.7), **RAI2** (FM 91.7) and **RAI3** (FM 93.7). These all feature both classical and pop music, talk shows and news reports and analysis. The two best commercial radio stations for international pop and dance music are **RTL** (FM102.5) and **Radio 105** (FM105),

although there are is a proliferation of others to suit all music tastes. The Vatican channel, **Radio Vatican**, AM1260, makes for interesting listening if you can speak a little Italian.

Newspapers

National newspapers include the independent centrist daily **La Repubblica** (w *www.repubblica.it*), and the reliable Milan-based **Il Corriere della Sera** (w *www.cds.it*) and Turin-based **La Stampa** (w *www.lastampa.it*). Minority national newspapers *L'Unità* and *Il Manifesto* are left-leaning; *Il Quadrifoglio* leans to the right. In central Milan, major foreign newspapers and magazines are available from most news-stands.

Fans of sport will not want to be seen without the daily, rose-pink *Gazzetta dello Sport* with all the latest on the shenanigans from Italy's football clubs, plus back pages on minor sports such as Formula 1 motor-racing.

There are also a number of local news-papers, available free from news kiosks, such as *City Milano*, *Hello Milan* and *URBAN*. These are particularly useful for listings on the latest films, plays and concerts.

TV

Italian television has three government-owned channels: **RAI 1**, **RAI 2** and **RAI 3** – the last covering regional news and with a good reputation for cultural programmes and interesting movies, especially late at night, rather than just the quiz shows, soap operas, talk shows and variety shows that are the staples of Italian TV. Prime Minister Silvio Berlusconi owns several media outlets, including **Canale 5**, **Rete 4** and **Telepiù Due** (a football channel). For TV news in English, most hotel rooms should offer either **CNN** or **BBC World**.

Money, Banks and Taxes

After an eternity of deliberation and debate, a single European currency is finally becoming a part of everyday life in Italy and most EU countries other than the UK. These countries will also share a single interest rate, set by the European Central Bank (ECB).

All non-cash transactions are now in euros, and the euro notes themselves, introduced on 1 January 2002, are used alongside eight denominations of coin, ranging from 1 cent to 2 euros (100 cents in each euro). The rate fixed for exchange of the Italian lira to the euro was 1936.27 lire to €1. At the time of writing, the euro is worth approximately £0.63, US$1 and CAN$1.60.

Note that because of the currency change, prices have mysteriously increased on the small things such as coffees, newspapers etc.

It is also worth pointing out that Italy, even Milan in parts, is still very much a cash culture, and several places do not accept credit cards.

Changing Money

The most convenient way to obtain money is to withdraw it from an ATM machine using a PIN code. You can also withdraw cash over the counter in a bank using a card and a passport as ID.

Check rates and commission before making any transaction. Banks tend to give better rates than kiosks. There are an increasing number of automatic exchange machines in the city for foreign banknotes.

If you have American Express or Thomas Cook travellers' cheques, it's worth going to the company's offices in Milan to save yourself €2.50 commission:

American Express, *Via Brera 3,* **t** *02 7200 3694;* **metro** *Cairoli.* **Open** *Mon–Thurs 9–5.30.*

Thomas Cook, *Via Dante 8,* **t** *02 8909 6459;* **metro** *Cordusio.* **Open** *Mon–Fri 9–12.30 and 1–6.30, Sat and Sun, 1–6.30.*

Credit and Debit Cards

Most banks and *bureaux de change* will give you cash on a credit card or Eurocheque with a Eurocheque card (taking little or no commission). ATMs (Bancomats/ Cashpoints) at nearly every bank spout cash

if you have a PIN number (Visa, Cirrus, Mastercard and Eurocard are the most widely accepted). Read the instructions carefully – you usually get a choice of English and other languages – so the machine does not devour your card.

Large hotels, expensive or tourist-oriented restaurants, larger shops, car hire firms and petrol stations will accept plastic as well; check the signs on the door.

American Express: *(international collect)* **t** *06 336 668 5110*

Diners Club: *(freephone)* **t** *800 864 034*
MasterCard: *(freephone)* **t** *800 870 866*
Visa/Eurocard: *(freephone)* **t** *800 018 548*

VAT Refunds

Value-added tax (VAT, or IVA in Italy) is charged at 20% on clothing, wine and luxury goods. On consumer goods it is already included in the amount shown on the price tag, whereas on services it may be added later. Non-EU citizens are entitled to a VAT refund on certain items under the Retail Export Scheme.

You can claim a tax refund as long as you have not been in the EU for more than 365 days in the two years before the date you buy the goods and you leave the EU with the goods within three months of buying them. Items excluded from the scheme are motor vehicles, boats you intend to sail to a destination outside the EU, goods for business purposes, goods that will be consumed in the EU, bullion and unmounted gemstones. You cannot get a refund on hotel and restaurant bills, except for business.

To get your refund, shop with your passport and ask for an invoice itemizing the article, price and tax paid. When you depart Italy, take the goods and invoice to the customs office at the point of departure and have the invoice stamped. You need to do this at your last stop in the EU. Once home, and within 90 days of the purchase date, mail the stamped invoice (keeping a copy) to the shop or store, which is legally required to send you a VAT rebate. You'll get around

16.5% back once post and admin are deducted. Shops that do not advertise tax-free services may be reluctant to get involved with official invoices, but the law entitles you to a refund.

For anyone who spends more than €150 at a go, many stores participate in the Tax Free Shopping scheme – you'll recognize the sign displayed in shop windows – which will do all the admin for you for a small fee. Get your invoices stamped at customs as above, then take them to one of the counters conveniently located at airports and your money will be refunded in cash on the spot, or as a refund to your debit or credit card.

Opening Hours and Public Holidays

Italy (except for bars and restaurants) closes down at 1pm until 3 or 4pm to eat and properly digest the main meal of the day. Afternoon hours are from 4 to 7, often from 5 to 8 in the hot summer months. Most of Milan closes down completely during August, when locals flee from the polluted frying pan to the hills, lakes or coast.

Banking hours vary, but core times in Milan and Lombardy are more or less Monday to Friday from 8.30am to 1pm and 3 to 4pm, closed weekends and on local and national holidays (see box). Outside normal hours, you will usually be able to find a travel office or hotel or even a machine in a wall to change money for a small commission.

Shops are usually open Monday to Saturday from 9.30am to 1pm and 3.30pm to 7.30pm, though hours vary according to season and are shorter in smaller centres. In Milan, Italy's shopping capital, the hours are understandly longer. A few supermarkets and department stores stay open throughout the day.

Italy's churches have always been a prime target for art thieves and as a consequence are usually locked when there isn't a sacristan or caretaker to keep an eye on things. All churches, except for the really

important cathedrals and basilicas, close in the afternoon at the same hours as the shops, and the little ones tend to stay closed. Always have a pocketful of coins for the light machines, or whatever work of art you came to inspect will remain shrouded in ecclesiastical gloom. Don't visit during services, and don't come to see paintings and statues in churches in the week preceding Easter – you will probably find them covered with mourning shrouds.

Many of Italy's museums are magnificent, many are run with shameful neglect, and many have been closed for years for 'restoration', with slim prospects of reopening in the foreseeable future. With two works of art per inhabitant, Italy has a hard time financing the preservation of its national heritage; it's as well to enquire at the tourist office to find out exactly what is open and what is 'temporarily' closed before setting off on a wild-goose chase.

In general, Sunday afternoons and Mondays are dead periods for the sightseer – you may want to make them your travelling days. Places without specified opening hours can usually be visited on request but it is best to go before 1pm. Entrance charges to Milan's star museums are quite steep, but others are fairly low, and some sights are completely free. For museums and galleries, the average is €2.50 to €4.50, for churches or cathedrals about €2, and for castles, palaces, villas and their gardens, around €3. EU citizens under 18 and over 65 get free admission to state museums, at least in theory.

Packing

It's hard to overdress in Italy; Italians may be a formal bunch but they also like to dress up with a gorgeousness that adorns their cities just as much as those old Renaissance churches and palaces. The few places with dress codes are the major churches and basilicas (no shorts, sleeveless shirts or strappy sundresses – women should tuck a light silk scarf in a bag to throw over their shoulders), casinos and a few smart restaurants.

After agonizing over fashion, remember to pack small and light: transatlantic airlines limit baggage by size (two pieces are free up to 1.5m in height and width; in second class you're allowed one of 1.5m and another up to 1.1m). Within Europe, limits are by weight: 20kg (44lbs) in second class, 30kg (66lbs) in first. You may well be penalized for anything larger.

If you're travelling by train, you will want to keep bags to a minimum: jamming big suitcases in overhead racks in a crowded compartment isn't much fun for anyone. Never take more than you can carry, but do bring the following: any prescription medicine you may need, an extra pair of glasses or contact lenses if you wear them, a pocket knife and corkscrew (for picnics), a flashlight (for dark frescoed churches, caves and crypts), and a travel alarm (for those early trains).

If you're a light sleeper, you may want to invest in earplugs. Your electric appliances will work in Italy if you adapt and convert them to run on 220 AC with two round prongs on the plug.

Photography

Photographic film is readily available in all the usual formats. In tourist areas the price of film is high, so it's a good idea to stock up before you go. Developing is much more expensive than in either the UK or the USA.

You are not allowed to take pictures in most museums and in some churches. Lombardy's light is less dazzling than in the vivid south, and clarity may be affected by Milanese air pollution or local mists.

VHS videotapes are readily available; all tapes use the same system as in other European countries.

Post and Fax

Dealing with *la posta italiana* has always been a risky, frustrating, time-consuming affair. One of the scandals that mesmerized Italy in recent years involved the minister of the post office, who disposed of tons of backlog mail by tossing it in the Tiber. When the news broke, he was replaced – the new minister, having learned his lesson, burned all the mail the post office was incapable of delivering. Not surprisingly, fed-up Italians view the invention of the fax machine and Internet as gifts from the Madonna.

Post offices are usually open Monday to Friday 8.30–1.50 and Saturday 8.30–12.30, or until 7.30pm (Mon–Fri) and 5.30pm (Sat) in the central and rail station offices of a big city.

To have your mail sent *poste restante* (general delivery), have it addressed to the central post office (c/o Uffico Posta Centrale and make sure you add the exact post code) and allow three to four weeks for it to arrive. Make sure your surname is very clearly written in block capitals. To pick up your mail you must present your passport and pay a nominal charge. Stamps (*francobolli*) may be purchased in post offices or at tobacconists (*tabacchi*, identified by their blue signs with a white T).

You can also have money telegraphed to you through the post office; if all goes well, this can happen in a mere three days, but expect a fair proportion of it to go on commission.

Postage rates: €.41 or €.52 for US and for Prioritria, €.62 or €.77 for US; over 2kg, €8.06 and for Prioritaria, €16.53. A useful tip: if you want your postcards to be treated as normal mail you should put them in an envelope. Otherwise they are downgraded by the Italian post and might as well be thrown in the river. For further information:

Information Poste Italiane, *t* 160, or w *www.poste.it.*

Smoking

Although smoking is not permitted in indoor public spaces, Italians have a tendency to disregard no-smoking laws, which are seldom enforced. If you ask someone not to smoke, even in an officially-designated no-smoking area, don't expect your request to be respected. Your best bet for a smoke-free environment is out of doors. All FS trains have no-smoking carriages. Specify when you reserve.

A packet of 20 cigarettes costs from €2.20– 4.40 (for imported brands). They can be purchased from tobacconists and bars with a T sign.

Strikes

Official strikes (the word to look out for is *sciopero*) are usually listed in newspapers, but lightning strikes are pretty common – so don't be surprised if you turn up at a bus stop, metro or railway station and discover there is no public transport.

Students and Seniors

Citizens under 18 and over 60 with ID get free entrance to most state museums. Students with international ID cards have some cheap housing options (*see* 'Youth Hostels', p.160) and can get some travel discounts by becoming members of student associations. The ARCI pass, which is necessary to get into some of Milan's

nightclubs and bars and which can be obtained on the door of one of these, will also allow you discounts of anything between 20–50% on entry to some cinemas, sites and museums.

Notices of items for sale, as well as special offers, are often posted in the University buildings in and around the Ca' Grande; it is a very useful starting point for visiting students wishing to do everything on the cheap or cut corners – an essential practice in Italy.

Telephones

Directory enquiries: *t* 12.
Collect calls: *t* 172
International directory enquiries: *t* 176

Italians are never knowingly not on the phone. When making calls in Italy, always dial the city's area code (Milan's is 02), followed by the number. For Italian mobile phones, dial the prefix and the zero in front.

As a whole, Milan is well supplied with telephones – seek them out on noisy street corners, in post offices, hotels or bars. There are phones in the offices of **Telecom Italia** (Galleria Vittorio Emanuele II, for the city centre office; open daily 8.30am–9.30pm).

Many places offering cheap international calls are mushrooming up in Milan, to serve the ever-growing population of immigrants and tourists:

AT&T USA Direct: *t* 172 1011
MCI Call USA: *t* 172 1022
Sprint XP: *t* 172 1877

Try to avoid phoning from hotels, which often add 25% to the bill. Telephone numbers in Italy change with alarming regularity. Nearly all take coins or phone cards (*schede telefoniche*) available in roughly €2, €5 or €10 amounts at tobacconists or news-stands; stock up for a long international call.

Local calls are most expensive on working days between 8am and 6.30pm. Once you call long distance, the phone gobbles your money. For reverse charges (*a erre*) dial

t 172 followed by the country code, which will connect you with the appropriate operator (e.g. 172 0044 for the UK). The telephone prefix for the UK is 0044, Ireland 00353, for the US and Canada 001, for Australia 0061, New Zealand 0064.

For help in English on international calls or to get a translation into Italian and vice versa, ring **International information**, (**t** 176; open Mon–Fri 8am–9pm). Calls are charged at €2 a minute plus €7.50 tax plus 20% VAT. If you're calling Milan from abroad, dial country code 39, then 02, then the number.

Time

Italy is always one hour ahead of Greenwich Mean Time, and generally six hours ahead of Eastern Standard Time in the USA. Summer Time (*ora legale*) starts on the last Sunday in March at 3am – when clocks are put forward one hour – and ends on the last Sunday in October at 3am – when clocks are set back one hour. Summer and winter opening hours of major tourist sights are usually changed at the same time as the clocks, unless Easter is very early.

Tipping

Service is almost always included in restaurant bills, but Italians customarily tip waiters unless the service gives them reason not to. Rather than a percentage of the bill, a tip of €2 per person for a meal at a moderately priced restaurant is enough to convey appreciation, less at cheaper places and pizzerias, more at fancy restaurants. A €0.20 coin on the *bancone* (counter)with your *scontrino* (receipt) will help to get your coffee served faster if standing at the bar.

Tip a generous 10% if sitting at a café. Italians tip taxi drivers and theatre ushers only if they are notably helpful. At a hotel, you might leave your chambermaid €15 for a week's stay, the bellhop €2–3 per trip. Tip the concierge only for personal services.

Toilets

Frequent travellers have noted a steady improvement over the years in the cleanliness of Italy's public conveniences, although you will only find them in places like train and bus stations and bars. Ask for the toilette or *gabinetto*; in stations and the smarter bars and cafés, washroom attendants will expect a few euros for keeping the place decent. Don't confuse the Italian plurals: *signori* (gents), *signore* (ladies).

Tourist Offices
Abroad

The Italian National Tourist Office (ENIT) can help before you leave home; in some countries, tourist information is also available from the offices of Alitalia or CIT (Italy's State Tourist Board).

Australia: *Level 26-44 Market Street, NSW 2000 Sydney,* **t** *(02) 92 621666,* **f** *(02) 92 621677,* **e** *lenitour@ihug.com.au.*

Canada: *175 Bloor St East, Suite 907, South Tower, Toronto, Ontario M4W 3R8,* **t** *(416) 925 4882/3725,* **f** *(416) 925 4799; 1 Place Ville Marie, Suite 1914, Montréal, Quebec H3B 3M9,* **t** *(514) 866 7667,* **f** *(514) 3921429;* **w** *www. italiantourism.com.*

UK: *1 Princes Street, London W1R 8AY,* **t** *(020) 7408 1254,* **f** *(020) 7493 6695.*

USA: *630 Fifth Av, Suite 1565, New York, NY 10111,* **t** *(212) 245 5095/4822,* **f** *(212) 586 9249; 12400 Wilshire Bd, Suite 550, LA, CA 90025,* **t** *(310) 820 1898,* **f** *(310) 820 6357,* **w** *www. italiantourism.com.*

In Milan

Tourist offices are known variously as EPT, APT or AAST, or more modestly as *Pro Locos*. They provide an updated list of accommodation, good city maps and other practical information:

EPT: *Piazza del Duomo on Via Marconi 1,* **t** *02 7252 4301/2/3,* **f** *02 7252 4350.* **Open** *Mon–Fri 8.30am–7pm, Sat 9–1 and 2–6, Sun 9–1 and 2–5.*

EPT: *Stazione Centrale.* **Open** *Mon–Sat 8am–7pm, Sun 9–12.30 and 1.30–6.*

EPT: *Gallerio V. Emmanuele, Piazza belle Scala,* **t** *02 869 0734.* **Open** *Mon–Sat 8am–7pm, Sun 9–12.30 and 1.30–6.*

Women Travellers

Milan is by and large a very safe city to walk in, even late at night. One area to avoid at night if walking alone, however, is the station and its immediate surrounds. If you have experienced sexual harassment or assault, ring **t** 02 7207 5787 for assistance.

Working and Long Stays

Registration and Residency

If you are planning to stay in Italy long term without working, and are not an EU citizen, you should register with the police within eight days of arrival and apply for a *permesso di soggiorno* from the Ufficio Stranieri (**t** 02 62261, Questura building, Via Fatebenefratelli 11; open mornings only). The *permesso* lasts for three months, after which time you will need to renew it. If you can prove you have enough money to live on, permission is usually granted. You should do all you can to appear calm and remain polite through the ordeal.

Anyone who wishes to be registered as a resident should apply to their local *Anagrafe* (registry office). There are plenty of these, easily located in the phone book or '*Pagine Gialle*' (Yellow Pages). If you are in Italy for work, your employer should help you with the red-tape. Many small businessmen will only employ unregistered foreigners (that way they don't have to declare them and pay tax).

Students

Students attending courses at Italian universities or private colleges must obtain a declaration from the Italian Consulate in their home countries before their departure, certifying their 'acceptability'. Ask your embassy about scholarships offered by the Italian Ministry of Foreign Affairs (many are never used for lack of requests).

Finding a Job

Finding a job in Milan can be difficult. EU residents may register at the nearest *Ufficio di Collocamento* (Manpower Office). Teaching English is the most obvious source of income; qualifications or some experience, while not always essential, may make the difference. *Hello Milano, Easy Milano , Seconda Mano* and *City Milano* newspapers are a good place to look for openings. It also never hurts to show up at a language school and ask for an interview. Some secondary schools take on mother tongue assistant teachers for their language classes. English-speaking *au pairs* are also in demand: try the papers or place an ad, either in one of the above papers or in the main university faculty buildings (leave paper strips with your telephone number, which interested parties can tear off). Other secretarial and catering jobs are generally available, but your chances are slim if you only speak English.

Ultimately, knowing or befriending someone is your best route.

Finding a Flat

The Wednesday edition of *Corriere della Sera* has an accommodation section, and it is worth checking out the local newspapers listed above, as well as noticeboards in the university faculty buildings. Expect to pay an average of around €300–400/month for a one-bedroom flat.

Most landlords insist on a deposit of two, and sometimes three months' rent in advance, and it can be the devil to get it back when you leave, even if you give the required three months' notice. If you find a flat through an estate agent their commission is usually 10% of a year's rent. Rental leases are signed through a *commercialista* or *notaio*, who represents both you and the landlord and is paid to know all the complicated legal niceties (landlords often have their lawyers along, so you may want to have one too, in case they try to pull a fast one because you're a foreigner). The lease (usually for one year) may specify that you are not to become a resident.

Cars

You have to be a resident to buy one second-hand and drive it in Italy; non-residents are only allowed to purchase a new car on the condition that they get a special EE plate (*escursionista estero*), valid for 365 days. Sales staff should be able to help with the papers. The law says residents have to change their driving licences over to Italian ones as soon as they become residents. Non-EU citizens are required to have an international driving licence. Non-residents are only allowed to keep a foreign car in Italy for 365 days.

The Centre

PIAZZA DEL DUOMO AND AROUND 70
The Duomo 70
Palazzo Reale and Museo del Duomo 73
San Gottardo 73
Piazza Fontana 73
Galleria Vittorio Emanuele II 73
Piazza Mercanti 74
Palazzo della Ragione 74
Corso Vittorio Emanuele II 74
San Carlo 74

PIAZZA DELLA SCALA AND AROUND 75
La Scala 75
Palazzo Clerici 76
Palazzo Marino 76
San Fedele 76
Casa degli Omenoni 77
Palazzo Belgioioso 77
Casa del Manzoni 77
San Giuseppe 77

THE FINANCIAL DISTRICT 78
The Borsa 78
The Ambrosiana 78
San Satiro 79
Palazzo Borromeo 80

1 Lunch

Ristorante San Tomoso, *Via San Tomaso 5*, **t** *02 874 510*; **metro** *Cairoli*. **Open** *Mon–Fri, and Sat eves*. **Cheap**. This place is popular with the working Milanese for its lunchtime self-service buffet; moderately priced in the evening.

2 Tea and Cakes

Antica Gelateria del Corso, *Galleria del Corso 4, off Piazza Beccaria*, **t** *02 799 961*; **metro** *Duomo*. **Open** *Mon–Fri 9am–1pm, and Sat–Sun brunch 12–4pm*. Three floors of saccharine paradise, including delicious ice creams, sandwiches, pastries and salads, as well as cocktails.

3 Drinks

La Banque, *Via Porrone 6, off Via Clerici*, **t** *02 8699 6565*; **metro** *Cordusio*. **Open** *Tues–Sun 6pm–2am*. Luxurious coloured marble surrounds bathed in soft light; this bar has a restaurant with comfy chairs, and is a dance mecca later in the evening.

The Centre

Piazza del Duomo in the city centre, with its surrounding interlinked baby piazzas, has always been the showcase of Milan's overweening ambition. In the centre of the square, old Vittorio Emanuele II on his horse looks ready to charge into action, trying to hold his own against the onslaughts of a thousand pigeons, while the extravagant mountain of the Duomo itself soars high overhead. To the south, the neoclassical Palazzo Reale, which housed Milan's rulers through the ages, from the Visconti to the Austrians, is now home to the Museo del Duomo.

To the north is the enormous 19th-century Galleria Vittorio Emanuele II, glittering symbol of Italian unification, as well as the world-famous but unprepossessing La Scala opera house, second home to the likes of Verdi and Toscanini.

Equally impressive piazzas surround La Scala; here vestiges of old-monied Milan survive in such buildings as the Palazzo Marino and the Banca Commerciale Italiano. There is a rich cultural history to be sought out in the centre's many preserved *palazzi*, such as those of Milanese author Alessandro Manzoni, and the 16th-century Casa degli Omenoni, home to the city's former Master of the Imperial Mint.

To the west, in what was once the heart of medieval Milan, is the still-thriving financial district, with the Borsa stock exchange glowering down on passersby, and the nearby Ambrosiana, home to one of world's most impressive collections of ancient manuscripts, as well as the 17th-century Cardinal Borromeo's eclectic art collection.

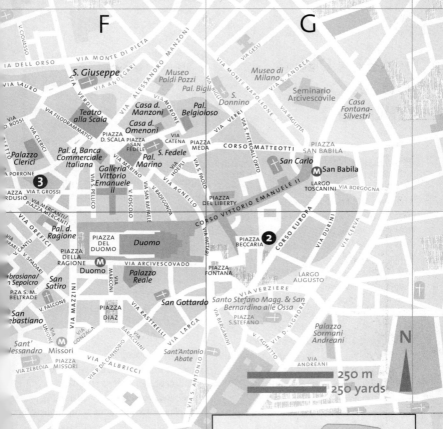

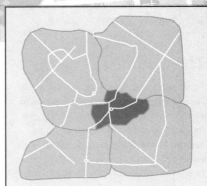

Highlights

Art City: Casa del Manzoni, the preserved 18th-century house of one of Italy's most revered authors, p.77

Architectural Milan: San Satiro, one of the marvels of the Italian Renaissance period, p.79

Bella Figura: The fine designer shops and elegant *caffès* in the glass-roofed arcade of the Galleria Vittorio Emanuele II, p.73

Trendy Milan: Cinemas, bookshops and chic boutiques along Corso Vittorio Emanuele II, p.74

Foodie Milan: The gastronomic delights of Peck, both the restaurant and its bountiful delicatessen nearby, p.164 and p.183

PIAZZA DEL DUOMO AND AROUND

Piazza del Duomo has been the city's religious and commercial centre since the 4th century, though much of that evidence has since been destroyed: the two churches that used to exist here were flattened in the 14th century to make way for the pompous cathedral, and, in accordance with the 19th-century fashion for Parisian-style boulevards, many medieval streets were knocked down and replaced. Unfortunately, even more space was created by the Allied bombing raids of 1943 – an air-raid shelter was recently rediscovered underneath the square itself – and the holes were soon filled in with unattractive, modern buildings.

Yet the piazza itself is never dull, constantly swarming with busy Milanese going to work, dawdling tourists and squirming Italian schoolchildren, as well as the usual con artists and vendors who come with such crowds, selling everything from sponges to sunglasses.

The Duomo F5

*Piazza del Duomo; **metro** Duomo. **Open** Tues–Sun 9.45–5.45; **adm** free; baptistry **adm** €1.50 (tickets at the bookshop, closed 1–3pm); treasury and crypt **adm** €1. Cathedral roof, **open** daily Nov–Feb 9–4.45, Mar–Oct 9–5.45; **adm** €3.30 by foot or €5 by lift. Note that the façade will be covered for restoration work until late 2004.*

In the exact centre of Milan towers its famous Duomo, a monument of such imposing proportions (third largest in the world after St Peter's and Seville Cathedral) that on clear days it is as visible from the distant Alps as the Alps are visible from its dome. Bristling with 135 spires, defended by 2,244 marble saints and one cheeky sinner (Napoleon, who crowned himself King of Italy here in 1805), guarded by 95 leering gargoyles, energized by sunlight pouring through the largest stained-glass windows in Christendom, the cathedral is a remarkable bulwark of the faith. And yet for all its monstrous size, for all the hubbub of its busy piazza, the Duomo is utterly ethereal, a rose-white vision of pinnacles and tracery woven by angels. In Vittorio de Sica's *Miracle in Milan* (1950) it serves its natural role as a stairway (or rather launching pad) to heaven for the broomstick-riding heroes.

Gian Galeazzo Visconti began the Duomo in 1386 as a votive offering to the Mother of God, hoping that she would favour him with an heir. His prayers for a son were answered in the form of Giovanni Maria, a loathsome degenerate assassinated soon after he attained power; as the Milanese wryly noted, the Mother of God got the better of the deal (*see* box, opposite).

The Interior

The remarkable dimensions of the interior challenge the eye to take in what seems like infinity captured under a canopy. Its tremendous volume is defined into five aisles by 52 pillars of titanic dimensions, unusually crowned by rings of niches and statues. Acres of **stained glass**, embellished with flamboyant Gothic tracery, provide the light; the oldest windows, from the 15th century, are along the naves at the crossing. All other decorations seem rather small (the better to emphasize the vast size), but you may want to seek out in the right transept Leone Leoni's fine Mannerist tomb of the Marquess di Marignano, Gian Giacomo de' Medici, or Il Medeghino, the pirate of Lake Como; it was erected by his brother Pope Pius IV. Fine bronze statues of Peace and Military Virtue sit on either side of the old buccaneer, portrayed with sword on hand, ready to go to war again. A relief of the *Adoration of the Magi* on top is the only nod towards religion, and its placement covers up part of the window. Il Medeghino's sarcophagus was originally here as well, until his nephew, St Charles Borromeo, took it away in accordance with the edict from the Council of

The Making of a Cathedral

Gian Galeazzo Visconti was the Man Who Would Be King – King of Italy, or whatever fraction of it he could snatch. A well-nigh psychotic ambition drove the frantic career of this paradigm of Renaissance princes, and such an ambition required a fitting symbol. Milan was to have a new cathedral, the biggest in the world, dedicated to the greater glory of God, Milan and the Visconti. The demolition of a huge part of the city centre made a space ready for it by 1386, when building began.

All Gian Galeazzo's schemes and aggressions came to nothing, as the little empire he built disintegrated after his death, but Milan did get its cathedral as a kind of consolation prize. From the beginning, the Duke called in all the most skilled builders of the day who were available. Their names are recorded: men such as Bonino da Campione and Matteo da Campione, two of the Campionese masters, and also a number of foreigners – Gamodia of Gmünd, Walter Monich and Peter Monich from Germany, and a Parisian known as Mignot.

In the court of the Duke, they argued over the sacred geometry appropriate to the task, over the relative merits of beginning the work *ad triangulum* or *ad quadratum*, that is, whether the plans and the measures should be based on the proportions of the equilateral triangle or the square. The latter, the more common form, was decided on, and in the lodge constructed for them the builders would have set up a large open space on the floor, for tracing out the detailed plan and elevation with compass and straight-edge. After that, over the years to come, they would work out all the details, every vault, column, buttress and pinnacle, from the same set of proportions.

There were other difficulties as well. Gothic may have been the international fashion in the 14th century, but the Milanese, like other Italian builders, wanted it on their own aesthetic terms. The huge size of the Duomo posed special problems; back when geometry was the only method architects had for figuring out problems of thrust, building a marble structure as high as it was wide wasn't obvious, and it was essential that the height of piers and vaults in the nave and the aisles be right on the money. Equally important to medieval builders, however, was the mystical accord of the numbers, the transcendant harmonies required in a house of God – which the Milanese were willing to adapt to create the effects they desired, much to the dismay of the experts brought in from Germany and France to pronounce on whether or not the Duomo would stand (most said no). Their quibbles were hashed out in a written debate known as the *dubia et responsiones* (questions and answers) that has come down to us, offering a rare glimpse into the medieval builder's concerns. The last expert, the Frenchman Mignot, predicted calamity and left in a snoot, writing, 'Art is nothing without science', to which the

---

Trent that 'receptacles and vain trophies' be removed from church interiors and buried under the floor. In the same transept you'll find one of the most peculiar of the cathedral's thousands of statues: that of San Bartolomeo holding his own skin, with an inscription assuring us that it was made by Marco Agrate and not by Praxiteles, just in case we couldn't tell the difference.

Other treasures include the beautiful walnut **choir stalls**, carved between 1572 and 1620, and the 12th-century bronze Trivulzio candelabrum by Nicola da Verdun, as well as medieval ivory, gold and silverwork in the **Treasury**, located below the main altar by the crypt, where the mastermind of the Counter-Reformation, St Charles Borromeo (1538–84) lies in state. He was lucky that he didn't die in the cathedral as well. When he returned to Milan as resident archbishop at the end of the Council of Trent he infuriated many members of Milan's then cosy clergy by making them toe the line to set a good example to other bishops. One dissendent priest shot him during Mass, but he was saved by the heavy brocade of his vestments.

Milanese made the famous reply, 'Science without art is nothing.'

The building would be a major drain on Gian Galeazzo's budget – almost as expensive as his endless wars. A normal, modest cathedral would have been a sufficiently difficult project. To get the Candoglia marble they wanted, for example, the master builders had to build roads and even canals, to bring the stone down from the quarries north of Lake Maggiore. The duke's passion for decoration made it even more difficult; he demanded angelic hosts of statuary – over 2,000 on the exterior and 700 more inside. As many as 300 sculptors found employment at one time in the Cathedral workshops. These too came from all over Europe; names like Pietro di Francia and Fritz di Norimberga on the pay lists are a reminder of the Christian, pan-European universality of the age. Men might speak different tongues, but at this time, the language of faith and art were the same.

How did Milan and the Duke pay for all this? The records mention a big campaign by local church authorities to sell religious indulgences, while the state contributed sums from a steep increase in fines in the courts. It wouldn't have been enough. The financing would have been a formidably complex matter, no doubt partially arranged by loans from the Lombard and Tuscan bankers, but no one can say exactly how deeply the Duke dug into his own pockets, how much he coaxed or squeezed out of the other great families, how much the pope, Milan's ally, threw in and how much was wrung out of the poor. New technology helped to lower the costs, especially the machines invented by a Master Giovanni da Zellino for hoisting stone more easily – it's often forgotten how the late Middle Ages was a time of dizzying technological progress, creating advances in everything from navigation to farming to the first mechanical clocks. For all the complexity, the duke and his builders knew what they were about; the cathedral was substantially complete by 1399.

However, by the time they got to the façade, the Gothic style – which the Italians never liked much to begin with – had become unfashionable. This bewildered front went through several overhauls of Renaissance and Baroque, then back to Gothic, with the end result, completed in 1809 under Napoleon, resembling a shotgun wedding of Isabelline Gothic with Christopher Wren. In the 1880s there were plans to tear it down and start again, but no one had the heart, and the Milanese have become used to it. Walk around, though, to the glorious Gothic apse, with its three huge windows (1389) to see what its original builders were about. The subjects of the bas-reliefs on the bronze doors are a Milanese history lesson: the Edict of Constantine, the Life of St Ambrose, the city's quarrels with Barbarossa and the history of the cathedral itself.

Throughout the Duomo you can see the alchemical symbol adopted as the Visconti crest, now the symbol of Milan: a twisting serpent in the act of swallowing a man. The story goes that in 1100, in the Second Crusade, the battling bishop Ottone Visconti (the founder of the family fortunes) fought a giant Saracen, and when he slew him he took the device from his shield.

Near the cathedral entrance a door leads down to the 4th-century remains of the **Baptistry of San Giovanni delle Fonti**.

Excavated in the 1960s, it contains the octagonal baptismal font where St Ambrose baptized St Augustine, as well as remains of the **Roman road** and other churches demolished to make way for the Duomo.

For a splendid view of Milan, take a walk through the enchanted forest of spires and statues on the **cathedral roof**. The 15th-century **dome** by Amadeo of Pavia, topped by the main spire with the gilt statue of *La Madonnina* (who at 12ft tall really isn't as diminutive as she seems when viewed from the ground 354ft below), offers the best view of all – on a clear morning, all the way to the Matterhorn.

Palazzo Reale and Museo del Duomo F5

Piazza del Duomo 12 and 14, t 02 7202 2656; metro Duomo. Open daily 9.30–12.30 and 3–6; adm for museum €5.16.

On the south side of the cathedral, the Palazzo Reale was for centuries the headquarters of Milan's rulers, from the Visconti down to the Austrian governors, who had the place redone in their favourite neoclassical style. In one wing, the **Museo del Duomo** contains art and artefacts made for the cathedral over the past six centuries, including some of the original stained glass and fine 14th-century French and German statues and gargoyles, tapestries, and a Tintoretto. Other rooms document the cathedral's construction, including a magnificent wooden model from 1519, designs from the 1886 competition for the façade, and castings from the bronze doors.

The main core of the **Palazzo Reale** used to accommodate the Civico Museo dell'Arte Contemporanea (CIMAC); though there are tentative plans to see the Palazzo Reale host all the city's contemporary art in the future, the museum is now closed for major restructuring, its collections divided between the Civica Galleria d'Arte Moderna (*see* p.91) and the Esposizione Permanente at the Società per le Belle Arti (*see* p.92), both of which are in the Giardini Pubblici area.

San Gottardo F5

Via Pecorari 2, t 02 8646 4500; metro Duomo, tram 12, 23 or 27, bus, 54, 60 or 65. Open daily 8–12 and 2–5.45; adm free.

Begun in the 1330s at the instruction of Azzone Visconti, this royal palace church still has its original 14th-century apse, though the remainder of the church has been incorporated into the Palazzo Reale since the 18th century. Its façade is primitive but the octagonal **medieval bell tower** is a

beautiful and popular icon of the city, known as the *campanile del duomo* since the cathedral, for all its bells and whistles, hasn't got one.

The **Gothic portal** was restored in 1929, while the neoclassical interior is a design of Piermarini, he of La Scala fame, with stucco decorations by Giocondo Albertoli. There is also a fragment of fresco attributed to the school of Giotto, depicting the Crucifixion. Left of the presbytery is the reconstructed funerary monument of Azzone Visconti by Giovanni di Balduccio. Giovanni Visconti was murdered on the steps of the church in 1412, in a bloody scene reminiscent of the murder of Thomas à Becket.

Piazza Fontana G5

Metro Duomo.

Set behind the Duomo, this little piazza was the target of a terrorist attack in 1969, when a bomb exploded in the nearby Banca dell'Agricoltura, killing 16 people; it was attributed to the *Brigate Rosse*, or Red Brigades. The **fountain** at its centre, one of more than 50 in the city, was designed in 1783 by Piermarini, who also designed the façade of the 12th-century **Palazzo Arcivescovile**, also known as Seminario Arcivescovile at No.2. If you can get a peek inside, it has a handsome *quattrocento* courtyard; a second one, in a muscular Mannerist style, was designed by Pellegrini.

Galleria Vittorio Emanuele II F4

Metro Duomo. Open daily; adm free.

The first king of Italy lent his name to Milan's majestic drawing room, or *salotto*, the elegant Galleria Vittorio Emanuele II, a glass-roofed arcade linking Piazza del Duomo and Piazza della Scala. It was designed by Giuseppe Mengoni, who tragically slipped and fell from the roof the day before its inauguration in 1878. For nine years, until Naples built its Galleria Umberto, it was the largest in the world, and over the years it has seen a number of historical events, including a parade of elephants on their way to play in a production of *Aida* at La Scala.

Inside are classic bars and some of the city's finest shops, while in the centre, under a marvellous 157ft **glass dome**, is a mosaic figure of Taurus; the Milanese believe it's good luck to step on the bull's testicles.

Piazza Mercanti F5

Metro *Duomo or Cordusio.*

This piazza was the centre of life under the *comune* in the 12th century, and is the only surviving medieval square in Milan. Other public buildings surround it, and at one time, they nearly enclosed it: flanking the square on the Via Mercanti side is the **Palazzo dei Giureconsulti** (1564), with its portico and richly designed windows by Seregni and Galeazzo Alessi; the building in black and white marble is the **Loggia degli Osii**, from 1316; to the right of this is the 17th-century **Palazzo delle Scuole Palatine**; on the left is the mid-15th-century **Casa Panigarola**.

Palazzo della Ragione F5

Piazza Mercanti; **metro** *Duomo.* **Open** *for exhibitions only.*

This was a typical medieval town hall, or Hall of Justice (1233), which was given an extra floor with oval windows by Austrian empress Maria Theresa. On the side facing Piazza Mercanti, look for a beautiful early 13th-century **equestrian relief**, with a single arch framing an equestrian statue of the *podestà* (or governor) Oldrado da Tresseno, erected in 1233 with the inscription *catharos ut debuit uxit* ('he burnt heretics as he ought to'). While facing Via Mercanti, don't miss the **bas-relief** of a sow partly clad in wool, discovered while digging the foundations for the *palazzo*. According to legend, a tribe of Gauls, under their chief Belloveso, defeated the local Etruscans in the 6th century BC and wanted to settle in the area. An oracle told them to found their town on the spot where they found a sow half-covered in wool, and

to name it after her. The sow was eventually discovered, and when the Romans conquered the Gauls, they translated the Celtic name of the town into the Latin Mediolanum, meaning 'half-woolly'.

Corso Vittorio Emanuele II F5–G4

Metro *San Babila.*

This busy pedestrian street, once chock-a-block with 19th-century buildings, had to be totally rebuilt after the Second World War. Now one of Milan's flashiest commercial thoroughfares, lined on one side by a classical arcade and on the other by the frilly flank of the Duomo, it sports cafés, cinemas and chic boutiques.

It was originally a Roman road and used to be called *Corsia dei Servi*, or 'servant street', due to the street's resident monks, or 'servants of God' in the former Monastery of Santa Maria (now the church of San Carlo), which is set back from its northern side on its own *piazzetta*. Manzoni's *I Promessi Sposi* (*The Betrothed*) contains a vivid description of the bread riots which took place in this street in 1628.

Piazza del Liberty G4

Metro *Duomo or San Babila.*

This square takes its Art Nouveau appella-tion from the façade of the building at No.8, which was restored after bombing in 1943 using the Liberty-style fragments from the former Hotel Rianon on Corso Vittorio Emanuele II.

San Carlo G4

Corso Vittorio Emanuele II 14, **t** *02 773 302;* **metro** *San Babila.* **Open** *daily 8–12 and 3–5;* **adm** *free.*

Built between 1838 and 1847, on a design by Carlo Amati derived from the Pantheon in Rome, this is an unusual example of neoclassicism conceived around a circular core. Set back from the bustle of Corso

Vittorio Emanuele II, the church is reached via a lovely **Corinthian arcade**.

PIAZZA DELLA SCALA AND AROUND

The site of Piazza della Scala represented the extremity of the town in the Middle Ages. Built in 1858 as part of the 19th-century urban planning project, this small and rather plain square does have fine buildings on each side, but it is really more of a prelude and passageway through to the more decorative Galleria Vittorio Emanuele II, and hardly worthy of the famous opera house for which it was created to provide an approach. An unloved **statue** of long-time Milanese resident, Leonardo da Vinci, made by Pietro Magni in 1872, pouts in the middle.

La Scala F4

Piazza della Scala; metro Duomo.
***Closed** for rebuilding, due to re-open December 2004. Museo Teatrale alla Scala has moved (see p.119).*

The Milanese have never been modest by nature, and La Scala lays no small claim as the world's most prestigious opera house. When Milan's old opera house, the Regio Ducal Teatro, burned to the ground, aristocratic box holders petitioned the Empress Maria Theresa for a new opera. It was built in a simple neoclassical style in 1778 by Giuseppe Piermarini, a pupil of Vanvitelli, and named after the 14th-century church of Santa Maria alla Scala (itself named after its founder, Beatrice della Scala, the wife of Duke Bernabò Visconti) which formerly stood on the site. Inaugurated in 1778 with Salieri's *Europa Riconosciuta*, La Scala started off specializing in Neapolitan opera *buffa*. But in those days, the music was often secondary – especially to the elite, who literally owned their boxes and rivalled one

another in their decoration, treating them as semi-public showcases. Each had an anteroom and a cloakroom, and noblemen used them for entertaining, even serving fancy suppers during performances.

La Scala started to find its destiny as the cathedral of Italian melodrama in 1781, with Gioacchino Rossini, whose *La Gazza Ladra* premiered here and who maintained a close relation with the theatre for two decades. La Scala later saw the premieres of a number of 19th-century classics of Italian opera: Doninzetti's *Lucrezia Borgia*, Verdi's *I Lombardi*, *Nabucco*, *Simon Boeccanegro*, *Otello* and *Falstaff*; Puccini's *Madame Butterfly* and *Turandot*. Occasionally politics intruded, as in 1859, when the crowded house at a performance of *Norma* took advantage of the presence of the Austrian governor to join in the rousing war chorus. Among 20th-century premieres were Poulenc's *Dialogues des Carmélites*, Bernstein's *A Quiet Place* and Berio's *La Vera Storia*.

In 1898, La Scala found a new artistic director in Arturo Toscanini, who made it one of the major opera houses in the world, the proving ground of singers. He broadened the horizons of the Milanese operagoers with innovative works such as *Pelleas et Melisande*, and invited composers such as Richard Strauss and Stravinsky to conduct their own works. Although Toscanini supported Mussolini when the dictator founded the Fascist party in Milan in 1919, he soon became disillusioned with it all and went to New York, forcing the opera house into a major slump.

Yet when bombs smashed La Scala in 1943, the Milanese, in a remarkable act of will and opera devotion, rebuilt it to its original grandeur in only three years. On 11 May, 1946 it reopened under the baton of Arturo Toscanini, who had returned to Italy one last time for the occasion. Nor was it long before La Scala re-established its pre-eminence: in the 1950s, it became home to such conductors as Tullio Serafin, Victor De Sabata, Antonio Guarnieri and Paul Sacher, and became famous for the prima donna rivalries between Maria Callas and Renata Tebaldi. In 1965 Franco Zeffirelli shot his first major film here, *La Bohème*, directed by Von Karajan, which is still rated as one of the best attempts to put opera on celluloid. Claudio Abbado and current director Riccardo Muti have kept standards high.

Since its reopening in 1946, La Scala has never closed, except now – for a major €49 million refurbishing of the stage, the dressing rooms and storage areas that is slated to be complete by the end of 2004. In preparation, and to assure that the show would go on, an alternative venue, the Teatro Arcimboldi was built out in the industrial suburbs (*see* 'Nightlife and Entertainment', p.178). There are hopes that La Scala's sojourn in the Arcimboldi will introduce it to a new, younger audience and give the company a breath of fresh air, which had become difficult to draw in its hallowed shrine.

For those who insist on seeing opera at the original La Scala however, half-hour operatic segments will be shown from a gigantic screen covering the building's façade throughout opera season.

Palazzo della Banca Commerciale Italiana F4

*Piazza della Scala; **metro** Duomo. **Open** during banking hours.*

Dominating the Piazza della Scala and in direct competition with the opera house for grandeur, the Palazzo della Banca Commerciale Italiana is at present the seat of one of the country's most important financial institutions, and a Milanese monument to '*capitalismo morale*'. Using German funds, the Palazzo was built in 1894 according to a design by Luca Beltrami Decolto alle Case Rotte, on the site of the former church of San Giovanni.

Palazzo Clerici F4

*Via Clerici 5, **t** 02 878 266; **metro** Cordusio. **Open** by prior arrangement only; **adm** free.*

The great Venetian wizard of the late Baroque brush, Giambattista Tiepolo, made two trips to Milan, in 1731 and 1740, to fresco palace ceilings. His first effort was destroyed in the Second World War, but his latter commisson in this 17th-century *palazzo* (now partly occupied by the Institute for the Study of International Politics) has survived in a splendid **Salone del Tiepolo**.

Palazzo Marino F4

*Piazza della Scala 2; **metro** Duomo. Courtyard only **open** to the public; **adm** free.*

Opposite the theatre, the imposing Palazzo Marino is a fine 16th-century building hiding behind a 19th-century façade. Now the Palazzo Municipale, the seat of the municipal council, it has one of the city's loveliest courtyards, designed in 1558 by Galeazzo Alessi.

The comparatively sombre ground floor of paired Doric columns sets up the theatre happening above – a beautiful, fantasy-filled blend of sculpture and architecture, designed to appeal more to the eye than to the mind.

San Fedele F4

*Piazza San Fedele, **t** 02 7200 8027; **metro** Duomo, **tram** 1 or 2, **bus** 61. **Open** Mon–Fri 8.30–2.30 and 4–7; **adm** free.*

Commissioned by Cardinal Borromeo, the church of San Fedele, with its austere single nave, side chapels, and altars, was conceived as a model of Lombard Counter-reformation style. It was begun by Pellegrini and completed only in the 19th century, after interventions by Martino Bassi and then Francesco Ricchino on the cupola.

The **façade**, however, has been restored to its original high Renaissance appearance. The interior contains 16th- to 17th-century Mannerist works by Barnaino Campi, and, more famously, a depiction of *St Ignatuis' Vision* by Giovan Battista Crespi, nicknamed 'il Cerano'.

The square in front of the church has a **monument to Alessandro Manzoni** (who died here after a fall on its steps), completed by Francesco Barzaghi in 1883.

Casa degli Omenoni F4

Via Omenoni 3; metro Duomo. Closed to public.

This Mannerist 'House of the Big Brutes' (1565) was built by Leone Leoni for his retirement. Leoni, originally from Arezzo in Tuscany, was a great goldsmith as well as a sculptor (see his monument in the Duomo) and he spent most of his career as Charles V's Master of Imperial Mint in Milan (when he wasn't in Spain with his son Pompeo, decorating the church of El Escorial with statues of the royal family).

He made his own house into a tribute to his hero, the philosopher emperor Marcus Aurelius; the six large and uncomfortable-looking telamones he sculpted for the **façade** probably represent members of the barbarian tribes subdued by the emperor.

Palazzo Belgioioso F4

Piazza Belgioioso 2; metro Duomo. Closed to the public.

This little corner of 18th-century Milan is named after the building which dominates the square's northeastern flank. Commissioned in 1772 from Piermarini by Prince Alberico XII di Belgioioso d'Este, it was finished in 1781. It is a typical piece of grandiose Lombard neoclassicism with three interior **courtyards**, the largest of which has pleasing Doric porticoed wings. The **façade** bears the heraldry of the Este family.

Casa del Manzoni F4

Via Morone 1, t 02 8646 0403; metro Montenapoleone, tram 1 or 2, bus 61. Open Tues–Fri 9–12 and 2–4; adm free.

Students and readers of the great Italian novelist Alessandro Manzoni (1785–1873) may want to visit the author's handsome old home, where he wrote his classic, *I Promessi Sposi (The Betrothed)*, one of Italy's greatest 19th-century novels.

The house is now a shrine, in the form of the **Museo Manzoniano**, which is filled with items relating to Manzoni's life and work, including illustrations from the *Sposi*, an autographed portrait of his friend Goethe, his bedroom and his perfectly preserved studio on the ground floor, where he wrote and also received the likes of Garibaldi and Verdi. The house also serves as a centre for Manzonian studies, containing a huge library of the novelist's work and criticism of it.

San Giuseppe F4

Via Verdi 11, t 02 805 2320; metro Duomo. Open Mon–Sat 9.30–12.30 and 3.30–6, Sun 9–1; adm free.

The church of San Giuseppe was a great architectural landmark in its day, and if it looks like hundreds of other churches in Italy, it proves the old adage that imitation is the sincerest form of flattery. Begun in 1607, it was the first independent project of Milan's most innovative Baroque architect Francesco Maria Ricchino, who began his career under Lorenzo Binago (*see* p.103) before his patron Cardinal Federico Borromeo sent him to Rome to finish his training. When he returned, this was the result: a church designed on the basis of two simple Greek crosses with very abbreviated arms.

The **dome** rises over the congregation on arches (Binago's innovation in Sant'Alessandro), but here, Ricchino added a high arch between the congregation and sanctuary to fuse the two spaces in a new and exciting way that would be endlessly repeated by later Baroque architects, who loved its rich possibilities for scenographic effects.

San Giuseppe's **façade**, designed at the same time as the church but not added until 1630, was another innovation. Previous Italian façades had been merely decorative, hardly related to the structure of the church itself. Here Ricchino strove for integration: the façade, designed as a pair of aedicules (compositions of a pediment over paired columns), one set inside the other, reflects the proportions and decorative style of the interior, and draws the eye to the other visible parts of the exterior rather than just the immediate 'show front'. The impression of unity is so immediate that Ricchino's aedicule façade became the favourite in the Baroque style – so common, in fact, that most people walk past this once cutting-edge church without a second glance. Originally a convent was attached to it, but it was demolished to allow La Scala to build a deeper stage.

THE FINANCIAL DISTRICT

Like London and New York, Milan has a sombre ghetto for its money men. Since the Middle Ages, this area between the Duomo and Sant'Ambrogio has been the headquarters of Milan's merchant guilds, bankers and financiers, concentrated in the bank-filled Piazza Cardusio, Piazza degli Affari and Via Mercanti, just off Piazza del Duomo.

The Borsa E4

*Piazza degli Affari; **metro** Cordusio. **Open** to the public for exhibitions only.*

Set in Piazza Affari (business square), Milan's Borsa (stock exchange) was founded by Napoleon's viceroy Eugène de Beauharnais. The current imposing Palazzo della Borsa dates from 1931, and

sits smack on the ruins of ancient Mediolanum's theatre; bits remain in the cellars and in the lower parts of the buildings along Via Vittore al Teatro.

The Ambrosiana F5

*Piazza Pio XI (off Via Spadari and Via Cantù), t 02 8645 1436; **metro** Duomo. Pinacoteca **open** Tues–Sun 10–5.30; **adm** €7.60; the **library** is open for study; occasional visits for special exhibits, ring for an appointment.*

The Ambrosiana is Milan's most enduring legacy of its leading family, the Borromei. Cardinal Federico Borromeo (cousin of Charles) founded one of Italy's greatest libraries here in 1609, and it now contains 30,000 rare manuscripts, including ancient Middle Eastern texts that were collected as part of the cardinal's efforts to produce a translation of the Bible; a 5th-century illustrated *Iliad*; Leonardo da Vinci's famous *Codex Atlanticus*, with thousands of his drawings; early editions of *The Divine Comedy*; and much, much more.

After years of restoration, the Cardinal's art collection, the **Pinacoteca Ambrosiana**, housed in the same building, has reopened. Although paintings have been added over the centuries, the gallery is essentially a monument to one man's taste – which showed a marked preference for the Dutch, and for the peculiar, and ranges from the truly sublime to some of the funniest paintings ever to grace a gallery. Here are Botticelli's lovely *Tondo*, and his *Madonna del Baldacchino* nonchalantly watering lilies with her milk; a respectable *Madonna* by Pinturicchio; paintings by Bergognone (including the altar from Pavia's San Pietro in Ciel d'Oro); a lovely portable altar by Geertgen tot Sint Jans; and the strange, dramatic *Transito della Vergine* by Baldassarre Estense.

Further along, an *Adoration of the Magi* by the Master of Santo Sangue is perhaps the only one where Baby Jesus seems properly thrilled at receiving the very first Christmas presents. A small room, illuminated by a pre-Raphaelite-style stained-glass window of Dante by Giuseppe Bertini (1865), contains the glove Napoleon wore at Waterloo, a 17th-century bronze of Diana the Huntress, so ornate that even the stag wears earrings, and entertaining paintings by the Cardinal's friend Jan Brueghel the Younger, who delighted in detail and wasn't above putting a pussycat in Daniel's den of lions.

These are followed by more masterpieces: a Page, perhaps by Giorgione, Luini's *Holy Family with St Anne* (from a cartoon by Leonardo), Leonardo's *Portrait of a Musician* (its attribution is now disputed, although it's hard to imagine who else might have painted it), a lovely portrait of Beatrice d'Este attributed to Leonardo's follower, Giovanni Ambrogio da Predis, and then Bramantino's *Madonna in Trono fra Santi*, a scene balanced by a dead man on the left and an enormous dead frog on the right. Challenging this for absurdity is the nearby *Female Allegory* by 17th-century painter Giovanni Serodine, in which the lady, apparently disgruntled with her lute, astrolabe and books, is squirting herself in the nose.

Raphael's magnificent *Cartoon for the School of Athens* is as interesting as the fresco itself, which is now in the Vatican; popular theory claims that Raphael used the faces of contemporary artists, such as Da Vinci for Aristotle, for this particular work. Here, too, is a copy of Leonardo's *Last Supper*, painted by order of the Cardinal, who sought to preserve what he considered a lost work (as with the original, the copy itself has recently been restored). A 16th-century *Washing of Feet* from Ferrara has one Apostle blithely clipping his toenails. Another room contains pages of drawings from Leonardo's *Codex Atlanticus*. The first Italian still-life, Caravaggio's *Fruit Basket*, is also the most dramatic; it shares the space with Alessandro Magnasco's *The Crow's Singing Lesson*. Further on is Titian's *Adoration of the Magi*, painted for Henri II of France, and still in its original frame.

San Sepolcro E5

*Piazza San Sepolcro; **metro** Duomo. **Open** Mon–Fri 9–12 and 3–5; **adm** free.*

This church was first built in 1030 and then rebuilt in 1100 at the time of the Second Crusade, in which the Milanese took part. The neo-Romanesque façade was added in 1897, and the very large crypt is now all that remains of the church's original construction. The mostly Baroque **interior** is correspondingly ornate, with impressive and delicate terracotta work by Agostino de Fondutis. Its piazza, and the space extending into the Piazza Pio XI, marks the site of Mediolanum's Forum, although not a trace of it exists.

San Satiro F5

*Corner of Via Spadari and Via Torino, t 02 7202 1804; **metro** Duomo. **Open** Mon–Sat 8.30–11.30 and 3.30–5.30, Sun 9.30–10.30 and 4.30–5.30pm; **adm** free.*

Hiding behind a bland 19th-century façade waits one of Italy's most remarkable Renaissance churches. The original San Satiro was built in the 9th century, and in 1476 Bramante was hired to build a new church next door. It was his first architectural commission, and to refer to the older church he opted for a Greek cross plan. However, the space he had to build on was squeezed because of the street, giving him room for a 'T' but not a cross. Back in his native Urbino, Bramante had trained with two of Italy's greatest perspectivists, Piero della Francesca and Francesco di Giorgio, and here, thanks to his training and a tricky bit of architecture, he created a perfect illusion of a deep choir extending back three bays under a coffered vault, in a space only a few feet long.

Bramante also designed the beautiful little octagonal **baptistry**, lavishly decorated to Milanese taste with terracottas by Agosto De Fondutis. To the left, the original 9th-century San Satiro, now the *Cappella della Pietà*, is one of the finest examples of Carolingian architecture in north Italy, though it was touched up in the Renaissance, with decorations and a *Pietà* by De Fondutis. San Satiro's equally antique **campanile** is visible on Via Falcone.

San Sebastiano E5

*Via Torino 28, **t** 02 874 263; **metro** Missori. **Open** Mon–Sat 8–12 and 3–5, Sun 9.30–12 and 3.30–7; **adm** free.*

A tall, attractive cylindrical church, designed by Pellegrini, San Sebastiano was built in 1576 and paid for by the city in thanksgiving for the end of a plague.

San Giorgio al Palazzo E5

*Piazza San Giorgio, **t** 02 860 831; **metro** Missori, **bus** 2, 3, 14 or 20. **Open** daily 8–7; **adm** free.*

Built in 750 and named after the ancient Roman Imperial Palace that once stood here, little remains of this church's original architecture. It was transformed in 1623 by Ricchino and then again by Cagnole between 1800 and 1821. Inside is a lovely

cycle of paintings with scenes from the *Passion* by Bernardino Luini (1516).

Palazzo Borromeo E5

*Piazza Borromeo 7; **metro** Cordusio. Courtyard only open, unless during exhibitions or by prior arrangement (ring tourist office).*

This once glorious 15th-century residence, still occupied by the Borromeo princes, was hit squarely during the 1943 Allied bombing raids, and the only architectural detail still intact is the **portal** depicting the coat of arms of the Borromeo family.

On the ground-floor hall is the **Sala dei Giochi** with wonderful frescoes depicting the games enjoyed by the aristocracy in the Renaissance, the work of an artist who became synonymous with this piece of work and is known simply as the 'Master of the Borromeo Games'. The strange red background was originally a blue sky, which has changed colour over the years, apparently due to chemical reaction.

Brera and the Northeast

BRERA 84
Pinacoteca di Brera 84
Palazzo Cusani 86
Santa Maria del Carmine 87
San Marco 87
Museo Minguzzi 87

CORSO GARIBALDI AND AROUND 88
Santa Maria Incoronata 88
Naviglio della Martesana 88

VIA MANZONI 88
Museo Poldi-Pezzoli 88
Archi di Porta Nuova 90

QUADRILATERO D'ORO 90
Palazzo Bolognini and Museo di Milano 91
Museo Bagatti Valsecchi 91

GIARDINI PUBBLICI AND AROUND 91
Villa Reale and Galleria d'Arte Moderna 91
Esposizione Permanente delle Belle Arti 92
Palazzo Dugnani and Museo del Cinema 92
Corso Venezia and Around 92

FURTHER NORTH 94
Stazione Centrale 94
Pirellone 94

1 Lunch

San Fermo, *Via S. Fermo della Battaglia 1*, **t** *02 2900 0901*; *metro Moscova or Turati*. **Open** *Mon–Sat*. **Moderate**. One of Milan's secrets, serving light, tasty lunches.

2 Tea and Cakes

Caffè Cova, *Via Monte Napoleone 8*, **t** *02 7600 0578*; *metro Montenapoleone*; **tram** *2 or 20*. **Open** *Mon–Sat 9am–2.30am*. A Milanese institution famous for its home-made pastries since 1837.

3 Drinks

Moscatelli, *Corso Garibaldi 93*, **t** *02 655 4602*; *metro Moscova*. **Open** *Tues–Sun 12.30–7.30pm, 9pm–1.30am*. A beloved Milanese oasis for the fashion-weary. At 150 years old, this is the city's oldest *bottiglieria*.

Brera and the Northeast

This is the most beloved and familiar district of Milan, its imposing Stazione Centrale often providing newcomers with their startling first look at the city. A stone's throw away stands another of Milan's temples to modern life, the Pirelli Tower, or *Pirellone*, designed by Milanese architect Gio Ponti. From here you are swept back in time, down Via Pisani and past the city's 18th-century public gardens to the remnants of the medieval Spanish walls at the Archi di Porta Nuova. One of the city's most prestigious avenues, Via Manzoni, begins here, its noble houses now converted to swish hotels, banks and shops. This part of Milan, more than any other, has preserved its original character, mostly in the winding lanes of the gentrified Brera district, home to the city's unmissable Pinacoteca di Brera.

To the east, in the grid of streets known as the Quadrilatero d'Oro, lie the formerly fashionable residences of Milan's 18th- and 19th-century aristocracy, which are now occupied by the designer boutiques of Italy's fashion nobility: Armani, Versace and Co.

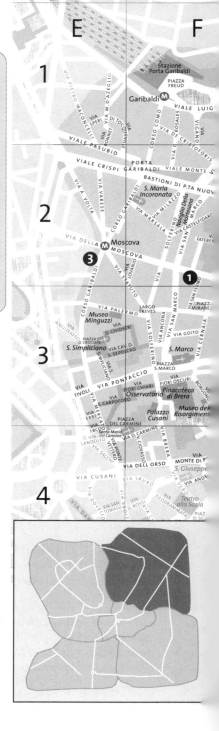

Highlights

Art City: Napolean's treasure, the Pinacoteca di Brera, p.84

Architectural Milan: The neo-Renaissance Museo Bagatti Valsecchi, long an inspiration for designers, p.91

Bella Figura: The glamorous Quadrilatero d'Oro, the grid of streets with catwalk designs and extortionate prices, p.90

Trendy Milan: The fashionable late-night bars and lounges near Porta Garibaldi in the northeast, p.174

Foodie Milan: The tiny Rossi gelateria, for a taste of what could be Italy's best ice cream, p.168

BRERA

The word Brera is derived from an old Germanic word, *braida*, meaning lawn – a reminder of Milan's historical ties with Germany (*see* 'Roots of the City', p.21) as well as the quarter's more verdant past.

The district has been ambitiously compared to Montmartre in Paris, or to London's Portobello Road, but, although hip and arty to a degree, it fails to quite measure up, partly because Italians never really let their hair down enough to be truly Bohemian.

Yet, in a city that was heavily bombed in the Second World War, Brera's cobbled and narrow streets were left relatively unscathed, retaining an appealing old-world artiness that the Milanese have enthusiastically cashed in on.

This is best seen in the atmospheric **Via Fiori Chiari** ('Street of Light-coloured Flowers'), which offers a very Milanese impression of *la dolce vita*, with its chic boutiques, small art galleries, and trendy bars and restaurants. The quarter's banner street, cobbled **Via Brera**, once poor and arty, is now lined with achingly exclusive bars and untouchable shops. But once a month, for those who would rather have a taste of what life used to be like in the district, it hosts a slightly more down-to-earth, though still pricey, antiques market.

Despite its present-day faux-Bohemian image, the Brera was once the real deal, and provided refuge for many influential Italian artists who were drawn in by the district's centrepiece, the art collection of the Pinacoteca di Brera. The Futurism of Boccioni and Marinetti is reputed to have taken seed in this quarter, and poets Eugenio Montale and Dino Buzzati spent much of their time here, often in the employ of Milan's national newspaper, the *Corriere della Sera*.

Pinacoteca di Brera F3

Corner of Via Brera and Via Fiori Oscuri, **t** *02 722 631;* **metro** *Lanza or Montenapoleone.* **Open** *Tues–Sun 8.30–7.15, may close at 6pm in winter;* **adm** *€6.20.*

One of world's finest hoards of art, especially of 14th–18th century northern Italian painting, the Brera's origins go back to 1773, when Pope Clement XIV banned the Jesuits, leaving their College in the Palazzo di Brera (1651–86, with a beautiful courtyard by Francesco Maria Ricchino) to the State. The Habsburgs converted the College into an art academy and gathered together a handful of paintings and sculptures from disused churches to inspire the pupils. Then along came Napoleon, whose bronze statue, draped in a toga, greets visitors as they enter; a believer in centralized art as well as central-ized government, he had northern Italy's churches and monasteries stripped of their treasures to form a Louvre-like collection in Milan, the capital of his Cisalpine Republic.

The result was the Brera; the gallery was first opened to the public in 1809, and stayed open even after Waterloo. It seems Milan rather enjoyed its role as the capital of northern Italy and didn't want to give the paintings back. In 1882, the academy and picture gallery were officially separated, putting the Brera into the sphere of Italy's national museums. A private collection, the **Donazione Jesi** has been added since, and there are plans to expand into the 18th-century Palazzo Citterio at Via Brera 12–14. Ongoing improvements and restorations since 1988 may lead to certain sections being closed.

Perhaps the best known of the Brera's scores of masterpieces is Raphael's *Marriage of the Virgin*, a Renaissance landmark for its evocation of an ideal, rarefied world, where even the disappointed suitor snapping his rod on his knee performs the bitter ritual in a graceful dance step, all acted out before a perfect but eerily vacant temple in the background. In the same room hangs Piero della Francesca's last painting, the

Pala di Urbino, featuring among its holy personages Federico da Monfeltro, Duke of Urbino, with his famous nose.

The **Venetian masters** are well represented: Carpaccio, Veronese, Titian, Tintoretto, Jacopo Bellini and the Vivarini, but especially Giovanni Bellini, with several of his loveliest Madonnas and the great *Pietà*, as well as a joint effort with his brother Gentile, *St Mark Preaching in Alexandria*. *The Flagellation,* by Luca Signorelli of Cortona, is his first documented work (it's signed *Opus luce cortonesis* on the building in the back-ground), and already shows his precocious talent and interest in the male nude that would culminate in his frescoes in Orvieto. There are luminous works by Carlo Crivelli (the golden, gorgeously dressed *Madonna della Candelletta*, in an arch made of Crivelli's trademark fruit and cucumbers) and *Cima da Conegliano*; Paris Bordone's famous *Venetian Couple* is here, too, complete with its mysterious man in the shadows.

There are several paintings by Andrea Mantegna, including his remarkable *Cristo Morto* (or *Cristo in scurto*), bathed in the wan light of the tomb. The abrupt foreshortening of the body on the stone slab puts the viewer in the scene, directly at Christ's feet; this immediacy and the relatively insignificant figures of the Virgin and St John mourning in the corner have been regarded as provocative in past centuries, but a recent study suggests that Mantegna's intentions were only the most pious; the dramatic composition was meant to emphasize an important relic much talked about at the time. According to Jewish ritual, Christ's body was anointed (see the pot of myrrh to the right of the pillow) and the slab he lies on, stained with his blood and the tears of the Virgin, was one of the holiest relics kept in Constantinople. It vanished in 1453 when the city was conquered by the Turks, only a few years before Mantegna was commissioned to paint the work (and just, coincidentally, when the popes were thumping the tub for another Crusade against the infidel). Mantegna's subdued colouring was an inspiration for Bramante, who was an elegant and graceful painter as well as an architect; see his *Christ at the Column* and his frescoes from the Casa Prinetti (1477), transferred to canvas. These include the *Colloquy of Philosophers*, 'weeping' Heraclitus and 'laughing' Democritus, discussing whether or not the earth is round; the figures' monumental, statuesque quality was a favourite Renaissance way of giving dignity to famous men of the past.

Other masterpieces include Caravaggio's striking *Supper at Emmaus*, the *Pala Sforzesca* by a 15th-century Lombard artist, depicting Lodovico il Moro and his family; a polyptych by Gentile da Fabriano; and fine works by the Ferrarese masters da Cossa and Ercole de' Roberti.

Outstanding among the non-Italians are Rembrandt's *Portrait of his Sister*, El Greco's *St Francis* and Van Dyck's *Portrait of the Princess of Orange*. When the Great Masters become indigestible, take a breather in the new 20th-century wing of the gallery, populated mainly by Futurists like Severini, Balla and Boccioni, who believed that to achieve speed was to achieve success, and the metaphysical followers of De Chirico, who seem to believe just the opposite.

Osservatorio Astronomico di Brera F3

Via Brera 28, t 02 805 7309; metro Lanza or Montenapoleone. Open Mon–Fri 9–4.30; adm €3.62 for guided tour, including dome, €5.16 on Fri eves.

Milan's observatory was established by the Jesuits in the 1760s as part of the Collegio di Brera, under the brilliant mathematician Father Ruggiero Boscovich from Dubrovnik – you can see a wooden model of his first observatory in Milan's Museum of Science and Technology (*see* p.122).

Under the Habsburgs in the 1780s, it helped to create an accurate cadastral survey of Lombardy well in advance of most of Europe

Made in Italy: the Martian Canals

The story of the canals is a genuine parable. It begins in 1858 at the Collegio Romano, the mouldering old Jesuit university a few blocks from Rome's Pantheon. Rome was entering its last decade of papal rule, the Inquisition was still in business, and Galileo and Copernicus were still on the blacklist.

Nevertheless, a few men in Rome were still wide awake. One of these was the Jesuits' chief astronomer, Pietro Angelo Secchi. In 1858, a Martian perihelic opposition year, Secchi took the opportunity to do some extended observations from the Collegio's observatory. He had a good look at the 'hourglass sea' (now Syrtis Major) and it seemed to him to resemble the narrow stretch of the Atlantic between Africa and the Americas. Like most astronomers of his time, Secchi was convinced that the dark patches were really water, and consequently called this one the *canale*, or channel. One of the great Martian myths was born.

A few years later, Giovanni Virginio Schiaparelli, was at work in Milan, making a name for his studies of Mars. He drew maps of the planet that were excellent (for the time) and designed fancy classical names for many of its surface features that are still used today. He was probably also the first person to observe the Martian dust storms.

Schiaparelli had an excellent eye for details, but he also happened to be colour blind. This seems to have actually helped him; the little handicap made it possible to pick out nuances of shading that others couldn't see. Ironically, though, it also helped him to see things that weren't really there.

In his long and careful observations of Mars, Schiaparelli discerned a number of long, straight streaks across the planet's surface, and following Secchi he called them *canali*. These were very faint and difficult to observe; the astronomer noticed that the planet had to be turned just the right way for the features on any one part of it to become manifest. Over the years, Schiaparelli built up a network of intersecting *canali* that girdled the red planet. By the 1870s he was talking about 'gemination' or twinning; many of the *canali* seemed to be made up of two fine parallel lines. When the first spectrographic observations revealed the presence of water vapour near the poles, for anyone with just a little imagination, the *canali* of Mars had become canals.

– the lobby has a collection of instruments from the period.

After a period of decline, the new Italian state revived the observatory, and in 1872 appointed astronomer Giovanni Virginio Schiaparelli the director. Schiaparelli discovered the orbit of double stars, as well as the periods of rotation for Venus and Mercury, and laid the foundations of modern astrophysics, but he is best known for his work on the canals of Mars in 1877 – a 'discovery' that earned the Brera observatory a state-of-the-art telescope in 1885, besides inspiring some wonderful science fiction (*see* box, above).

Palazzo Cusani F3

Via Brera 15; metro Lanza, tram 3, 4, 12 or 14, bus 61. Closed to the public.

Though the origins of this *palazzo* date back to the 1500s, the building was substantially rebuilt in 1719 by Giovanni Ruggeri when the Baroque façade, windows and balconies were added; the neoclassical façade which gives onto the garden is the work of Piermarini. Legend has it that the Cusani brothers commissioned the two entrances as a sign of equality. Inside is a Madonna fresco by the Tiepolo school. The palace was the Austrian Ministry of War in the 19th century and still plays a military function today as headquarters of the Third Army Corps.

Santa Maria del Carmine F3–4

Piazza del Carmine 2, t 02 8646 3365; metro Lanza, tram 1, 3 or 14, bus 61. Open daily 7.15–11.30am and 3.30–7pm; adm free.

This Gothic-style church was in fact built in 1447 on the site of a Romanesque church, using material from the partially demolished Castello Sforzesco. Like many of Milan's churches, it underwent several additions and refurbishments in the Baroque period; in 1880, the façade was added by Carlo Macciachini. The beautiful wooden **interior** contains a fine Baroque sacristy, and the statues in the wooden choir are the models for the Duomo's spires, created by 19th-century artists. The tilt in the first set of piers is due to the absence of a supporting façade for so many years. The beautiful **Cappella del Rosario** by Gerolamo Quadrio is decorated with canvases by Camillo Procaccini depicting the *Life of Mary*.

Museo del Risorgimento F3

Via Borgonuvo 23, t 02 8846 4176, w www.museidelcentro.mi.it; metro San Babila or Montenapoleone. Open Tues–Sun 9–5.30; adm free.

Set inside a neoclassical *palazzo*, this museum is dedicated to the Unification of Italy in 1860 and the period leading up to it, a story told in manuscripts and artifacts from the Napoleonic era up until 1870.

San Marco F3

Via Fatebenefratelli, Piazza San Marco 2, t 02 2900 2598; metro Montenapoleone, bus 41 or 43. Open 7.30–12 and 4–7.30; adm free.

This 13th-century church stands at the top of Via Fatebenefratelli, which runs over Milan's original but now covered canal, the Naviglio Grande (*see* p.110). Founded by an Augustine monk, Lanfranco Settala, the church was dedicated to Mark the evangelist,

the patron saint of Venice, as a gesture of thanks to the Venetians for their help in defeating Frederick II Barbarossa. On 22 May, 1874, the church saw the first performance of Verdi's *Requiem* (*see* box, p.89).

Parts of the church's medieval structure survive – the portal and some of the statues adorning the front, part of the transept and the handsome **campanile**, although the neo-Gothic façade was added in 1871 by Carlo Macciachini. Inside, in the right transept, are some fine medieval marble tombs and **frescoes** from the *trecento*, including good ones by Paolo Lomazzo, and the *Foundation of the Augustine Order* by the Fiammeghini brothers.

The **presbytery** has a fine depiction of the *Legend of St Augustine* by Camillo Procaccini and Cerano, and the wonderful 17th-century *Geneological Tree of Order* by Genvesino. The fragment of a fresco in the left aisle, discovered in 1975, has been attributed by some to Leonardo da Vinci.

Nearby Via dei Giardini, laid out in 1938, is lined with handsome mansions with gardens.

San Simpliciano E3

Piazza San Simpliciano 7, t 02 862 274; metro Lanza. Open daily 7–12 and 3–7; adm free.

Possibly founded by St Ambrose, this church retains its palaeo-Christian form in a 12th-century wrapping, with an octagonal drum. The apse has a beautiful fresco of Bergognone's *Coronation of the Virgin* (1515), and the larger 16th-century **cloister** has especially charming twin columns.

Museo Minguzzi E3

Via Palermo 11, t 02 805 1460, e museominguzzi@tin.it; metro Moscova. Open Wed and Thurs 10–6, or by request; adm €5.16.

This small museum celebrating the life and work of the Bolognese sculptor has around a hundred pieces by the artist on display, accompanied by a chronology and memorabilia from his life.

Convento di Sant' Angelo F2–3

Piazza Sant'Angelo; **metro** *Turati.* **Open** *daily 8–12 and 3–5;* **adm** *free.*

This 16th-century Franciscan convent has a chapel with a two-layered façade, begun in 1552 following a design by Domenico Giunti. The best art is in the **sacristy** – canvases by Antonio Campi, the Fiammenghini brothers, Giulio Cesare and Camillo Procaccini. The original convent, demolished in 1931, was replaced by the current, not very attractive building designed by Giovanni Muzio and built in 1939–47. It's best to visit on Easter Monday, when the pretty Piazza Sant'Angelo hosts its annual flower market.

CORSO GARIBALDI AND AROUND

Santa Maria Incoronata F2

Corso Garibaldi 116, **t** *02 654 855;* **metro** *Moscova.* **Open** *daily 8–12 and 3–5;* **adm** *free.*

From the exterior it is possible to see that this church was originally conceived as two separate designs, then merged in 1468 to form one church for the Augustine order. The Sforza family used it as a mausoleum, and several of their funerary monuments survive. There are also traces of frescoes in the right-hand apse.

Naviglio della Martesana F2

Metro *Moscova.*

Now dry and weed-ridden, this narrow **canal** once flowed along what is now Via San Marco, linking the river Adda to Milan. It was used to carry food and building materials for the expansion of the city, and was one of the medieval canals dug for

the building of the Duomo. The wooden gates at either end are a lock, known as the *Trombone di San Marco.*

VIA MANZONI

Named after Milan's famous novelist when he died in 1873, Via Manzoni was one of Mediolanum's original Roman roads. In the past it was called *la Corsia del Giardino*, as it was not only the most direct route to the city's public gardens, but it was also lined with *palazzi* fronting many a hidden garden. If you are lucky you may be able to sneak a peek at one: two fine examples are the Palazzo Brentani at No.6 and Palazzo Anguissola at No.10.

Yet it was the opening of La Scala opera house at its southern end that kick-started Via Manzoni's life as a chic boulevard – and it is still lined with those original, elegant *palazzi*, some of which are now museums, galleries and expensive hotels. At No.29 is the esteemed **Grand Hotel et de Milan**, where Verdi lived and died (*see* box, opposite). As with many of Milan's central boulevards, the street has an extraordinary amount of green clocks – not altogether too surprising as the first public clock to strike the hours was made and erected in Milan in 1335.

Museo Poldi-Pezzoli F4

Via Manzoni 10, **t** *02 796 334,* **w** *www.museo poldi-pezzoli.it;* **metro** *Montenapoleone.* **Open** *Tues–Sun 10–6;* **adm** *€6.*

Here you'll find the lovely 17th-century palace of Gian Giacomo Poldi-Pezzoli, who rearranged his home to fit his fabulous art collection, then willed it to the public in 1879 Repaired after bomb damage in the Second World War, the Museo Poldi-Pezzoli retains its owner's designs.

His exquisite collection of 15th- to 18th-century paintings includes one of Italy's best-known portraits, the 15th-century *Portrait of a Young Woman* by Antonio

Verdi in Milan

Giuseppe Verdi (1813–1901) was from Busseto near Parma but lived for years in a room in the Grand Hotel et de Milan at Via Manzoni 29. The name of the street is apropos: Verdi's great *Requiem* Mass was composed for the first anniversary of the death of Manzoni, of whom Verdi once said: 'If men worshiped men I would have knelt before him.'

Verdi has achieved similar status in Italy, and today holds a position akin to that of Shakespeare in England. His relationship with La Scala wasn't always smooth sailing, but when the young composer reached the lowest ebb of his career, when his son, daughter, and wife (his childhood sweetheart) all died within a year, it was the director of La Scala who convinced him to return to composing.

The inspiration was a *libretto* which included a lament of captive Jews in Babylon. The result was his first big success, *Nabucco* in 1842; his rendition of the lament, a rousing chorus in praise of freedom, instantly became an anthem for those fighting in the Risorgimento for national unity; many Italians would still like to see it replace their present national anthem. By the 1850s, crowds at his operas would shout 'Viva Verdi!' – not just as a tribute, but as a not-too-subtle demand for Vittorio Emanuele, Re D'Italia (*see* 'Roots of the City', p.29).

But Verdi did try. Right from the beginning, he was a sincere patriot and progressive, though he was forced to work political themes into his operas in the most careful ways to get them past the vigilant Austrian censors. He used distant periods of Italian history such as *I Lombardi* and *I Due Foscari* as vehicles to inject a little politics into every opera season. The censors did their best to annoy. In an absurdity of truly operatic proportions, they forced him to transfer the setting of *Un Ballo* in Maschera from the royal court of Sweden to, of all places, Puritan Boston, since the original *libretto* dealt with the taboo subject of regicide. After Italian reunification, Verdi often turned to Shakespeare, whose plays were translated into Italian in 1838.

Verdi was such an icon that at the end of his life, as he lay on his death bed in his hotel room, straw was scattered in Via Manzoni to mute the sound of passing carriages – an act of kindness repeated for the centenary of his death in 2001. He was buried in Milan, in the chapel of a rest home founded for poor musicians, the Casa di Riposo dei Musicisti on Piazza Buonarroti 29 near the Fiera di Milano. 'He wept for and loved everyone' is his epitaph.

Pollaiuolo, depicting an ideal Renaissance beauty. She shares the most elegant room of the palace, the *Salone Dorato*, with the museum's other jewels: Mantegna's Byzantinish *Madonna*, Giovanni Bellini's *Pietà*, Piero della Francesca's *San Nicolò* and, from a few centuries later, Francesco Guardi's beautiful, dreamlike visionary *Grey Lagoon* (c. 1790).

Other outstanding paintings include Vitale da Bologna's *Madonna*, a polyptych by Cristoforo Moretti and works by Botticelli, Luini, Foppa, Turà, Tiepolo, Crivelli, Lotto, Cranach (including portraits of Luther and wife) and a crucifix by Raphael.

The collection is also rich in **decorative arts**, with Islamic metalwork and rugs (note the magnificent 16th-century Persian carpet depicting a hunting scene in the Salone Dorato), medieval and Renaissance armour, Renaissance bronzes, Flemish tapestries, Murano glass, lace and antique sundials.

Palazzo Borromeo d'Adda F4

*Via Manzoni 39; **metro** Montenapoleone.*
Closed to the public.

This 18th-century *palazzo*, now a private residence, was once a literary hangout for artists and novelists, including the Italophile, Henri Stendhal. Note the perfectly proportioned neoclassical façade.

Archi di Porta Nuova G3

Near the intersection with Via della Spiga; **metro** *Montenapoleone,* **bus** *94.*

These huge stone arches, dating from 1171, are a rare survival of Milan's medieval walls. On the inside of the arches are Roman tombstones – used as building stone – as well as a Gothic tabernacle with statues of the saints. The moat that once went around the walls was enlarged into a canal; like many of the city's medieval canals, it was covered in the 1880s (*see* p.110).

QUADRILATERO D'ORO

East of Via Manzoni lies the entrance to Milan's high-fashion vortex, nicknamed the Quadrilatero d'Oro, or 'grid of gold', for its pricey boutiques concentrated in the *palazzi*-lined Via Monte Napoleone and the elegant Via della Spiga to the north. Even if you're not in the market for astronomically priced clothes by Italy's top designers, these exclusive lanes make for good window-shopping and perhaps even better people-watching.

It's hard to remember that up until the 1970s Florence was the centre of the Italian garment industry. When Milan took over this status – it has the airports Florence lacks – it added the essential ingredients of business savvy and packaging to the Italians' innate sense of style, creating a high-fashion empire rivalling Paris, London and New York. Besides posing as Italy's fashion headquarters, these gilded streets also tell a history of their own. Via Monte Napoleone follows the line of the city's old Roman walls, and the grid of streets still reflects the original Roman ideas of town planning. Many of the *palazzi* now house boutiques of the fashion aristocracy, but they were once home to Milan's 'real' aristocrats such as the Melzi di Cusano and Bagatti Valsecchi families, who commissioned their neoclassical lines and porticoed courtyards. In the times of Sforza rule, the building at No.12 was a private

---

La Filiera

In the last 50 years, Italy, and in particular Milan, has become the yardstick of high-quality fashion. But Italian design hardly came out of the blue; Milan became famous in the Middle Ages for its luxury silks, cotton fustians, and woollens (all beautifully modelled on the Madonnas in the Brera), and to this day, the Lombard textile industry is the locomotive pulling the train of *la filiera*, a phrase that covers the 10,000 companies that make up the fashion industry from thread to finished garment.

La filiera netted €47.8 billion in 2001, making it the most important income earner in Italy. Most firms are three or four generations old, and most attribute this success to their dedication in maintaining artisanal roots and resisting Anglo-American models of producing goods at the lowest possible price and moving factories to other countries.

For most Italians in *la filiera*, such practices are anathema; to maintain control over their famous quality and craftsmanship, they believe it's essential to keep an eye on all stages of production from thread to sales in the smart boutiques. Como still produces the silk, and Biella still provides the wool, each small company trying to outdo the next. Only recently have a few companies given in to bottom-line economics and moved their textile factories to Central and Eastern Europe, although they are quick to point out that they own and control the whole affair from top to bottom.

The second factor, of course, is the art. With about 70 per cent of the world's art, Italy supplies its designers with limitless inspiration, and a very appreciative national market always striving to cut a suave *bella figura*. After all, this is a country where a group of friends going out for the evening will ring one another up to see what colour the others are wearing – to make sure no one clashes.

residence; it was subsequently transformed by Piermarini in 1782 and in 1804, and during Napoleonic rule it was taken over, becoming 'Monte Napoleone', giving rise to the street's name.

Palazzo Bolognini and Museo di Milano G4

Via S. Andrea 6; metro Montenapoleone. **Closed** *for restoration until 2003.*

There are three museums in the sumptuous 18th-century Palazzo Morando Bolognini: the **Museo di Milano** and the **Museo di Storia Contemporanea**, the first with paintings of old Milan, the second devoted to Italian history between the years 1914 and 1945; the third, the **Museo Marinaro Ugo Mursia**, has a collection of nautical models, figureheads, and mementoes.

Museo Bagatti Valsecchi G4

Via Santo Spirito 10, t 02 7600 6132, **w** *www.museobagattivalsecchi.org;* **metro** *Montenapoleone.* **Open** *Tues–Sun 1–5.45;* **adm** *€6.*

This was the life's work of two brothers, Fausto and Giuseppe Bagatti Valsecchi, who built a neo-Renaissance palace to integrate the period fireplaces, ceilings and friezes they had collected, carefully disguising such 19th-century conveniences as the bathtub. Some of the city's top designers have made unique creations inspired by the museum's displays, which are sold in the shop in the lobby.

Palazzo Bigli F–G4

Via Bigli 6; metro Montenapoleone. **Open** *for exhibitions only.*

Entered by way of a fine **Renaissance portal** with bas-reliefs depicting the Annunciation, this *palazzo*, open occasionally for exhibitions, is decorated with frescoes attributed to artists of the school of Luini.

San Donnino alla Mazza G4

Via Bigli 14; metro Montenapoleone.

Only one wall survives of this demolished 14th-century church, which can be seen by going under the *Portico del Lattèe*, or 'the milkman's portal'.

GIARDINI PUBBLICI AND AROUND

Although Milan can seem a city of unrelenting stone, its main municipal gardens provide rare, but welcome, relief. Designed by Piermarini in 1786, they were enlarged in 1857 by Giuseppe Balzaretto, who incorporated the gardens of Palazzo Dugnani. This shady arcadia, equipped with artificial rocks to compensate for Milan's flat terrain, is a good place for children, with its zoo, swans, playgrounds and a Natural History Museum. The Giardini Pubblici have a natural extension in the romantic Giardini di Villa Reale, laid out in 1790 for the Belgioioso family by Leopoldo Pollak, who later built the Villa Reale within the gardens.

Villa Reale and Galleria d'Arte Moderna G3

Giardini di Villa Reale, t 02 7600 2819; **metro** *Palestro.* **Open** *Tues–Sun 9.30–5.30;* **adm** *free.*

The neoclassical Villa Reale, once Napoleon's residence, is now the Civica Galleria d'Arte Moderna, which includes the ground floor **Vismara collection** of paintings (works by Picasso, Matisse, Modigliani, de Pisis, Tosi, Morandi and Renoir) and the Marino Marini sculpture collection. Marini (d. 1980), generally acknowledged as the top Italian sculptor of the 20th century, spent most of his career in Milan, and in 1973 he gave the city many of his sensuous, acutely observed bronzes, as well as paintings and graphic works.

The gallery's first floor hosts a collection of 17th-century Italian art, which includes the famous painting of *The Fourth State* by Pelizza da Volpedo. Also on display are the fine paintings of the self-consciously romantic *Scapigliati* (the 'Wild-Haired Ones') of Milan, as well as Italian Impressionists. The second floor hosts the Grassi collection of **French painters** Gauguin, Bonnard, Manet and Toulouse Lautrec and paintings by **Italian Futurists** Balla and Boccioni, including the latter's *Spiral Construction* of 1913.

Museo di Storia Naturale H3

*Giardini Pubblici, **t** 02 8846 3280; **metro** Palestro. **Open** Tues–Fri 9–6 and Sat–Sun 9–6.30; **adm** free.*

Another victim of the Second World War, the museum has been rebuilt in its original medieval style. Look for the Canadian cryptosaurus, the colossal European lobster, the Madagascar aye-aye and the 40kg topaz.

Planetarium H3

*Corso Venezia 57, **t** 02 2953 1181, **w** www.brera. mi.astro.it/~planet; **metro** Porta Venezia or Palestro, **tram** 9, 29 or 30. **Open** Mon–Fri 9–12.30 and 2–5.30; **adm** free.*

Children may like to visit the city's classical-style Planetarium, built in the 1930s as a gift to the city from its famous publisher-son, Ulrico Hoepli. It even has swivelling seats for the admiration of the heavens.

Esposizione Permanente delle Belle Arti G2

*Via Turati 34, **t** 02 659 9803; **metro** Turati. **Open** Tues–Fri 10–1 and 2.30–6.30, Thurs until 10pm; Sat, Sun and hols 10–6.30; **adm** €6.20.*

In a classy palace of the 1800s, the Esposizione Permanente delle Belle Arti temporarily displays 100 sculptures and paintings of the 20th century from the Civico Museo dell'Arte Contemporanea, including paintings by Boccioni, De Chirico, Modigliani

and Fontana, as well as 40 contemporary works of the **Jucker collection**, with paintings by Picasso, Klee, Kandinsky, Boccioni, and Modigliani.

Palazzo Dugnani and Museo del Cinema G3

*Via Manin, Giardini Pubblici, **t** 02 655 4977; **metro** Palestro. **Open** Fri–Sun 3–6; **adm** €2.58. (Palazzo Dugnani: only the 'Tiepolo' rooms are open to the public).*

The **Palazzo Dugnani** is a late 17th-century building, formerly a private residence, but belonging to the city since 1846. It is famous for two damaged but still very fine frescoes, *The Allegory of the Dugnani Family* and *The Legends of Scipio and Massinissa*, painted in 1731 by Giambattista Tiepolo during his first visit to Milan in 1731.

Also within the *palazzo* is the **Museo del Cinema**. As well as displaying movie posters, this museum traces the development of the moving image from its 18th-century magic lantern beginnings to the Lumière brothers and the invention of sound.

Corso Venezia and Around G4–H3

Corso Venezia is one of Milan's most attractive streets, lined with neoclassical and Liberty-style *palazzi* – most remarkably, the 1903 Palazzo Castiglione at No.47 and the neoclassical Palazzo Serbelloni, Milan's press club on the corner of Via Senato. Other notable *palazzi* are the theatrical 19th-century **Palazzo Rocca-Saporiti**, a former nobleman's house designed by Giovanni Perego; note the grandiose Ionic columns and the friezes on the upper loggia of the façade depicting scenes of Milanese history. Neighbouring **Casa Fontana-Silvestri** is a rare survivor of Renaissance Milan, allegedly built to a design by Bramante, and with a façade of typical Lombard teracotta figurines.

Down the road is also the **Seminario Arcivescovile**, originally the Collegio Elvetico, and one of the most important secular Baroque buildings in Milan. Begun by the Milanese architect Fabio Mangone in 1608, it has an austere classical courtyard of Doric and Ionic columns in two tiers, with an equestrian statue in the centre. The beautiful façade was later added by Francesco Maria Ricchino.

The district just west of the Corso Venezia was the city's most fashionable in the 1920s, and there are also a smattering of rewarding buildings here, including the **Casa Galimberti** with a colourful ceramic façade at Via Malpighi 3, off the Piazza Oberdan; a good Art Deco foyer at Via Cappuccini 8; the eccentric houses on Via

Gio Ponti, the Universal Designer

If credit for Milan's current vocation as the design capital of Europe could go to one man, it would be Gio Ponti (1891–1979), who was born and educated in Milan, and spent all of his workaholic life here, designing everything from light fixtures and forks and knives to stage sets for La Scala and skyscrapers. Sent off to fight in the First World War in the Veneto, he returned captivated by Palladio. In 1923 he was the art designer for Ginori ceramics, and by 1925 he was building his 'Domus' houses in Milan (also the name of his influential architectural magazine, founded in 1928, which he edited until his death); the plain exteriors hid gorgeous interiors full of innovations.

His writings in *Domus* about modernizing the national architectural style found a keen audience among Mussolini and the Fascists. Ponti (who loved Italy and its art, but had no interest in its politics) built a number of works in the Fascist 'stripped neoclassical style', most notably the Faculty of Mathematics for Rome University (1934). In 1936 he showed his personal side in the first and more delicate of the two Montecatini towers (1936) on Milan's Via Turati, one of the first buildings to use aluminium.

After the war, Ponti was one of the key figures in Italy's post-war renaissance. 'Industry is the style of the 20th century, its mode of creation,' he wrote. His stylish La Pavoni coffee machine (1948) became the Italian bar classic. In *Domus* he promoted the rebuilding of Northern Italy's war-damaged industries, but with the stipulation that has become the mantra of all Italian design – not

to lose sight of Italy's great art and artisan roots, while staying in control of production in order to stay in control of quality.

Ponti travelled around the world and built several buildings abroad, many showing the innovations possible in a mind not hampered by the dogma of a 'style'. In Taranto he built a cathedral (nicknamed 'the sail'), its façade filled with holes to admit light; he also built the revolutionary Villa Planchart, in Caracas (1955), where gaps in the walls, illuminated from behind, make the walls and ceiling appear to float – an idea picked up by designers in the 1980s and 90s, who have otherwise ignored Ponti as being too 'decorative'. He also designed the Museum of Art in Denver.

In 1957, Ponti designed one of his most famous works, the delicately detailed *Superleggera* ('ultralight') chair with a rush seat, and began work on the building that would symbolize Italy's rebirth – the 34-storey steel and glass Pirelli Tower, Europe's tallest building (415ft) when it was completed (*see* p.94). While everyone else was building shoe boxes, Ponti, with the assistance of the great engineer Nervi, came up with this slender, sophisticated stream-lined six-sided slab that tapers to diamond points – one of his favourite motifs.

Ponti's inventiveness and his lack of any immediately identifiable personal style or dogma have left him difficult to place – his pro-decoration stance also left him out of fashion amongst late 20th-century minimalists. Recently, however, he has returned to fashion both abroad and in Milan – witness the restoration of his Fernet Branca Tower (*see* p.115).

Mozart (especially No.11); and the romantic Palazzo Fidia at Via Melegari 2.

Bastioni di Porta Venezia G2–H3

Porta Venezia; **metro** *Porta Venezia or Repubblica.*

This street, now part of the busy inner ring road, originally marked the city's second ring of walls, built by the Spanish in the 16th century. In the late 18th century, with the creation of the public gardens, these walls turned from a defence into an area for leisurely perambulation.

The 20th century saw the creation of the two squares at either end: Piazza Repubblica, on the site of the city's original main railway station; and Piazza Oberdan, whose central monument is the Porta Venezia, itself a reconstruction of the original Spanish fortified gate, the **Porta Orientale**.

FURTHER NORTH

Stazione Centrale H1

Via Pisani; **metro** *Centrale.*

Train passengers arriving into Milan via the Stazione Centrale are greeted in style. The Mesopotamian-style station, blocking the end of Via Pisani, is the largest in Italy; it was designed by Ulisse Stacchini in 1912 and built between 1925 and 1931. This station is as essential to Milan's urban psyche as Grand Central station in New York; the announcements of train arrivals and departures that echo around its cathedral-like halls resemble Papal supplications, and it is always swarming with life, be it hordes of schoolchildren, expectant friends and relatives, or departing lovers. Close inspection of the architecture reveals unsuspected Art Nouveau detail, including a fantasy of winged creatures along its façade.

In front of the station is the **Albi di Milano**, a sculpture designed by British architect Ian Ritchie to celebrate and mark the turning of the Millennium – the rays of lights are meant to convey Milan's fame as a hub of design and innovation.

Pirellone H1

Piazza Duca d'Aosta; **metro** *Centrale.*

The Milanese are particularly proud of this skyscraper, the Pirelli Building, or *Pirellone* (Big Pirelli), built in 1959 by Gio Ponti (*see* p.93), its concrete structure designed by Pier Luigi Nervi. Now the seat of Lombardy's regional government, you can see most of the city from its terrace. It made headlines in April 2002, when a small, private plane flew into the top of it – subsequent investigation interpreted the action as suicide.

University and the Southeast

CA' GRANDE AND AROUND 98
Ca' Grande 98
Corso di Porta Romana 98
San Nazaro Maggiore 98
Torre Velasca 99
Sant'Antonio Abate 99
Santo Stefano and San Bernardino alle Ossa 99
Largo Augusto 100
Palazzo Sormani Andreani 100

PALAZZO DI GIUSTIZIA AND AROUND 100
Palazzo di Giustizia 100
Rotonda della Besana 101
San Pietro in Gessate 101
Santa Maria della Passione 101
Conservatorio di Musica Giuseppe Verdi 102
Palazzo Isimbardi 102

CORSO ITALIA AND AROUND 102
Sant'Alessandro 102
San Paolo Converso 103
Santa Maria dei Miracoli/San Celso 103

FURTHER OUT 103
Abbazia di Chiaravalle 103

1 Lunch

Al Penny, *Viale Bligny 42*, **t** *02 583 21230*; **tram** *15*. **Open** *daily exc Mon eve*. **Moderate**. Rustic Tuscan cuisine served in a cheerful and friendly atmosphere.

2 Tea and Cakes

Acerba 2, *Via Orti 4*; **metro** *Crocetta or Porta Romana*. **Open** *Tues–Sun*. Excellent choice of cakes in an old carriage garage.

3 Drinks

Martinique Café, *Via P. da Cannobio 37*; **metro** *Missori*. **Open** *Tues–Sun, happy hour 6–9pm*. Standing jazz and soul bar with over 100 distilled labels; happy hour offers sushi.

University and the Southeast

Southeast Milan is a rather neat pie wedge defined by the busy north–south Corso Italia and the east–west Corso di Porta Vittoria. Part of the city since the 17th century, its modern aspect dates from the 19th, when the Milanese elite left the city centre to litter the suburbs with their neoclassical *palazzi*. Spread amongst these are many fine churches and monasteries, all of which are veritable galleries of Lombard art, though most notable is the beautiful Santa Maria della Passione.

The defining monument of the district, however, is the enormous Ca' Grande, formerly Milan's hospital (Ospedale Maggiore) and now the main building of the city's university. The legacy of the Ca' Grande's past and present roles permeates the neighbourhood: firstly with memories of the great plague that afflicted the city – remembered in the cemetery of the Rotonda Besana and the Colonna Verziere in Largo Augusto – and more happily in the bubbly and buzzing university cafés, craft shops and old-fashioned bookshops that now characterize the area.

Further afield are two monuments to contrasting eras of Milan's history: the brutal, Fascist architecture of the city's Law Courts in the Palazzo di Giustizia, and an oasis of tranquillity at the Cistercian Abbey of Chiaravalle.

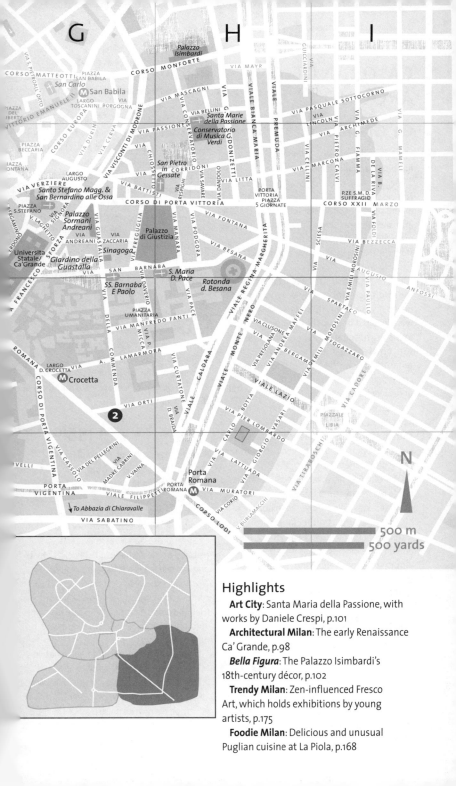

Highlights

Art City: Santa Maria della Passione, with works by Daniele Crespi, p.101

Architectural Milan: The early Renaissance Ca' Grande, p.98

Bella Figura: The Palazzo Isimbardi's 18th-century décor, p.102

Trendy Milan: Zen-influenced Fresco Art, which holds exhibitions by young artists, p.175

Foodie Milan: Delicious and unusual Puglian cuisine at La Piola, p.168

CA' GRANDE AND AROUND

Ca' Grande G5

Via Festa del Perdono 5; tram 12, 20 or 27, bus 94. Open for exhibitions only.

The Ospedale Maggiore was the idea of Francesco Sforza, who decided to consolidate all the small hospitals scattered across Milan into one big one (hence Casa Grande, meaning big house or home, which was then shortened by the Milanese dialect to Ca' Grande).

In 1456, he asked Filarete to design it, and the result, now the centrepiece of the city's university, is a beautiful early Renaissance work inspired by Brunelleschi's pioneering foundling hospital in Florence, combined with ornate Lombard brickwork and terracotta. It was the first hospital to have cross-shaped wards, and over the years underwent a number of improvements: Francesco Maria Ricchino added the large aedicule **façade** of the monumental entrance in 1631, and collaborated on the large courtyard. Inside are over 900 portraits of hospital benefactors since 1602.

After building his masterpiece, Filarete wrote an architectural treatise on an imaginary ideal city called *Sforzinda* in honour of his patron, a curious, rather fantastical illustrated work that included everything, right down to the brothel. It was widely studied during the Renaissance, and notably inspired the Gonzaga to build their own ideal city, Sabbioneta, near Mantua.

Corso di Porta Romana F6–G7

Metro *Missori or Crocetta, **tram** 24, **bus** 77.*

One of Milan's oldest radial streets, Corso di Porta Romana was lined with porticoes and punctuated by arches in Roman times; of these arches, only the 16th-century Porta Romana remains. Signs of Milan's prehistoric ancestors have also been found around nearby Piazza S. Nazaro, and in more recent times, the road was given a procession of elegant buildings.

Of particular interest is Palazzo Annoni at No.6, built in 1631 by Francesco Maria Ricchino and containing an art collection that includes the odd Rubens and Van Dyck, and Casa Bettoni at No.20, which is recognizable for the statues of *Bersagliere*, Italian marksmen, on either side of its entrance. The *Bersagliere* formerly used arrows (hence the nod to Sagittarius), though they are now the élite troops of the Italian army.

At the top of Corso di Porta Romana is Piazza Missori, with a monument to Garibaldi at its centre, and at the south end stands the classical Roman style **Porta Romana** gate itself, wth its Doric columns, built in 1598 after a design by Aurelio Trezzi to celebrate the marriage of Maria Margherita of Austria to Philip III of Spain. Here are also fragments of the old Spanish walls.

San Nazaro Maggiore F6

Piazza San Nazzaro, off Corso di Porta Romana, t 02 5830 7719; tram 12, 20 or 27, bus 94. Open daily 7.30–12.15 and 3.15–6; adm free.

A church that has undergone several rebuildings since its 4th-century dedication by St Ambrose, San Nazaro was last restored in the Romanesque style. Its most original feature is the hexagonal *Cappella Trivulzio* (1512–47) by Bramantino, built to contain the tomb of the *condottiere* Giangiacomo Trivulzio, who wrote his own epitaph, in Latin: 'He who never knew rest now rests: Silence.'

Trivulzio did have a busy career; a native Milanese who disliked Lodovico Sforza enough to lead Louis XII's attack on Milan in 1499, he became the city's French governor, then went on to lead the League of Cambrai armies in thumping the Venetians at Agnadello (1509).

Milan's Plagues

Like Italy's other densely populated cities, Milan lost a third to half of its inhabitants in the Black Death (1347–8). Unlike other cities, however, Milan made a serious effort to contain future outbreaks. Physicians were ordered to file detailed reports on their patients' symptoms as well as causes of death, over a century before the rest of Europe, and when the diagnosis was plague, the house of the victim would be marked with a red cross and boarded up, quarantining both the patient and their households. Often entire families perished together, untended by doctors or priests. Only the men in charge of collecting corpses could enter, making themselves drunk to stand the horror, then taking their pay by plundering the houses of the dead. Draconian as such measures were, fewer died of plague in Milan than elsewhere.

Yet on two occasions, Milan's princely archbishops acted heroically to comfort their flocks. In the outbreak of 1576, Carlo Borromeo (who had predicted the city was doomed to be punished for its licentious behaviour) defied all advice to stay away, and during the four months that the plague lasted, he tirelessly visited deathbeds and hospitals, while giving funeral Masses every day in the Duomo. It was considered one of the future saint's miracles that the only two of the 30 members of his household who died were the ones who had stayed indoors.

The next outbreak, in 1630, happened during the tenure of his nephew, Archbishop Federico Borromeo, who was already popular in Milan – three years previously he had fed thousands daily at his residence during a famine. When the plague struck, he followed his uncle's lead in tending to the ill, only this time nearly a hundred of his clergy perished in the epidemic. This time the outbreak was so virulent that rumours spread that *untori* ('anointers') were going about the city deliberately spreading the plague by wiping ointments they received from the devil on houses, city walls and churches; as Milan's Spanish rulers succumbed to panic, suspected *untori* were subjected to horrific tortures and death. The story is well known in Italy – the *untori* and plague figure prominently in Alessandro Manzoni's *I Promessi Sposi* (1825–6), based on the harrowing first-hand account in Federico Borromeo's unpublished memoirs, which rest in the Biblioteca Ambrosiana.

Torre Velasca F5

Piazza Velasca 5; **metro** *Missori, tram 4, 12, 15, 24 or 27, bus 65 or 94.* **Closed** *to the public.*

Sometimes referred to as *il fungo*, or 'the mushroom', for its shape and debatable contribution to the city's aesthetics, this tower of offices and flats was built between 1956 and 1958 by the architects Enrico Peressutti and Ernesto Nathan Rogers.

Meant to symbolize Milan's modernism and post-war recovery, it is 27 storeys tall and stands 106m high, while the design of the bulging summit is a nod to the shape of medieval towers still found elsewhere in Italy. It shows that the Milanese were no slouches in mastering the then latest technologies in construction – without which its top section would have been impossible.

Sant'Antonio Abate G5

Via Sant'Antonio 5; **metro** *Missori, tram 12, 20 or 27.* **Open** *8.30–12.30 and 3.30–6;* **adm** *free.*

Almost completely rebuilt in 1582, this church has frescoes by several 17th-century Milanese artists, in particular Bernadino Campi and Ludovico Carracci.

Santo Stefano and San Bernardino alle Ossa G5

Piazza Santo Stefano; **tram** *12, 20 or 27,* **bus** *54, 60 or 65. Santo Stefano Maggiore,* **t** *02 7600 6222.* **Open** *9–12 and 4–6. San Bernardino alle Ossa,* **t** *02 7602 3735.* **Open** *8am–2pm;* **adm** *free.*

Occupying the northeastern flank of the market square of Santo Stefano, the basilica from which it takes its name is in fact a reconstruction of an old church which went up in flames in 1075; the church was then completed in 1584, after a design by Aurelio Trezzi. No longer a functioning church, it instead serves as the home of the diocesan archive. In the sacristy are canvases by, or at least attributed to, Camillo Procaccini.

Next door is the extraordinary and rather macabre church of **San Bernardino alle Ossa**. Its Cappella Ossario chapel, built in 1695, is covered in the bones of Milanese citizens, all recovered from city cemeteries that were closed in the 1600s; many of the bodies were victims of the plague (*see* box, previous page). There is, however, a particularly lovely antidote to this eerie shrine, in the form of a dome frescoed by Sebastiano Ricci of Venice, his very first commission (1695).

Largo Augusto G5

Metro *Duomo,* **tram** *12, 20 or 27,* **bus** *94.*

Whereas many of the squares away from the original core of Milan are the product of 19th-century urban planning, this one, really more of a widening at the end of Via Durini, has stood here for centuries. A high-rent district in Baroque times, at its centre stands the **Colonna del Verziere**, a monumental column designed by Francesco Maria Ricchino, erected here to mark the end of the plague of 1576. This is one of the city's few surviving monuments belonging to the church, as most religious monuments were suppressed during Napoleon's reign. On one side of the square, along Via Durini, is the vast and majestic Baroque **Palazzo Durini** (1628) at No.24 – another work by Ricchino. At No.20 is the Casa Toscanini, former residence of the great Italian conductor.

Palazzo Sormani Andreani G5

Corso di Porta Vittoria 6, t 02 782 219; **tram** *12 or 27,* **bus** *94.* **Open** *Mon–Sat 9–7.30;* **adm** *free.*

This is an 18th-century noble house with a wonderful Baroque façade, with balconies

added in 1736 by Francesco Croce. The interior was completely refurbished after the Second World War, and since 1956 the building has housed the main **municipal library**, which the Milanese simply refer to as *la Sormani*. The library contains many important old manuscripts and books, including the private library of the French novelist and Italophile, Henri Stendhal.

Exhibitions are occasionally held in the building's other rooms, one of which, the **Sala del Grechetto**, is almost completely wallpapered in canvases by the eponymous and excellent Genoese painter, who is perhaps better known these days by his real name, Giovanni Benedetto Castiglione (1610–65). His *Orfeo che ammansisca gli animali* is particularly worth a look if you manage to coincide with an exhibition.

Giardino della Guastalla G5

Via Francesco Sforza and Via San Barnaba; **tram** *12, 23 or 27,* **bus** *37, 60, 73, 77, 84 or 95.* **Open** *daily 8–5.*

This garden, Milan's oldest public park (laid out in 1555), is one of the most understated and pleasing spots in the city to stop for a break. It is adorned with an array of monuments, including a neoclassical **temple** designed by Luigi Cagnola.

PALAZZO DI GIUSTIZIA AND AROUND

Palazzo di Giustizia G–H5

Corso di Porta Vittoria; **tram** *12, 23 or 27,* **bus** *37, 60, 73, 77 or 84.* **Closed** *to public.*

Occupying the entire island between Corso di Porta Vittoria, Via San Barnaba, Via Freguglia and Via Manara are Milan's law courts, set in a monolithic marble building in the Mussolini Modernist style. Suffice to say that it is not one of the Milanese's most loved buildings, possibly because of this connection, as well as because it symbolizes the intrusion of Rome's bureaucracy into this supposedly more enlightened city.

That said, the image of the building is one familiar to most Italians, if for no other reason than because in the early 1990s it appeared every day on television as the scene of Milan's infamous counter-corruption trials, the result of the 'Clean Hands' investigation (see 'Roots of the City', p.32). All this has tended to obscure the building's many works of art, in the form of sculptures, reliefs, frescoes and mosaics that decorate its 65 rooms, 13 courtyards and some of its 1,200 offices.

Rotonda della Besana H5

Corner of Via Besana and Via San Barnaba; **tram** *9, 29 or 30,* **bus** *77 or 84.* **Open** *only for exhibitions and summer cinema.*

South of Porta Vittoria, and along the road which follows the Spanish walls, stands the Rotonda della Besana, built between 1698 and 1725 to serve as the cemetery church for the Ospedale Maggiore. It is an intriguing anomaly in the city's predominantly angular appearance; its singular round building is divided into eight segments around a church in the form of a Greek cross. In the centre is the tranquil ex-church of **San Michele ai Nuovi Sepolcri**, designed by Attilio Arrigoni in 1713. The church is now used for temporary exhibitions, while the surrounding cemetery is transformed to a cinema *al fresco* in the summer.

San Pietro in Gessate H5

Piazza San Pietro in Gessate, **t** *02 545 0145;* **tram** *12, 20 or 27,* **bus** *37, 77 or 84.* **Open** *daily 9.30am–6pm;* **adm** *free.*

This 15th-century church was named after the first apostle and attributed to one of the Solaris, either Pierantonio or Guiniforte. It is Milan's finest example of the transition from Gothic to Renaissance, though the façade was added in 1912 as part of a 'restoration' project that also managed to destroy many of the interior decorations from the 17th and 18th centuries. In the fifth chapel on the right is a detached fresco on the *Funeral of St Martin* by Bergognone, and the chapels along the left side of the nave have *quattrocento* paintings and frescoes by the Lombard school. Most remarkable of all though is the **Cappella Grifi** in the left-hand transept. Here in the 19th century, underneath the layers of plaster that were put on the walls in misguided attempts to disinfect the church during the plague, restorers uncovered a cycle of beautiful frescoes by Bernardino Butinone and Bernardino Zenale, depicting scenes from the *Life of Saint Ambrose* (see p.120). The frescoes have undergone many attempts at restoration, sadly not all successful, so that the effect is rather patchy and uneven, but splendid nonetheless.

Santa Maria della Passione H4

Via Bellini 2, **t** *02 7602 1370;* **metro** *San Babila,* **tram** *9, 20 or 23,* **bus** *61 or 94.* **Open** *7–12 and 3–6.15;* **adm** *free.*

This is Milan's second largest and arguably most beautiful church, built on a design by Cristoforo Lombardo and funded by the patron and then prelate of the city, Daniele Birago. Begun as a Greek cross in 1482, with a fine octagonal dome added in 1530, Santa Maria della Passione seemed rather old fashioned to the Laternesi monks who worshipped here, and by the end of the century they had converted it into a Latin cross. In doing so, they lengthened it westwards and added semi-circular chapels down the nave, the work of Martino Bassi. Between 1692 and 1729, Giuseppe Rusnati added the Baroque façade. The church's most distinctive feature is its lovely octagonal **cupola**, which rises to a height of 50m. The Renaissance interior is particularly fine and uplifting, a veritable treasure-trove of works by Daniele Crespi and his school, most notably those depicting the *Passion* hanging from the piers (the *Christ Nailed to the Cross* is particularly impressive); Crespi's *St Charles Borromeo at Supper* (1628), the one picture of the saint that best shows his austere devotion, is generally held to be his masterpiece. The two magnificent organs, dating from the 16th and 17th centuries, are still used for concerts; the left hand one has been beautifully decorated by Crespi.

Other fine paintings include *Christ at the Pillar* by Giulio Procaccini in the third chapel, and the *Madonna di Caravaggio* by Bramantino in the sixth chapel. The right transept contains a magnificent *Deposition* by Bernardino Luini, completed in 1515, while another, less famous version of the *Last Supper* is also on show, painted by Gaudenzio Ferrari in 1543. Further on, the **chapterhouse** contains the 15th-century *Redeemer and the Apostles* by Bergognone, while in the gallery there are more paintings by both Camillo Procaccini and Daniele Crespi, the latter of whom also did the paintings on the pretty frescoes on the wood panels in the 15th-century sacristy.

Conservatorio di Musica Giuseppe Verdi H5

*Via Conservatorio 12, t 02 762 110; **tram** 9, 20 or 23, **bus** 61 or 94. **Open** for concerts only.*

The young Giuseppe Verdi was in fact rejected by the music conservatory that now bears his name. As the delicate, cloistered courtyards denote, the building was originally a monastery and convent attached to Santa Maria della Passione. In 1808, after its religious inhabitants were evicted under Napoleon, his viceroy, Eugène de Beauharnais, founded the city's principal music college in the buildings. Apart from continuing to be Milan's most prestigious musical conservatory, the academy also contains a rich library of scores, including many original works by Rossini, Mozart and the improved Verdi himself, as well as a fine collection of old stringed instruments. The

interior was refurbished by Ferdinando Reggiori after it suffered heavily in the bombing raids of the Second World War. The 1,800-seat auditorium is used for concerts.

Palazzo Isimbardi H4

*Corso Monforte 35, t 02 7740 2973; **metro** San Babila, **tram** 9, 20 or 23, **bus** 54 or 61. Visits by prior arrangement; **adm** free.*

This former nobleman's house, built in the 15th century and inevitably added to and much refurbished since, takes its name from the Isimbardi family, who bought it in 1775. The seat of Lombardy's provincial government since 1935, it has recently been opened to the public, allowing access to a number of unusual works of art, such as a wooden 17th-century globe by Jacopo de Rossi.

The vault of the **Sala delle Giunta** has a large canvas by Tiepolo depicting the *Trionfo del Doge Morosini*, which was originally painted for the Palazzo Morosini in Venice. The Sala dell'Antegiunta is illuminated by a resplendent Venetian chandelier from the glassworks at Murano. The **Sala degli Affreschi** is appropriately decorated with many lovely frescoes, while the other rooms are fine examples of later, neoclassical decorative styles.

CORSO ITALIA AND AROUND

The shops and hotels of this grandiose street have been a feature of Milan since the 19th century. Yet Corso Italia's modern intrusion into the city's fabric is betrayed by the strange angles at which the smaller, older streets intersect it.

Sant'Alessandro F5

*Via Zebedia 2, t 02 8645 3065; **metro** Missori. **Open** 8–12 and 3–6; **adm** free.*

This large church, begun in 1601, was designed by Milan's architect-monk Lorenzo

Binago (or 'Biffi'), and completed by Francesca Maria Ricchino in 1659. In many ways it was the precursor to San Giuseppe (see p.77). In 1601, Bramante and Michelangelo's St Peter's was the rage, and Biffi's design reflects many of its features, but with several proto-Baroque twists: the arrangement of two different-sized domes (completed only in 1694); the revolutionary emphasis on the longitude created by the two centres; and the fact that the arches of the crossings are supported by freestanding columns.

The interior decorations offer a good overview of 17th- and 18th-century Milanese painting, with outstanding works by Camillo Procaccini (in the third chapel on the right-hand and in the first chapel on the left) and by Daniele Crespi, also in the chapel on the right.

San Paolo Converso F6

Piazza Sant'Eufemia; tram 15, bus 65 or 94. Open 8–12 and 3–6; adm free.

This former church, built in 1580 according to a design by Domenico Giunti, was completed in 1613, with a façade by Cerano. The interior is intriguingly decorated in a mixture of stucco, canvases and frescoes, many of which are *trompe l'oeil* scenes by the Campi family, Antonio, Giulio and Vincenzo from Cremona. Opposite the church stands a 17th-century **column**, moved here from Piazza Bertarelli.

Santa Maria dei Miracoli/San Celso F6

Corso Italia 37, t 02 5831 3187; tram 15, bus 65. Santa Maria dei Miracoli open 7–12 and 4–6.30; adm free. San Celso open for exhibitions only .

Santa Maria dei Miracoli (1490–1563) offers a fine example of the Lombard love of ornament, with its handsome, lively façade by Alessi. Beyond an attractive atrium within, the interior is paved with an exceptional marble floor and decorated with High Renaissance paintings by Paris Bordone, Bergognone and Moretto; on the day of their marriage Milanese brides and grooms traditionally stop by to pray in the chapel of the Madonna. The adjacent 10th-century church of **San Celso** has a charming interior restored in the 19th century and a well-preserved original portal.

FURTHER OUT

Abbazia di Chiaravalle Off maps

Via Sant'Arialdo 102, Chiaravalla Milanese, t 02 5740 3404; metro Corvetto, bus 77. Open Mon–Sat 9–11.30 and 3–5.30, Sun 3–4.30; adm free.

If you become weary of the unrelenting stone of the city centre, a visit to this abbey will reward with you a great sense of serenity. Founded in 1135 by the Cistercians following a commission from Bernardo de Calirvaux, the abbey has nearly gone the way of all worldly things. All that remains is its French Gothic church, the cemetery and the ruins of the Gothic cloister – which was pulled down to make way for a railway in 1858, then partially restored in 1952 using the one surviving wall as a model. Also remaining is a beautiful, tall **bell tower** with delicate marble columns, added in 1349 by Francesco Pecorari. Despite its bare bones, the whole complex is once again a functioning abbey.

The interior is rather sparse – decoration and paintings (of which there are a few) were considered a distraction from devotion by the Cistercians' founder St Bernard, though the wooden choir has lovely carvings by Carlo Garavaglia dating from 1645. One of the few sacrifices to pictorial temptation is the *Madonna della Buonanotte* (1512) by Bernardino Luini; so-called as it was the last image the monks saw before they retired to bed – as they passed her, it was as if she was wishing them 'good night'.

There are more frescoes in the transept dating from the 14th century, and also works by the Fiammeghini and Campi families. The nave has something rather unusual for Lombardy – 17th-century Flemish frescoes; there are also a few by the school of Giotto. The 15th-century chapterhouse by Bramante has graffiti depicting the city's church of Santa Maria delle Grazie and the Castello Sforzesco.

At the centre of the complex – in tune with the Cistercian motto of *ora et labora* (prayer and work), and with the fact that the Cistercians were instrumental in reclaiming Milan from its setting on the edge of a swamp – is an appropriately well-tended and fruitful garden.

Ticinese and Navigli

TICINESE DISTRICT 108
San Lorenzo Maggiore (alle Colonne) 108
Piazza della Vetra 108
Parco delle Basiliche 108
Santa Maria della Vittoria 108
Amfiteatro Romano 108
Sant'Eustorgio 109
Museo Diocesano 109
San Vincenzo in Prato 109

NAVIGLI 110
Santa Maria delle Grazie al Naviglio 110
Vicolo Lavandai 110
San Cristoforo al Naviglio 110

06

1 Lunch

Osteria delle Vigne, *Ripa di Porta Ticinese 61*, **t** *02 857 5617*; *metro Porta Genova*. **Open** *Tues–Fri 12–2pm and 8pm–1am, Sat 8pm–1am*. **Moderate**. A chilled out, good-value, friendly restaurant with delicious food; the pick of many in this buzzing district.

2 Tea and Cakes

Le Biciclette, *Via Torti, off Conca di Naviglio 10*; **tram** *2 or 14*. **Open** *Mon–Sat 6pm–2am, Sun 12.30–4.30 and 6pm–2am*. Trendy café in an old bicycle shed.

3 Drinks

Yguana, *Via Papa Gregorio XIV 16, behind Piazza della Vetra*, **t** *02 8940 4195*; **tram** *2, 3 or 8*. **Open** *Wed–Mon 11am–3pm and 6pm–3am*. This tropical bar, decorated like a Henri Rousseau canvas, is a favourite for after-dinner drinks in a mellow atmosphere.

Ticinese and Navigli

Southwest of the city centre, Via Torino leads into the artsy Ticinese district, named after the Ticino river, which is traversed by the main thoroughfare, Corso di Porta Ticinese. Though not immediately apparent, this part of modern Milan reveals many traces of Roman Mediolanum, from the newly reopened Roman Amphitheatre, which stands on Via E. De Amicis, to the basilica of San Lorenzo, where the city's landmark Roman columns are now better known as a trendy *aperitivo* hangout.

Further south are a few survivors of Milan's once-essential medieval *navigli* (canals), which used to lace through the city, using diverted water from nearby rivers. Although most of them are covered over today, the *navigli* were responsible for Milan's success as a growing medieval metropolis, not only allowing the city's dukes to import the marble for the Duomo and other grandiose civic buildings, but also making it possible for the Milanese to have fresh water, as well as vital trading routes with Italy's other medieval city-states.

Nowadays, this district is better known for its rising status as Milan's hotspot, with an ever-growing number of trendy bars and late-night lounges, as well as smaller designer shops, inexpensive restaurants, and its buzzing monthly antiques market on the Naviglio Grande.

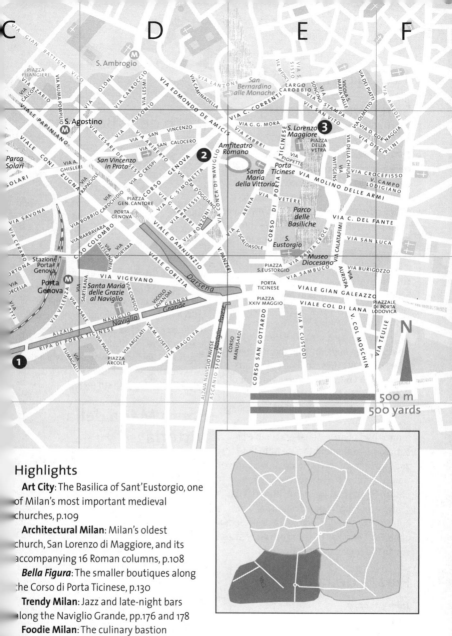

Highlights

Art City: The Basilica of Sant'Eustorgio, one of Milan's most important medieval churches, p.109

Architectural Milan: Milan's oldest church, San Lorenzo di Maggiore, and its accompanying 16 Roman columns, p.108

Bella Figura: The smaller boutiques along the Corso di Porta Ticinese, p.130

Trendy Milan: Jazz and late-night bars along the Naviglio Grande, pp.176 and 178

Foodie Milan: The culinary bastion of exquisite gourmet restaurant la Scaletta, p.169

TICINESE DISTRICT

San Lorenzo Maggiore (alle Colonne) E6

Corso di Porta Ticinese 39, t 02 8940 4129; tram 3, 15 or 20. Open daily 7.30–6.30; adm free. Cappella di Sant'Aquilino; adm free.

This is Milan's oldest surviving church, dating from the 4th century. Carefully spared by Barbarossa in the sack of Milan in 1164, it has since suffered severe fires. In the 16th century, when it was near total collapse, it was rebuilt, with much of its original structure conserved. Luckily, the beautiful octagonal **Cappella di Sant'Aquilino** has survived intact, with 4th- or 5th-century mosaics of Christ and his disciples and an early Christian sarcophagus. Below are blocks from a Roman building from the 2nd century.

One of Milan's most striking ornaments is the set of 16 **Corinthian columns** in front of the basilica of San Lorenzo. It is now a favourite location for the Milanese to lounge about and sip cocktails, but it originally formed part of an Imperial-era temple or bath complex thought to date from the 2nd–3rd century AD; the columns were then transported here in the 4th century as a portico for the basilica of the church. At its centre is a bronze copy of a statue of Emperor Constantine, placed there in honour of his Edict of Milan of 313, which ordered an end to the persecution of Christians.

Piazza della Vetra E6

Tram 3, 15 or 20.

This small square behind the basilica of San Lorenzo once marked the confluence of a number of the city's *navigli*, in the form of a small dock. Much debate surrounds the origins of its name, which could derive from the Latin *castra vetera*, signifying a type of military defence camp, or from the *vetere*, or tanners, who gave their name to the small street that leaves the park's western flank. Subsequently filled in, it then hosted public executions before it became a favourite with photographers seeking award-winning views of the nearby San Lorenzo church.

Parco delle Basiliche E6

Piazza della Vetra; tram 3, 15 or 20.

This open green space, beginning in Piazza della Vetra, is the third largest park in central Milan, cultivated on the site of heavy bombardments suffered in the Second World War. It also, incidentally, opened up the view between two of the city's most ancient and prestigious basilicas, San Lorenzo to the north and Sant'Eustorgio to the south. While there, note the nearby **Portoni di Porta Ticinese** at the northern end of the park. The 12th-century gate was redone in the 14th century, then made into three arches in the 19th century. The tabernacle on the outside has reliefs of saints, sculpted by Giovanni di Balduccio's workshop while they were working on the Arca di San Pietro in the adjacent Basilica di Sant'Eustorgio.

Santa Maria della Vittoria E6

Via E. De Amicis 11; tram 3, 15 or 20, bus 94. Open Mon–Fri 10–5; adm free.

The crypt of this 16th-century church is now an exhibition space for shows devoted to displaying the latest Roman and Lombard archaeological finds. The original church was built by Cardinal Luigi Omodeo, and is now the residence of the Milan branch of the Romanian Orthodox church.

Amfiteatro Romano E6

Via E. De Amicis 19, t 02 8515 4434; tram 3, 15 or 20, bus 94. Open to the public by prior arrangement only.

The remains of Milan's Roman Amphitheatre are preserved in the basement of the **Camera del Commercio** (Chamber of Commerce). It has been reopened for group visits, thanks to efforts by the local archaeological society.

Sant'Eustorgio E6

*Piazza Sant'Eustorgio, **t** 02 5810 1583;*
***tram** 3, 15 or 20. **Open** Tues–Sun 9.30–12 and
3.30–6; **adm** free. Cappella Portinari
adm €6.*

The Basilica of Sant'Eustorgio, one of the
most important medieval churches in Milan,
was rebuilt in 1278 along the lines of
Sant'Ambrogio, with a lofty campanile (1309).
The pillars along the naves are crowned with
good 11th-century capitals, and the
chapels, added in the 15th century, are finely
decorated with early Renaissance art; in the
first chapel on the right, look for a triptych by
Bergognone. The transept has a chapel
dedicated to the Magi, where a large Roman
sarcophagus held the relics of the Three
Kings until Frederick Barbarossa hauled them
off to Cologne. On the altar, the vivacious
marble triptych on the *Story of the Magi* is by
an unknown hand, although it has been
attributed to the sculptor who assisted
Giovanni di Balduccio on his relief of *St Peter
Curing the Dumb*.

The highlight of the church, however, is
behind the apse; the pure Tuscan
Renaissance **Cappella Portinari** (1468), built
for Pigello Portinari, an agent of the Medici
bank in Milan. Attributed to Michelozzo and
often compared with Brunelleschi's Pazzi
Chapel in Florence in its elegant cubic
simplicity and proportions, the chapel is
crowned by a lovely dome, adorned with
painted stucco reliefs of angels.

This jewel of architecture is dedicated to
the Dominican Inquisitor St Peter Martyr
who was axed in the head on the shores of
Lake Como in 1252, whose life of intolerance
was superbly frescoed on the walls by
Vincente Foppa – a painter who never did
anything finer. The Inquisitor's remains are
buried in the marble **Arca di San Pietro
Martire**, signed in 1339 by the Pisan sculptor
Giovanni di Balduccio.

The tomb, inspired by Nicola Pisano's Arca
di San Domenico in Bologna, has five tiers of
figures: the *Seven Virtues,* plus *Obedience,*
standing on their attributes, support the
marble casket, carved with relief panels of
the life of the saint, with figures of other
saints in between. Above them are
members from the eight choirs of angels –
each with slots in its back for now-missing
metal wings.

The tabernacle above them holds the
Virgin and Child flanked by SS Dominic and
Peter Martyr, crowned in turn by Christ with
two Seraphim. Originally details were picked
out in blue and gold paint. Although many of
the higher figures on the tomb are by
Giovanni's workshop, the master's deft hand
is evident in the caryatid Virtues, especially
the lovely and gracious *Temperance* pouring
from her jug, and the vivid relief on the
sarcophagus of a ship in a storm.

Museo Diocesano E6

*Corso di Porta Ticinese 95, **t** 02 8940
4714, **w** www.museodiocesano.it;
tram 3, 9 or 15. **Open** Tues, Wed, Thurs–Sun
10–6; **adm** €6.*

This newly reopened and refurbished
museum displays a rich collection of religious works of art collected from convents,
churches and the private collections of
Cardinals. It contains an eerie collection of
icons, Madonnas and crucifixes, copies of
famous drawings by Titian and Raphael,
and also a few priceless originals such as
the 17th-century *Christ and the Adultress*
by Tintoretto.

San Vincenzo in Prato D6

*Via Daniele Crespi 6, **t** 02 835 7603; **metro**
San Agostino. **Open** daily 7.45–12.45 and
4.30–7; **adm** free.*

This church has suffered a colourful life
since its construction in the Middle Ages,
first as a pagan, then a Christian necropolis.
It was appropriated by the Benedictines until
the 16th century, when it was sacked by
Napoleon's troops and used as a storehouse.
In the early 19th century, it was used as a
chemical factory, earning it the nickname
'The Magician's House'.

NAVIGLI

Santa Maria delle Grazie al Naviglio D7

Alzaia Naviglio Grande; **metro** *Porta Genova.* **Open** *8–12 and 3–5;* **adm** *free.*

This rather unattractive 19th-century church sits Venetian style, its façade almost flush with the Naviglio Grande.

Vicolo Lavandai D7

Tram *2 or 9.*

This little street was once the area's laundrette and takes its name from the women who used to wash clothes in the river here. On the towpath, the old washing stations – like cattle troughs sheltered by wood – are still visible (*see* 'A Walk Through the Navigli', p.126).

San Cristoforo al Naviglio Off maps

Naviglio Grande, Via S. Cristoforo 3, **t** *02 4895 1413.* **Open** *8–6.30;* **adm** *free.*

Out of town, this rather enchanting asymmetrical church sits prettily by a bridge on the banks of the Naviglio Grande. It is in fact the fusion of two buildings, one from the 12th century and one from the 14th. The inside is decorated with various frescoes by artists of the Lombard school.

The Navigli Canals

The colourful Navigli district is named for its navigable canals, the Naviglio Grande (linking Milan to the River Ticino, Lake Maggiore and the Candoglio marble quarries) and Naviglio Pavese (to Pavia) that meet to form the docks, or Darsena, near Porta Ticinese. The Naviglio Grande, built in 1239 and stretching for 50 kilometres, was once the canal that connected Milan commercially with Lago Maggiore and central Europe beyond. The narrower Naviglio Pavese, which flows due south for 33km, was built in the late 14th century, but was only made navigable in 1819. Up until the 1950s, Milan, through these canals, handled more tonnage than seaports like Brindisi. And like any good port, the Navigli was then a working-class district of warehouses, workshops, sailors' bars and public housing blocks, notorious home to the red-light district and the city's most thieving and shadowy streets.

Much has changed since, however, and this district has now been developed into a relaxed and fashionably bohemian zone. In fact, the Navigli district is fast becoming Milan's most innovative and contemporary quarter, with a growing number of artists and newly-opened clubs, bars and exhibition spaces reclaiming old industrial sites. Here, you will also see the best example of Milan embracing the *aperitivo* lifestyle that is more natural to Italians from further south. From 6pm onwards, the hard-working Milanese seem to descend on the area *en masse*, to relax after a long day by feasting on *prosecco* and abundant delicious snacks in the surrounding bars.

Further north is the rather stagnant-looking piece of water known as the Darsena, which is in fact supplied and drained by the Olona River, a tributary of the Ticino. Built in 1603 by the Spanish ruler Count Fuentes, the Darsena was enlarged to its current shape and size in 1920, though it remains only a metre and a half deep. The docks themselves once stood along Viale d'Annunzio – the Conca del Naviglio, which connected the Darsena to the rest of Milan's inner waterways has been filled in by a road of the same name.

Debate has raged periodically as to whether the old waterways should be reopened; the idea has been championed by the far-right Lega Nord political party, which sees the canals' restoration as part of their larger northern-secessionist dream. Also *see* 'A Walk Through the Navigli', p.126.

The West End

CASTELLO SFORZESCO AND AROUND 114
Civici Musei d'Arte e Pinacoteca del Castello 114
Parco Sempione 115

CORSO MAGENTA AND AROUND 116
Santa Maria delle Grazie 116
Museo Teatrale alla Scala 119
Palazzo Litta 119
Museo Archeologico 119
San Maurizio 119

SANT'AMBROGIO AND AROUND 119
Sant'Ambrogio 119
San Vittore al Corpo 121
Leonardo da Vinci Museo Nazionale
della Scienza e Tecnica 122
San Bernardino alle Monache 122

FURTHER OUT 123
Fiera di Milano 123
Cimitero Monumentale 123
Meazza Stadium (San Siro) 124
Certosa di Garegnano 124

1 Lunch

La Brisa, *Via Brisa 15*, *t 02 8645 0521*;
metro Cordusio. *Open Tues–Sat, and Mon
eves*. **Expensive**. A favourite with celebs, with
abundant classic regional dishes and a menu
geared towards seasonal specialities.

2 Drinks

Roialto, *Via Piero della Francesca 55*,
*t 02 3493 6616; **bus** 57 or 94*. **Open** *daily
6pm–2am*. A former garage, now one of the
city's best lounges, with eccentric furnishings
and friendly service.

The West End

Milan's west end is anchored by the
enormous and outrageous 14th-century
Castello Sforzesco, a medieval testament
to pride and vanity that now stands somewhat incongruously in the modern city. The
presence of Milan's equally vain master-for-
a-day, Napoleon, is also most tangible here;
he sought to recreate the views of the centre
of his empire in Paris by transforming Corso
Sempione into a wide avenue, a would-be
Champs-Elysées, lined with trees and leading
up to a triumphal arch. Along elegant Corso
Magenta hides one of the world's most
famous works of art, Leonardo da Vinci's *Last
Supper*, which resides, in something
approaching its original form, in the refectory of Santa Maria delle Grazie, itself one of
northern Italy's most beautiful Renaissance
churches. Further along still is Milan's
treasure-laden basilica, founded by and
dedicated to her patron saint, Ambrose.

Highlights

Art City: Da Vinci's unmissable *Last Supper*,
in Santa Marie delle Grazie, p.117

Architectural Milan: The beautiful medieval
church of Sant'Ambrogio, p.119

Bella Figura: Operatic finery on display in
the Museo Teatrale alla Scala, p.119

Trendy Milan: Gio Ponti's re-opened Fernet
Branca Tower in Parco Sempione, p.115

Foodie Milan: Antica Trattoria della Pesa, for
perfected traditional Italian dishes, p.172

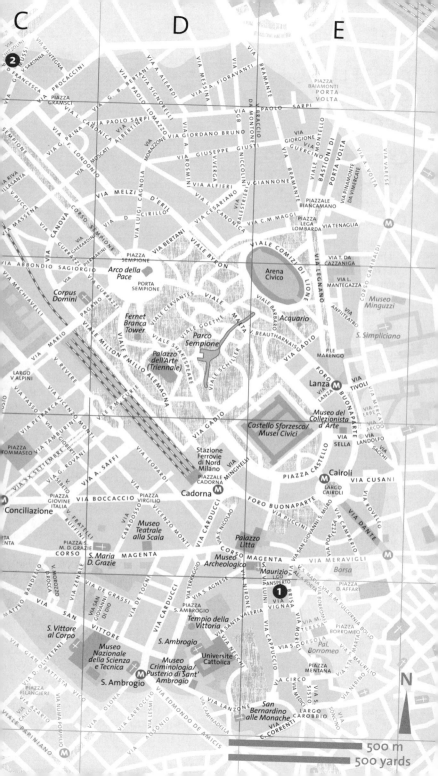

CASTELLO SFORZESCO AND AROUND

Castello Sforzesco and Civici Musei d'Arte e Pinacoteca del Castello E3–4

Parco Sempione; **metro** *Lanza.* **Open** *Tues–Sun 9–5.30;* **adm** *free.*

The mighty Castello Sforzesco is one of Milan's best-known landmarks. It replaces an even older fortress that stood here within the city walls; the Visconti made it their base, and as a hated symbol of their power it was razed to the ground by the Ambrosian Republic in 1447. Three years later, under Francesco Sforza, it was rebuilt in grandiose style. The castle stood pretty much intact until air raids in the Second World War damaged it and its treasures; it was rebuilt again, this time disguising water cisterns in its stout towers.

Today the castle houses several excellent museums, the **Civici Musei d'Arte e Pinacoteca del Castello**. The entrance, by way of a tower rebuilt to a design by Filarete (1452) and then the huge Piazza d'Armi, is through the lovely Renaissance **Corte Ducale** and the principal residence of the Sforza. There are intriguing fragments of Milanese history here: a beautiful 14th-century monument of the Rusca family; reliefs showing Milan's triumph over Barbarossa; the intricate, delicate *Voghera Monstrance* (1406) marking the epitome of Lombard Gothic goldsmithery; and the city's gonfalon.

Also in the collection is the powerful equestrian tomb of Bernabò Visconti (d. 1385), who for a long time shared power in Milan with his brother Galeazzo II, dividing the lands they inherited from their uncle Giovanni Visconti, Archbishop of Milan. Chaucer's 'God of delyt and scourge of Lumbardie', Bernabò was famous for his coarse, cruel, braggart nature and numerous children. When his brother withdrew from politics, Benabò became the strongest man in northern Italy, and tried to domineer his nephew Giangaleazzo, until the latter beat him at his own tricks, and without the slightest scruple, had him seized and thrown in prison and usurped his half of the family turf. Bernabò died soon after, but fortunately for him he had ordered his tomb from Bonino da Campione some 29 years earlier. Once covered with gold and silver, it originally stood rather alarmingly, one imagines, on the altar of the now ruined church of S. Giovanni in Conca.

Leonardo Da Vinci designed the ilex decorations of the **Sala delle Asse**; the next room, the **Sala dei Ducali**, contains a superb relief by Agostino di Duccio from Rimini's *Tempio Malatestiano*. The **Sala degli Scarlioni** contains the two finest sculptures in the museum: the *Effigy of Gaston de Foix* (1525) by Bambaia and Michelangelo's unfinished *Pietà Rondanini*, a haunting work that the aged sculptor worked at off and on during his last nine years, repudiating all of his early ideals of physical beauty in favour of blunt, expressionistic figures; the difference between this and his *Pietà* in St Peter's couldn't be greater.

Upstairs, most notable among the fine collection of Renaissance furnishings and decorative arts are the 15th-century *Castello Roccabianca* frescoes illustrating the popular medieval tale of Patient Griselda. The Pinacoteca contains a tender *Madonna with Child* by Giovanni Bellini, his brother-in-law Mantegna's more austere, classical *Madonna* in the Pala Trivulzio, and the lovely *Madonna dell'Umiltà* by Filippo Lippi. Lombards, not surprisingly, predominate: Foppa, Solario, Magnasco (a Genoese who spent most of his life in Milan), Bergognone (especially the serene *Virgin* with SS. Sebastian and Gerolamo) and Bramantino, with an eerie *Noli me tangere*. There's a room of Leonardo followers, and then the *Primavera*, a woman face made up entirely of flowers, by the first rrealist, Milanese Giuseppe Arcimboldo 527–93). From 18th-century Venice, ancesco Guardi's *Storm* looks ahead to other school – Impressionism.

The castle's third court, the beautiful **rtile della Rocchetta,** was designed by the orentines Bramante and Filarete, both of hom worked for several years for Francesco orza. The basement of the courtyard is led with an extensive Egyptian collection funerary artefacts and the prehistoric llection of items found in Lombardy's n Age settlements, most notably the h-century BC bronzes from the tomb of the arrior of Sesto Calende.

The first floor houses the **Museum of usical Instruments** with a beautiful llection of over 600 stringed and wind struments, and a spinet that was played by ozart. The Sala della Balla, where the Sforza ed to play ball, now contains Bramantino's *pestries of the Months.*

arco Sempione D3

etro Cadorna, Cairoli or Lanza. **Open** *ily 6.30am–8pm, until 11.30pm in mid- mmer.* **Triennale,** *Viale Alemagna 6, 2 724 341.*

Behind the Castello stretches the Parco mpione, Milan's largest park. Originally the rden of the ducal palace in the Middle ges, the Viscontis enlarged it to turn it into hunting reserve – although it takes a good agination to evoke deer and hounds once unding through these 'woods'.

The Spaniards largely ignored the area, and en Napoleon turned it into a parade ound for his regiments; its current form is anks to landscape architect Emilio emagna, who gave it a distinct English untry-house garden look in 1890. In the esperate times of the Second World War, e area was reputedly used to cultivate heat to feed the city, but is now, once ain, a favourite place for the Milanesi to me and take their evening strolls, arrange norous trysts, and in summer attend the ark's numerous musical events.

Within the park grounds, you can find: De Chirico's **Metaphysical Fountain**; the 1930s Palazzo dell'Arte, used for exhibitions, especially the Milan **Triennale** of Modern Architecture and Design; the Arena, designed in 1806 after Roman models, where 19th-century dilettantes staged mock naval battles; and an imposing triumphal arch, the **Arco della Pace**, a lesser Arc de Triomphe originally intended to glorify Napoleon (though the Austrians changed the dedication to peace), which marked the terminus of Napoleon's highway (Corso Sempione) to the Simplon Pass.

Acquario Civico E3

Parco Sempione, Via Gadio, **t** *02 8646 2051;* **metro** *Lanza.* **Open** *Tues–Sun 9.30–5.30;* **adm** *free.*

Milan's Art Nouveau aquarium, built in 1906, is the only surviving building from that year's National Exhibition. Much smaller than its more modern competitor in Genoa, its 30 or so tanks exhibit over a hundred species of predominantly Mediterranean fish and sea creatures.

The building features original and enter-taining tiles and reliefs depicting various aquatic animals by master ceramicist Richard Ginori. Fittingly, a statue of Neptune by Oreste Labo stands atop the building.

Fernet Branca Tower D3

Parco Sempione; **metro** *Cadorna.* **Open** *Wed–Thurs and Sat–Sun 11–6;* **adm** *€3.*

The panoramic steel Fernet Branca Tower, reminiscent of the Eiffel Tower in Paris, was designed by **Gio Ponti** (see p.93), and erected in 1933, in the record time of two and a half months, in time for the Triennale. Only recently reopened to the public after closing in 1972 for safety reasons, the tower no longer has a café at the top, but the views are still lovely and there is a nearby café/restau-rant in the park.

Corso Sempione B1–D2

Tram 1, 14 or 33, **bus 94.**

Commissioned by Napoleon in the early 19th century, this tree-lined avenue was modelled on the Champs-Elysées in Paris, and certainly resembles it in its view up to the Arco della Pace. It is now home to glitzy shops, chain restaurants and cinemas. At Corso Sempione No.36, the **Casa Rustici** (1931), designed by Giuseppe Terragni of Como on the proportions of the Golden Section, is often considered Milan's finest modern building and an interesting example of rationalist architecture.

Foro Buonaparte E3–4

Metro Cairoli.

With the roundabout of Largo Cairoli at its fulcrum, this semi-circular street of imposing neoclassical buildings and low, leafy trees marks the starting point of the Napoleonic urban development that saw the Castello Sforzesco enveloped in the landscaped Parco Sempione. In a piece of classical symmetry, Foro Buonaparte has a mirror image to the north, in **Via Melzi d'Eril**, on the other side of the Arco della Pace.

Via Dante E4

Metro Cairoli or Cordusio.

Named after Italy's most famous poet, this street leading out south from Parco Sempione is a typically grand and elegant boulevard – but since cars are banned on it, it affords a chance, rare in traffic-mad Milan, to sit out on the street and soak up some of Italy's fabled café life.

Museo del Collezionista d'Arte E4

Via Quintino Sella 4, **t** 02 7202 2488; **metro** Cairoli or Lanza. **Open** Mon–Fri 10–6 and Sat 10–2; **adm** €6.

This unusual venue is a fascinating cross between museum and laboratory. Its studios serve to help collectors identify fakes from genuine collectors' items, but as a by-product, the collection effectively displays a history of art and fakes, accompanied by a thorough bilingual explanation of 'how to fake it' and how to recognize a fake.

CORSO MAGENTA AND AROUND

Metro Conciliazione.

This elegant street forms the main art west of Piazza del Duomo and is lined v historic buildings. The neoclassical **Pala: delle Stelline** at No.65 incorporates the remains of the Atellani residence, where Leonardo Da Vinci is reputed to have live while working on the *Last Supper*. The interior gardens contain vines reputedly given by Ludovico il Moro to the artist. Two-thirds of the way along, Corso Mag meets **Via Carducci**, one of Milan's form *navigli* (canals), now filled in to make a the crossroads marks the site of the old Vercelliana and the extremity of what w once the second ring of city walls. Just c Corso Magenta is **Via Brisa**, a street not; for the Roman ruins revealed by post-w excavations; archaeologists believe they belonged to Emperor Maximiian's palac The raised columns are thought to be an example of early central heating, to let v air flow under the ground floor paving.

Santa Maria delle Grazie D4

Piazza Santa Maria delle Grazie, **t** 02 894 1146, must book (for a fee); **metro** Cadorna. **Open** Tues–Sun 8.15–6.45, may extend in summer, Thurs and Sat until 10pm; **adm** refectory (for the Last Supper) €7.24. Only 15 visitors admitted at a time.

Milan's greatest painting, Leonardo da Vinci's *Last Supper* (the *Cenacolo*), is in t refectory of the convent of this Dominic church. But before entering, get into the proper Renaissance mood by walking a the 15th-century church and cloister. Bu Guiniforte Solari, with later revisions by Bramante, it is perhaps the most beauti Renaissance church in Lombardy, its ext articulated with fine brickwork and terracotta that respects the local delight in a bit of fancy stuff – Bramante would never do anything as lavish again. His greatest contribution, however, is the majestic **tribune**. It was added in 1492 – inspired by Brunelleschi in Florence, but with an eye towards the imposing style of the ancient Romans.

In the next decade, Bramante would take this style back to Rome itself. Nearly every element in the tribune is based on a circle, from the decorative motifs, to the play of geometric forms, to the great cupola that crowns it all. Bramante also designed the choir, the sacristy and the elegant little cloister, all simple, geometric and pure.

The *Last Supper*

Leonarda da Vinci painted three of his masterpieces in Milan, the two versions of the mystery-laden *Virgin of the Rocks*, and the *Last Supper*. The former two are in London and the Louvre; the latter would have been in Paris too, had the French been able to figure out a way to remove the wall.

Ever since the 14th century, it had been the fashion in Italy to paint a *Cenacolo*, or scene of the Last Supper, on the walls of monastic refectories, and as the Dominicans at Santa Maria were special favourites of Lodovico il Moro, he sent them his special favourite artist to make their *Cenacolo* the last word on the subject. For Renaissance

Leonardo's Horse

'Of the horse I shall say nothing, because I know the times,' wrote Leonardo in 1497, expressing his regret at not being able to complete the largest equine statue ever conceived. The statue was commissioned by Galeazzo Maria Sforza to honour his father Francesco. During the 17 years that followed the initial request, the artist worked on the *Last Supper* and a series of portraits of Italian nobles, and his talent for engineering produced a city plan for Milan, new weapons designs and a defence system for the castle. And if that wasn't enough, the Duke expected Leonardo to create stage sets, manage gala parties and compose rhymes and puzzles for the ladies of the court. Finally, a 24ft clay model of the horse was erected in a vineyard near the castle. But after the French seized Milan in September 1499, their archers used it for target practice, reducing it to a mound of clay. Legend has it that Leonardo never ceased mourning over his lost horse. Many of the working sketches, along with a revolutionary method to cast the statue in bronze, were detailed in his notebooks. These were lost for centuries, though one set of notebooks, known as the Windsor Collection, came into the possession of the British royal family; another was discovered in Madrid's Biblioteca Nacional in 1966, the now famous *Codex Madrid II*. Then in 1977, a retired airline pilot, artist and art collector from Pennsylvania, Charles Dent, wrote an article in *National Geographic* proposing that Leonardo and Italy should have a horse as a gesture of appreciation from the American people for all that the Renaissance has meant to culture. He initiated the Leonardo's Horse Foundation, though he died in 1994, before the project was completed.

Five hundred years after Leonardo's clay model was destroyed, the 24ft horse reappeared in Milan cast in bronze by US sculptor Nina Akamu. The imposing animal stands firmly on its back legs on a white Carrara marble pedestal mounted on a large, classic Milanese Montorsano granite base, the same stone used in the Duomo. The horse, which weighs 12 tons, is engineered to withstand windshear and earthquakes. After some initial embarrassment over where to put such a cumbersome gift, the *Comune* of Milan placed the horse in its natural setting, in the grounds of the city's Ippodromo del Galoppo racecourse, near the San Siro stadium. Just one month after its inauguration in September 1999, a second cast appeared in Grand Rapids, Michigan: once the spell is broken, it appears the horse can gallop anywhere.

painters, the special challenge was to represent the expressions and gestures they imagined on the faces of the Apostles when Christ announces, 'One of you will betray me.'

When Leonardo unveiled his *Last Supper* (1494–8), it was immediately acclaimed as the greatest of them all, praised as the greatest work of the greatest living artist, a masterful psychological study, and an instant caught in time. The apostles' gestures of disbelief and dismay had been captured almost photographically by a keen student of human nature. Everything about it, from its composition to its colouring, added meaning. In the 16th century, Vasari wrote in his *Lives of the Artists* 'In all the faces one can read the fearful question: who will betray the Lord? And each expresses in his own way not only his love for Jesus, but also fear, anger and indeed sorrow, because they cannot understand his words.' According to Vasari, Leonardo left the portrait of Christ purposely unfinished, believing himself unworthy to paint divinity; Judas, the isolated traitor, also posed a problem, but the artist eventually was able to catch the expression of a man caught guiltily unawares but still nefariously determined and unrepentant.

Unfortunately for posterity, damp was a problem even as Leonardo worked on the fresco, the ever-experimental genius wasn't content to use proper, established fresco technique (where the paint is applied quickly to wet plaster), but painted with tempera on glue and plaster as if on wood, enabling him to return over and over to achieve the subtlety of tone and depth he desired. Leonardo knew even as he painted his masterpiece that it wouldn't last, that it would be soon be changed and damaged, but the fact only stimulated his restless mind, which was fascinated with the unfinished and the transitory. Almost immediately, the moisture in the walls began its deadly work of flaking off particles of paint. Although it was considered a 'lost work' by the 17th century (in 1620 it was so dark that the Spaniards cut a doorway into its centre), various restorers and repainters

have tried their hand at it, with mixed success. In the Second World War, the monastery received a direct hit from a bomb, and the *Last Supper* was only preserved thanks to piles of mattresses and other precautionary measures. In 1953, master restorer Mauro Pelliccioli covered what remained of the now dingy work with a rock-hard protective shield of clear glue; by then, only an estimated 20 per cent of what was visible was by Leonardo's own hand.

In 1977, the Ministry of Arts decided to let Italy's communications company Olivetti pay €3.5 million to make the *Last Supper* a showcase restoration project to highlight Italy's state-of-the-art restoration techniques (not surprisingly, the Italians are acclaimed as the world experts in the field). The leader of the project, Pinin Brambilla, was given the job of chipping off Pellicioli's protective coating, cleansing the work of its previous restorations and repaintings, then stabilizing the wall to prevent further damage, and finally painting in the gaps. In May 1999, when the last scaffolding was taken down (the restoration took over five times as long as it took Leonardo to paint it), Brambilla's work was displayed to howls of fury by art critics around the world.

Italians for the most part have tried to hold their chins up (the then Minister for the Arts, Giovanna Melandri, called it 'the restoration of the century'), while one of the harshest critics, James Beck from the Department of Art History at Columbia University, countered: 'This woman has simply produced a new Brambilla. What you have is a modern repainting of a work that was poorly conserved. It doesn't even have an echo of the past. At least the older over-paintings were guided by Leonardo's work.' Brambilla (who was quoted as saying she communed daily with Leonardo's ghost while working on the project) notoriously even went where the living Leonardo feared to tread and put some finishing touches on Christ's face.

Museo Teatrale alla Scala D4

Corso Magenta 71, t 02 805 3418; metro Cadorna. Open Tues–Sun 9–6; adm €5.

The La Scala Museum (moved here to this new, larger abode) has an excellent collection of opera memorabilia including scores (some by Verdi), letters, portraits and photos of legendary stars, and set designs; there's even an archaeological section related to ancient Greek and Roman drama, and a great collection of costumes on the top floor.

Palazzo Litta D–E4

Corso Magenta 24; metro Cadorna. Open for expos only.

Surely few national rail companies can boast such fine headquarters, in one of Milan's most sumptuous *palazzi*. Since 1905 it has been home to Italy's Trenitalia. The original *palazzo* was constructed in 1648, commissioned by Count Bartolomeo Arese and designed by Mario Ricchini. The rose-red rococo **façade** was added in 1763 by Bartolomeo Bolli, and it has a lovely courtyard surrounded by twinned columns. If your visit coincides with one of the *palazzo*'s exhibitions, visit the ornate and velvety **Sala Rossa** (Red Room), which has a pearl embedded in the floor, apparently to mark a tear shed upon the meeting of the Duchess Litta with Napoleon. The **Sala degli Specchi** (Room of Mirrors) is a dazzling optical frenzy of light, and the **Salotto della Duchessa** retains all of its original furnishings, including the wallpaper. The **Teatro Litta**, next door, is the oldest theatre in the city, now a venue for experimental work (*see* 'Nightlife and Entertainment', p.173).

Museo Archeologico D4

Corso Magenta 15; metro Cadorna. Open Tues–Sun 9–5.30; adm free.

A former Benedictine convent linked to the church of San Maurizio houses the city's Etruscan, Greek and Roman collections. As important as Milan was in the late Roman Empire, relatively little has survived the frequent razings and rebuildings: on display is the **3rd-century tower** in the garden, Roman altars, sarcophagi, stelae, glass, ceramics, bronzes and mosaics. Other sections are Greek, Etruscan, Indian (from Gandhara), Goth and Lombard.

San Maurizio E4

Corso Magenta 15; metro Cadorna. Open Sept–June daily 4–6; adm free.

The Monastero Maggiore's church of San Maurizio is a pretty example of Lombard Renaissance, completed in the early 1500s and decorated with exceptional frescoes by Bernardino Luini and his students; the master himself painted the scenes from the *Life of St Catherine* in the third chapel on the right, as well as the story of the *Passion*, and lovely frescoes on the partition that divides the two naves. Boltraffio added the figures of the saints on the loggia.

SANT'AMBROGIO AND AROUND

Sant'Ambrogio D5

Piazza Sant'Ambrogio; metro Sant'Ambrogio. Church open daily 9–12 and 2–8. Museo della Basilica di Sant'Ambrogio open Mon and Wed–Fri 10–12 and 3–5, Sat and Sun 3–5; adm free.

The Pusteria, a towered gate that contains its own museum (*see* 'Museo della Criminologia', p.121), guards the last resting place of Milan's patron saint, Ambrose, in the beautiful church of Sant'Ambrogio. Founded by Ambrose himself in 379, the church was enlarged and rebuilt several times (most notably by Archbishop Anspert in the 870s, when it became the prototype of the Lombard Romanesque basilica). Its current appearance dates from the 1080s.

St Ambrose (Sant'Ambrogio)

No sooner had Christianity received the imperial stamp of approval than it split into two hostile camps: the orthodox, early-Catholic traditionalists and the followers of the Egyptian bishop Arius, who denied that Christ was of the same substance as God. Arianism was widespread on the fringes of the Roman Empire, and although Milan was then at the core, one early bishop was an Arian and persecutor of the orthodox, and a schism seemed inevitable when he died in 373. When the 34-year-old consular governor Ambrose spoke to calm the crowd during the election of the new bishop, a child's voice suddenly piped up: 'Ambrose Bishop!' The cry was taken up, and Ambrose, who hadn't even been baptized, found himself in a new job.

Christianity, although only officially tolerated for 60 years, was well on its way to becoming the religion of the establishment, attracting members of the Roman ruling class to which Ambrose belonged; his father, the Praetorian Prefect of Gaul, was one of the most powerful men in the Empire. Born to rule, Ambrose would almost single-handedly set the tone for the princely medieval church. According to his biogra Paulinius, when Ambrose was an infant Rome, bees had flown into his mouth, attracted by the honey of his tongue. Hi eloquence would serve him well as bish (374–97), and it has been given much of credit for preserving the unity of the Ch His goal was to see the Church rise 'like growing moon' above the ruins of the R Empire, and he helped it along by makin attractive for the erudite and educated deftly substituting the heroes of Rome Old Testament saints as role models and transmitting Greek philosophy into theo He mined the works of the Neoplatonist particular, borrowing their mystical ima for his sermons, which, composed in the perfect classical phrasing of a Cicero, are this day regarded as masterpieces of Lat 385, when the widow of Emperor Valent demanded a Milanese basilica for Arian worship, Ambrose and his supporters he the basilica through a nine-day siege, converting the empress's soldiers in the process. His most famous convert was

The church is entered through a porticoed atrium, which in 1140 replaced the original Carolingian paved court, or *parvis*. It sets off the simple, triangular façade with its rounded arches and towers; the one to the right, the Monks' Campanile, was built in the 9th century, while the more artistic Canons' Campanile on the left was finished in 1144.

The bronze doors, in their decorated portals, date from the 10th century. In its day, the finely proportioned, if shadowy, interior was revolutionary for its new-fangled rib vaulting; arches divide the aisles and support the women's gallery or *matroneum*. On the left, look for the 10th-century bronze serpent (the ancient symbol of health, or perhaps representing Moses' staff) and the richly sculpted pulpit, a vigorous masterpiece carved in 1080, set on an enormous late Roman sarcophagus.

The apse is adorned with 10th- and 11th-century mosaics of the Redeemer a saints, while the sanctuary contains two ancient treasures: the 9th-century *Cibor* on columns, and a magnificent gold, silv enamel and gem-studded altarpiece (83 both signed by 'Wolvinus magister phab

In the **crypt** below moulder the bones Saints Ambrose, Gervasio and Protasio. A end of the south aisle, the 4th-century Sacello di San Vittore in Ciel d'Oro ('in the of gold') contains brilliant 5th-century mosaics in its cupola and a presumed authentic **portrait** of St Ambrose.

After working on Santa Maria delle Gra (*see* p.116), Bramante spent two years on Sant'Ambrogio, contributing the Portico Canonica and the two cloisters, now incorporated into the adjacent **Universit Cattolica**; these display Bramante's new interest in the ancient orders of architec an interest he was to develop fully when

Augustine of Hippo, a professor of rhetoric, who had come to hear his eloquence (and who noted with astonishment that Ambrose read silently to himself, without moving his lips). The future doctor of the Church left Milan baptized, and always honoured Ambrose as a 'perfect bishop.' Back home, he would take the Neoplatonism in Ambrose's sermons and make it into a philosophical base that would transform Christian theology in his *City of God*.

'Perfect' or not, no previous bishop or pope had assumed as much power as Ambrose, who continued to dress in the robes of a Senator. Viewing emperors as 'dutiful sons of the Church' he intervened to an unprecedented extent in the affairs of state and set what was to become the standard in relations between Church and Empire. In 384, when Roman Senators wanted to erect an altar of Victory, he entered into a public debate with their spokesman, his relative, Quintus Aurelius Symmachus, and won an appeal against tolerance of any lingering paganism. In 388 he publicly rebuked the Emperor Theodosius for having punished a bishop who had burnt a Jewish synagogue, and got him to countermand his order. Ambrose then excommunicated the emperor until he had done penance for ordering a civilian massacre in Thessalonica. He made sure that Theodosius' Edict outlawing paganism, its schools of philosophy, its festivals, and games was extremely strict; all but the most beautiful temples were to be smashed. Yet Ambrose was notably against capital punishment, and intervened to have a number of condemned men spared.

The basilica Ambrose built in Milan became his headquarters in combatting Arianism, not through persecutions (those came later) but by convincing Arians that Trinitarian Christianity was the superior product. Saintly relics were one of his trumps. Although Theodosius had condemned their traffic, Ambrose, who sincerely believed the world was haunted by evil demons, was a tireless promoter of the cult (which the Arians found ridiculous). To make up for Milan's lack of relics, he just happened to find the bodies of SS Gervaius and Protasius in his basilica as he

moved to Rome. In the upper section of the Portico della Canonica is the **Museo della Basilica di Sant'Ambrogio**, housing illuminated manuscripts, the saint's bed, Romanesque capitals, ancient fabrics and vestments called the Dalmatiche di Sant'Ambrogio, dating from the 4th century, tapestries, and frescoes by Luini and Bergognone.

Tempio della Vittoria D5

Piazza Sant'Ambrogio; **metro** *Sant'Ambrogio.*

Standing alongside the church of Sant'Ambrogio is the Temple of Victory, a memorial (1930) designed by Giovanni Muzio and erected to honour the 10,000 citizens of Milan who died in the Pyrrhic victory of the First World War.

Museo della Criminologia D5

Piazza Sant'Ambrogio; **metro** *Sant'Ambrogio.* **Open** *daily 10–7;* **adm** *free.*

This museum within the stern towers of a 12th-century gate bristles with armour, antique weapons and torture instruments.

San Vittore al Corpo C5

Via San Vittore 25, **t** *02 4800 5351;* **metro** *Sant'Ambrogio.* **Open** *7.30–12 and 3.30–7;* **adm** *free.*

This paleo-Christian church is one of Milan's less-vaunted treasures, built on the original site of the 4th-century Roman mausoleum of Emperor Valentinian II, and rebuilt in the 11th and 12th centuries during the residence by Benedictine monks. It was only in 1560 that the church was given its dedicated it, and spread the story that they once enabled a blind man to see – a success he topped off with finding a few other holy bodies lying around Milan, including SS Nazarius and Celsus. He introduced splendid priestly vestments and a liturgy with theatrical touches; he was the first to hold daily masses and regular prayer services during the day, and special feast days for saints. One of his greatest weapons against the Arians were antiphonal psalms and hymns he composed himself (he was the first one in the West to do so), sung by choirs and the congregation. Four of Ambrose's hymns are still used in the Church today .

Ambrose also became the first to write extensively on sex; according to him, celibacy was still best, harking back to the implied New Testament models of Jesus, John the Baptist, Peter and Paul, but marriage was to be tolerated for the propagation of the species – but certainly not for bishops, who would be distracted from higher things (also, Ambrose feared a hereditary caste of priests). Women, he thought, ideally should be virgins, to redeem the sin of their parents in conceiving them; they should also be silent and fast for a week or more at a time – it reached the point that noble families kept their marriageable daughters away from his sermons. His pure Virgin Mary would become the medieval ideal. As for the economy, Ambrose declared that agriculture was the only honest way to make a living, claiming that all trade was tainted. Churchmen could be content with giving to charity rather than giving away all their possessions. 'Just as riches are an impediment to virtue in the wicked, so in the good they are an aid to virtue,' he said.

Ambrose also believed that Milan was Rome's equal: 'All we bishops have in the blessed Apostle Peter received the keys of the kingdom of heaven,' he wrote. To this day genuine Milanese are called *Ambrosiani*. Their church, which remained practically independent from Rome until the 11th century, still celebrates Mass according to the Ambrosian rite; his feast day on 7 December is a citywide holiday, as is the carnival of Sant'Ambrogio in March.

current orientation, and filled with fine works of art. The Baroque chapel designed by Gerolamo Quadrio in 1668 is exquisite, as is the right-hand apse decorated with scenes depicting the *Life of St Gregory* by Camillo Procaccini (1602). Don't miss the **chapel of Sant'Antonio Abate**, entirely frescoed in 1619 by the hand of Daniele Crespi.

Leonardo da Vinci Museo Nazionale della Scienza e Tecnica C–D5

*Via San Vittore 21, t 02 4855 5330; **metro** Sant'Ambrogio. **Open** Tues–Fri 9.30–5 and Sat–Sun 9.30–6.30; **adm** €6.20.*

The Olivetan convent of San Vittore was repaired after the Second World War to house this museum. Most of the vast and diverse collection, still arranged in its original 1950s format, is rather mysterious for the uninitiated, and if you're not keen on smelting and the evolution of batteries you may want to head straight for the Leonardo da Vinci Gallery, lined with pretty wooden models and explanations of his machines and inventions (*see* box, opposite).

Other rooms include musical instruments and displays on optics, radios, computers, clocks and astronomy; downstairs you can push buttons and make waterwheels turn. Another building is devoted to trains, and another to ships and naval history.

San Bernardino alle Monache D–E5

*Via Lanzone 13, t 02 645 1948; **metro** Sant'Ambrogio, **tram** 2, 3 or 14. **Open** 8–12 and 3–5; **adm** free.*

Recently restored, this church is the only surviving building from a mid-15th-century

Franciscan convent built on this site. It is named after the great Franciscan preacher Bernardino da Siena, whose powers of persuasion were such that, suitably enough, he's now the patron saint of advertising. The building was partially rebuilt in 1922, and inside there are some lovely 15th- and 16th-century frescoes, especially the *Madonna and Child* by Vicenzo Foppa.

FURTHER OUT

Fiera di Milano A1–B2

Largo Domodossola 1, t 02 499 771; metro Amendola Fiera. Open for exhibitions.

Milan's exhibition centre was founded in 1920 in a move to give the post-war economy a catalyst. Most of its beautiful 1920s pavilions were destroyed in bombing raids in the Second World War, but some Liberty-style buildings have survived, particularly near the entrance from Via Domodossola. Nowadays, the Fiera di Milano hosts a variety of international trade fairs, making it one of Europe's prime exhibition venues, particularly for the staple Italian industries of fashion, cars and interior design.

Cimitero Monumentale Off maps

Piazzale Cimitero Monumentale, tram 14. Open Tues–Sun 8.30–5; adm free.

This is the last rendezvous of Milan's well-to-do. Their lavish monuments – Liberty-style temples and pseudo-ancient columns and obelisks – are just slightly less flamboyant than those of the Genoese, the Italian champions of post-mortem splendour.

The cemetery keeper has guides to the tombs – Manzoni, Toscanini and Albert Einstein's father are among the best-known names. The central structure, called *The Temple of Fame*, hosts other

Da Vinci the Scientist

In 1481 Leonardo wrote to Lodovico il Moro (*see* p.26), applying for a job in his court. He had been recommended to the Duke as a musician (he played a beautiful lyre that he had made himself, of silver, in the shape of a horse's head). In his letter of introduction, Leonardo boasts of his other talents as a military engineer, as a designer of war machines and fortifications, a canal builder, an arranger and festival decorator, a sculptor, a caster of bronzes, and mentions only at the end of the letter that he could paint too, if required. In fact, exactly what he did and for whom seemed to matter little. 'I work for anyone who pays me,' he once said, and as if to prove it, right after his Milan period he worked with the nefarious papal love child Cesare Borgia. For Leonardo, at any rate, the results of his genius weren't half as important as the quest. In Milan he filled notebook after notebook (many are on display in the Ambrosiana, *see* p.78) with studies of nature, weather and anatomy, and ideas for inventions in the applied sciences. His most practical work in Milan, however, was in hydraulic engineering – working on the city's numerous canals. He painted occasionally; besides the *Virgin of the Rocks* and the *Last Supper*, he did a range of portraits including one of Sforza's mistress, Cecilia Gallerani, called the *Lady with an Ermine* (now in Cracow). Yet Leonardo was chiefly interested in solving composition problems and, once solved, he often left the painting unfinished. Though he seemed to disdain painting, more than any other painter he was responsible for the intellectualizing of what had hitherto been regarded as a mere craft. This culminated the Renaissance evolution towards the use of mathematics in art, the study of the nude form, and the taste for illusion that had motivated the great artists of ancient Greece – as explained by the Elder Pliny, whose works had been rediscovered and published in Italian in 1473.

illustrious citizens. More recent arrivals include Italian novelists Eugenio Montale and Elio Vittorini, along with opera singer Maria Callas. The memorial to the 800 Milanese who perished in German concentration camps is very moving.

Meazza Stadium (San Siro) Off maps

Via Piccolomini 5, t 02 400 92175; metro Lotto, tram 24. Open for matches.

Most football fans around the world know the name San Siro, but they could be forgiven for not knowing Milan's famous stadium by its real name, Meazza. The name is in honour of Italian footballing legend, Giuseppe Meazza, who played for both Milan's teams, Internazionale and AC Milan. San Siro is truly one of Milan's great modern temples, where the *tifosi*, or fans, come in their thousands every Sunday to worship their teams. The first stadium was built here in 1926, renovated in 1950 to increase capacity, and then worked on again in 1990, when the retractable roof was added for Italy's hosting of the World Cup. The stadium now seats 85,000 people, and curiously looks as if it were built on springs. In between the football stadium and the nearby running track, a huge sculpture of a **horse** has been erected, a large-scale version of an original design by Leonardo Da Vinci (*see* box, p.117).

Certosa di Garegnano

Off maps

Via Garegnano 28, t 02 3800 6301; tram 14. Open 7.30–12 and 3–6; adm free.

Though Milan's **charterhouse** was founded in 1349 by Archbishop Giovanni Visconti, it has attracted most of its fame for the uproar surrounding the construction of the A4 motorway to the northwest of the city, which effectively went all but through its front garden.

Only the 14th-century cloister on the right of the entrance remains from the original building, which was given a Renaissance face-lift in 1562 and a façade in 1698, when the birthday-candle obelisks were stuck on. The central courtyard was conceived on a grand scale and you can still see where the monks' accommodation, kitchen and gardens would have been. The church has a beautiful cycle of **frescoes** by the Lombard master Daniele Crespi; most of them were painted in the 17th century, a year before he died at age 31, and depict *The Legend of the Foundation of the Carthusian Order*. This was reputedly a gift by the artist to the monks for offering him refuge after he had been accused of murder. In the first bay of the cycle, the servant blowing a horn is a self-portrait of Crespi, who inscribed the date of the fresco, 1629, in one of the scrolls.

Walks

A WALK THROUGH THE NAVIGLI 126

A SHOPPING TRIP 130

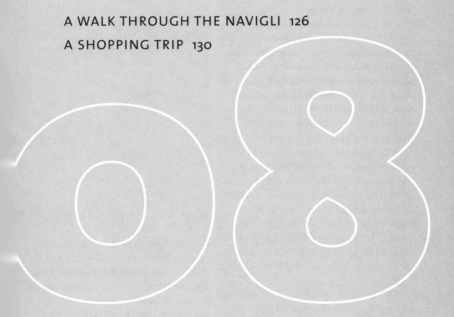

A WALK THROUGH THE NAVIGLI

There's no denying Milan lacks the river that could give it the proper majestic air of the world's great cities such as Paris or London. And as no city can survive without a constant supply of fresh water, Milan had to get hers through crafty diversion.

Milan lies north of the Po River, between two of its Alpine tributaries: the Ticino, which flows down from Lake Maggiore; and the Adda, which flows down from Lake Como. Both of these rivers ignore Milan and instead irrigate the nearby Lombard Plain, making the surrounding area a wonderfully fertile and occasionally swampy place, well known for its rice paddies.

As early as the 12th century, the Milanese set out to change this, partially diverting the two rivers through man-made canals, thus providing Milan with its essential fresh water source, as well as important trade and transport routes. It is hard to believe now, but the inner circle of the modern city, which runs along Via Molino delle Armi and Via Santa Sofia right round to Via Fatebenefratelli, was once a ring of water in the form of a navigable canal. In fact, this medieval ring road is still known as the Cerchia dei Navigli (Ring of the Canals).

The ring was fed by the Naviglio Grande and Naviglio Pavese, from the Ticino in the southwest, and by the Naviglio Martesana (now Via Melchiorre Gioia), from the Adda in the northeast. It was said that in the Middle

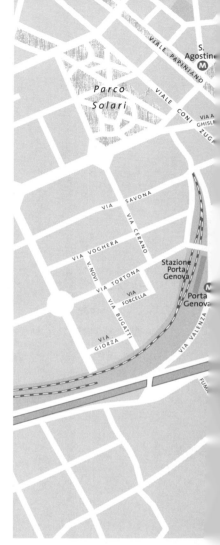

Ages and right up to the 1930s, when the majority of canals were filled in, Milan resembled Amsterdam. In that time, these dock areas were the industrial heartland of the city, home to the factories (primarily textiles and arms) which built Milan's fortune, and with them the dwellings of the city's workers.

Nowadays, only the southwestern section of Milan's canal system, officially known as *il quartiere dei navigli*, survives to any great extent (the last boat to unload cargo on the Darsena was in 1979), and as with many post-industrial cities around the world

Start and finish: San Lorenzo's Roman columns (metro Missori, or tram 3, 15 or 20).
Walking time: 3 hours, depending on how much time you spend browsing in the market and shops.
Lunch and drinks stops: Ponte Rosso, *see* p.169; Blues Canal, *see* p.171; Trattoria Toscana, *see* p.170; Officina 12, *see* p.169.
Info: Amici dei Navigli Tours, *see*, p.187; Associazione Naviglio Grande, *see*, p.187.

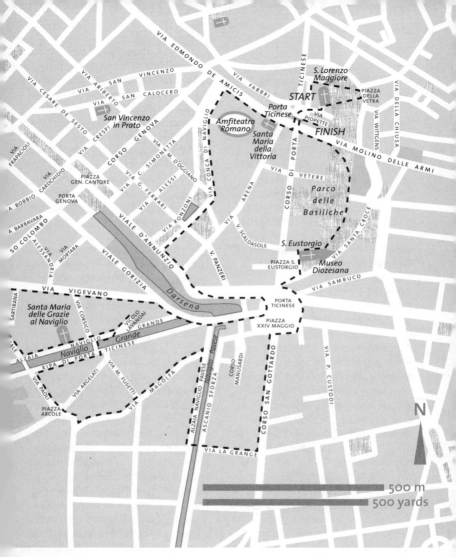

today, this characterful area has undergone
extensive gentrification and regeneration,
which has turned disused warehouses and
factories into one of the most lively and
artistic parts of the city. This walk will take
you through the memory of Milan's watery
past, to reveal its vibrant, new future as the
city's artistic quarter.

And in a city whose traffic-laden
streets can seem a disheartening
obstacle to pedestrians, this walk reveals
a more calm and ambling side to
hard-working Milan.

We start at the 16 3rd-century **Roman
Corinthian columns** that have stood in front
of the church of San Lorenzo since the 5th
century, imported from outside the city to
form what was once a four-sided atrium. The
late 16th-century basilica of San Lorenzo,
with its beautiful octagonal dome flanked by
an intricate set of chapels, apses and
rectories, is best viewed from behind in the
adjacent **Piazza della Vetra**. This square took
its current aspect in the 1930s during the
major urban-planning overhaul that
destroyed much of old Milan, and covered up
its canals in the name of progress (and the

motor car). Yet Piazza della Vetra once marked the confluence of a number of canals. Now return to the Roman columns to inspect the nearby red brick **Porta Ticinese**. In the 13th century, this city gate marked the southern entrance into Milan; water from the *navigli* system would then have flowed around its outside, along what its now Via E. de Amicis and Via Molino delle Armi. The gate and the whole Ticinese district takes their name from the fact that water was brought into the city here, along the Naviglio Grande from the river Ticino. The gate has undergone a number of facelifts; what you see now is the work of Camillo Boito, completed in 1865.

The southern tranche of **Corso di Porta Ticinese** is in the process of being pedestrianized, a development which will certainly fuel the already buzzing café and bar life of the district. However, this road is a 19th-century intrusion onto the cityscape; if you want to follow the course of the water in ancient times, you must instead turn right onto Via E. de Amicis, itself a filled-in waterway, until you reach a street on the left called **Via Conca del Naviglio**. Walk the length of this pair of narrow alleys, once the tributary that connected the Cerchia dei Navigli ring of waterways to the Darsena.

You are now at the **Darsena** harbour, still home to the odd barge and pack-boat, which was the nearest Milan ever had to a port. Although not of the same nature and import as Venice or Genoa, Milan at one stage took pride in the fact that it was Italy's 13th-largest port. The Darsena's northern bank was once the city's commercial docking area, and would have been prickled with cranes and strewn with ropes and containers – it was paved over in the 1930s, and is now a parking lot and part of Viale G. d'Annunzio. Though hard to imagine now, ships and barges would arrive here from the Naviglio Grande in one direction, carrying supplies and materials such as the marble that helped build much of the Duomo, while Milanese products such as grain, iron and fabrics would be exported out down the

Naviglio Pavese. This transport system enabled Milan to trade with other Italian city-states and move goods across the Alps and into Europe via Lake Como and Lake Maggiore, in the process securing its future as an affluent urban centre.

If it is Saturday you will be able to soak up the colours and smells of one of Milan's best food markets around the banks of the Darsena, the **Mercato della Darsena** (*see* 'Shopping', p.184). Once you are on the Darsena's northern bank, turn left at the Viale d'Aunnunzio to reach the busy crossroads of **Piazza XXIV Maggio**, once a historic marketplace for the medieval Milanesi, and the junction between the city and the countryside. At the centre of the square is Milan's second **Porta Ticinese**, this one built by the Spanish as part of the fortifications which encircled the city in a second ring of walls. The gate you see is not the original, but a monumental atrium built in its place in 1804, a neoclassical structure with Ionic columns and an imposing granite structure on top. Vestiges of this area's past commercial role as a port remain in the form of the two customs houses near the atrium.

Turn right on Alzaia Naviglio Grande to reach the banks of the **Naviglio Grande**, the largest and most important of all the waterways. It was begun in 1177, predating the city's inner system of smaller canals by 300 years; it, too, was expanded in the 1400s, allegedly a commission to Leonardo da Vinci from Ludovico 'il Moro' Sforza. The banks and back streets of the Naviglio Grande are home to some of Milan's most evocative buildings; if you have arrived early in the morning and caught the mist rising off the water, this area can seem beautifully lost in time. If you are lucky and it is the third Saturday in the month, you will catch the large **antique/flea market** set up along the Naviglio Grande, with stalls selling anything from priceless furniture to secondhand reading glasses and out-of-date Barbie dolls, attracting Milanese and people from 'the provinces' in their thousands (*see* 'Shopping', p.184).

Take a little tour starting down **Via Vigevano**, where you can admire a number of large 19th-century residential buildings interspersed with interesting shops and galleries. At the end of Via Vigevano is the **Porta Genova train station**, surrounded by old warehouses and factories that have been earmarked for regeneration.

Return towards the canal along Via Casale, to **Alzaia Naviglio Grande**. This street, together with its opposite number on the other side, the busy **Ripa di Porta Ticinese**, were formerly the towpaths used by the horses which brought the barges up and down the canals. The street's railings have visible signs of friction left by the ropes which were used to pull the boats on their return journey against the stream. Along this stretch of the canal you will find many arts and crafts shops in old *case di ringhiera* (houses with railings), selling anything from fine candles and secondhand and antique books to specialist papers and old furniture. Crossed at regular intervals by pretty bridges with iron railings, this area is very soothing and picturesque, even vaguely Venetian. One particular jewel of a street, preserved as if intended as an open-air museum, is the **Vicolo Lavandai** – the 'street of the launderers' – not referring to the modern Milanese malaise of money-laundering, but instead to the washer-women who used to rinse and string out their clothes here, in wash-houses that have been immaculately preserved with their canopies. Crossing over the Naviglio Grande down the little Via Paoli you come out into another picturesque little corner in the form of the **Piazza Arcole**. To the south of this square lies another stretch of Milan's dormant waterways. This is known as the *conca fallato*, the failed sluice; it was part of a project to improve the nearby Naviglio Pavese, but it was never finished due to lack of funds. Beyond this, along Via Magolfa, you reach Alzaia Naviglio Pavese and the **Naviglio Pavese** itself. This is the second most important of Milan's old canals, and was the system's outflow pipe. It was begun much later in 1359 and cynics report that it was

commissioned by Gian Galeazzo Visconti merely in order that his hunting reserve near Pavia (from which it takes the name Pavese) could be better irrigated. Various engineering works were conducted over the centuries to improve the Pavese; the French under Napoleon really took the bull by the horns, and by 1819 the canal was deemed more important and took more traffic than the Naviglio Grande.

Crossing the Pavese, take Via Lagrange and head north into the old Roman road of **Corso San Gottardo**. The little area used to be called *el borgh d'i formaggiatti*. It was here that cheeses – including Milan's famous gorgonzola and other dairy products – were left to season and mature. In the 19th century, the Milanese could recognize the area blindfolded, simply by its aroma. Arriving back at Piazza XXIV Maggio, cross over, and instead of heading up Corso di Porta Ticinese, turn right and return instead via the elegant, Parisian-style **Parco delle Basiliche**. This will take you past the church of **Sant'Eustorgio**, to finish where you started, at **San Lorenzo Maggiore (alle Colonne)**, where you will have earned yourself a restorative meal or drink at one of the square's trendy and popular bars.

This walk covers only the metropolitan tracts of the two canals, but both the Naviglio Grande and Pavese canals stretch further south, making for very pleasant longer walks or bicycle exursions into the beautiful Lombard countryside. Also on the banks of the Naviglio Grande is the rather unusual and pretty little church, actually two churches put together, of San Cristoforo, the patron saint of all boatmen.

The canals can now be visited by **boat** tours, which leave the Darsena on a 20km round trip (*see* box, p.126). The proposed restoration of the canals has become a political football in recent local elections, with many Milanese wanting to see the canals restored (and some of the old ones uncovered), in hopes of returning their city to something of the form it enjoyed before the aberrations of 1930s urban planning.

A SHOPPING TRIP

Those who don't like shopping will unfortunately find this past time very hard to avoid in Milan. Those who do may already have demoted the city's traditional art and architectural treasures to the elegant background in favour of more sartorial considerations.

This walk will take committed consumers down many of Milan's most elegant and oldest surviving streets, which are lined with 18th- and 19th-century *palazzi* formerly belonging to old Milanese institutions, now owned by Milan's rags-to-riches designer fashion barons. The shop windows themselves are the modern equivalent of Milan's many Baroque and neoclassical façades, their displays and lighting put together with such artistic flair that they deserve a look for their own sakes.

We start in the famous Quadrilatero d'Oro, along the well-trodden boards of Via Monte Napoleone and Via della Spiga, then take you away from the major fashion brands to a different type of shopping in the Brera. Here, you will find a charmed retail universe of unique boutiques offering wonderful curios of all kinds, as well as pleasant cafés. From here, we will move down to the hipper, younger trends being plied in the Ticinese district to the south.

> **Start**: Metro Duomo.
> **Finish**: Porta Ticinese (metro Duomo, or tram 3, 15 or 20).
> **Walking time**: 3–4 hours (depending on purchases, trying-on times), 5 hours if Ticinese district included.
> **Suggested start time**: Early morning for less crowded shops. Note that some shops may be closed on Sundays and Mondays. Business hours are usually 8.30–1 and 3–7 or 7.30.
> **Lunch and drinks stops**: Caffè Sant'Ambroeus, *see* p.164; Armani Caffè, *see* p.165; Latteria San Marco, *see* p.165; L'Exploit, *see* p.176.

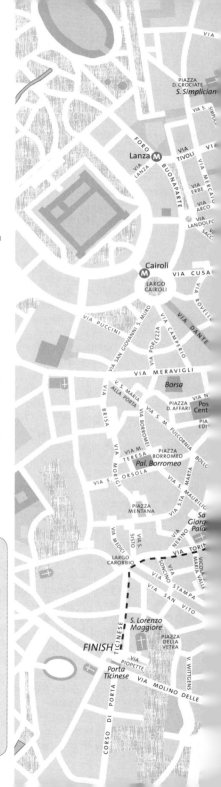

First of all, get up early – the dedicated follower of fashion must be prepared for a long search for that certain item. And this will, of course, be interspersed with many skinny cappuccino breaks, darling. So be prepared to cover some distance – and do not fret about wearing out your soles, as you'll most certainly be buying plenty more foot leather along the way.

Start by stretching your legs and warming up your plastic by taking a stroll in **Piazza Duomo**. If you can, hang on before having breakfast. Breathe in some rare fresh air and inspire yourself with the ultimate in accessories (the Duomo's frills) and the elegance of the arcades as you walk along the northern flank of the square, past the entrance to the Galleria Vittorio Emanuele II.

Just as you might be tempted to look in at some of the high street stores on Corso Vittorio Emanuele II, turn left into Via San Paolo and, not missing the Cacharel store at No.1, walk up to the **Piazza Liberty**. Here, you can admire the elegant curves on the Art Nouveau façade of the *palazzo* at No.8, then proceed to Corso Matteotti. While on this street, collect a coffee and croissant from Sant'Ambroeus, a Milanese favourite and one of the classiest breakfast spots in town; after all, a wallet cannot open on an empty stomach.

At this point you might want to continue down Corso Matteotti to the **Galleria San Carlo**. Reason: designer bargain-hunting at Diffusione Tessile (*see* box, below). Although Milan prices on designer labels can be as much as 20–30% cheaper than in the UK, this is still hardly cheap. They may not be this season's, but this outlet stocks surplus of women's clothes and shoes from the MaxMara brand (incorporating Marina Rinaldi and Sport Max) at knock-down prices. This may provide room in your bank balance for more adventurous purchases later in the day, and there's nothing like an early catch to set the ball rolling.

Triumphantly or otherwise, take the next left into Via San Pietro all'Orto, turn left on Via Verri and back into Via Catena. This street curves round to the right, finishing in the quiet little square of Piazza San Fedele, the site of two important secular buildings in central Milan: the **Casa del Manzoni**, former home to 19th-century novelist Alessandro Manzoni (*see* p.77), and 18th-century **Palazzo Belgioioso** at No.2, with its heraldic façade (*see* p.77).

If you take Via Morone, you then come out onto **Via Manzoni**, long-since one of the most important, majestic and exclusive streets of Milan. Its beginnings as a chic address started with La Scala theatre at its southwestern end, and with hotels such as the Grand Hotel et de Milan, where artists and composers lived (and died in the case of Verdi). Today, its modern chic status continues in the form of Giorgio Armani's latest fashion temple, **Armani**, at Via Manzoni No.31.

Opened as a shop in October 2000, its home is a building from the Fascist era, appropriately reflecting his slightly autocratic and outsize billboard adverts plastered throughout the city. If you like Armani's sleek and shiny greys and blacks this is a one-stop shop, with all the various Armani offshoots under one roof. There's even an Armani Caffè for your second caffeine dose of the morning. While ladies might be captivated by Giorgio, their other halves might want to slip across the street to Paul Smith at No.30.

Bargain-hunting

Before you embark on your retail roller-coaster ride, perhaps you would do well to check out a couple of the city's under-advertised bargain designer-label outlets first:

Diffusione Tessile, *Galleria San Carlo 6*, *t 02 7600 0829*; *metro Duomo*. Specializes in clothing under the MaxMara umbrella label.

Salvagente, *Via Fratelli Bronzetti 16*, *t 02 7611 0328*; *metro Lima*, **bus** 54, or on *Via Balzaretti 28*, *t 02 2668 0764*; *metro Piola*, **bus** 62, **tram** 11 or 23. 'Lifebelt' in Italian.

If you had a late start and are already in the mood for some lunch, you could restore yourself at Armani's **Nobu**, a flash sushi restaurant supervised by designer chef supreme, Nobuyuki Matsuhisa.

By now you might be laden down with a number of beautiful stiff card bags; alternatively you could ask shops to look after your purchases for you to pick up later that day. Either way, proceed further up Via Manzoni and turn right into the famous **Via Monte Napoleone**, the beginnings of the official fashion quarter; this street, and its parallel, **Via della Spiga**, is an A–Z of designer stores, each more minimalist and more cryptic than the next in its attempt to merely exude by inference the style of its contents. Fashion in Milan is not worn on the sleeve, so to speak.

Where to start? On Via Monte Napoleone, **Prada** is at No.6 or 8, depending on whether you're a boy or a girl; **Etro** is opposite at No.5; **Versace** is at No.11 and **Louis Vuitton** is at No.14; **Alberta Ferretti** is at No.19, and the famous **Gucci** is to be found at No.27.

For a rest from the boutiques, duck into the quiet street of Via Santo Spirito and take in the **Museo Bagatti Valsecchi** at No.10, making time to note its beautiful 16th-century façade. Its 19th-century art collection contains many Renaissance works, including a *Santa Giustina* by Giovanni Bellini.

If you can stomach – or afford – some more of the same achingly high-end fashion, then the lords and ladies of *la moda* can certainly finish you off. Continue walking to the end of Santo Spirito, turning right in to Via della Spiga; continue down this street and turn right on to Via Sant'Andrea. This grid of streets comprises the entire **Quadrilatero d'Oro** – goldmine of the *fashionistas*.

Those who didn't go for the sushi could be tempted by the bars of the fashion district, but don't be. Instead, head a little off the beaten track, away from designer boutiques and into a more humble and down-to-earth past. One such haven is only a short walk away; cross back over Via Manzoni and head up Via Borgonuovo to Via Fatebenefratelli.

Turn left, then immediately right onto Via San Marco. At No.24 is the **Latteria San Marco**, an old-style authentic 'dairy shop' serving bumper Milanese dishes with wine at very wallet-friendly prices.

You are now perfectly positioned to head into a shopping paradise of a different kind. Parallel to Via San Marco is Via Solferino; head south on this street, to eventually meet up with **Via Brera**. Here, ladies in particular will be allured by old-world boutiques selling the possibility of a return to la Belle Epoque in the form of sought-after cosmetics, lingerie, jewellery, furniture, lamps and stationery. Via Brera is the main artery of this pseudo-Bohemian quarter, an Italian, more clinical version of Portobello Road, home to the Brera art gallery at its northern end and the world-famous La Scala at its southern end.

Reaching **Piazza della Scala**, it is only a short retail ride through the **Galleria Vittorio Emanuele II** and back to Piazza Duomo, where you started out.

If you want to continue, the shopping trip is far from over. So far, you have seen the untouchable stuff of high fashion and the marketed elegance of a bygone age. Tired of labels, pretence and formality?

Look no further than **Corso di Porta Ticinese**. You may want to hop on a tram (no.3, 15 or 20) to get there – or else it's about a 10-minute walk southwest along Via Torino from Piazza Duomo, but it's worth the effort. Recently pedestrianized as part of a plan to make Milan more friendly for the favourite city pursuit of walking and talking, Corso di Porta Ticinese is one of Milan's trendiest streets.

This is where young designers, dot-com survivors and media types hang out. Here, creativity has not yet been bottled and labeled, and experimentalism, influence and flair remain untrammelled by corporate chic. Check out the woven silk clothes on display at No.76 in **Fatto a Mano** (literally 'Made by Hand'), as well as the weird and wonderful bazaar of antique and modern design objects at **Studio 1950**, No.68.

More importantly, you will now be in just the right spot to take full advantage of the relatively recent Milanese habit of the *aperitivo*. A serious bunch at heart, the industrious Milanese have taken slowly to this blatant misuse of time, but having done so, they have launched themselves at it with inimitable panache and attention to detail.

For your final destination, head to the **Roman coloumns** in front of the basilica of San Lorenzo, off Corso di Porta Ticinese. Once here, you can rest your feet, sip a *caipirinha* cocktail from any of the trendy bars on the square, and contemplate your purchases in the evening sunlight.

Day Trips

MONZA 136

LAKE MAGGIORE 138

LAKE COMO 139

BERGAMO 141

CITIES OF THE LOMBARD PLAIN 144
Pavia 145
Cremona 147
Mantua (Mantova) 150

09

Milan owes much of its wealth and its appeal to its surrounding areas: nearby Monza; the Italian Lakes, with their palatial villas lining the shores; the unique cultural heritage of Bergamo; and the Lombardy plain, with historic Pavia, violin-loving Cremona and Mantua, former capital of the Gonzaga dukes.

MONZA

Only a hop and a skip from Milan, Monza attracts throngs in September when it hosts the Italian Grand Prix; otherwise you may have its venerable monuments to yourself.

Getting There

Monza is 15 minutes by **train** from Milan's Garibaldi Station, or 20 minutes by ATM **bus** from the same place. Less frequent trains also depart from Stazione Centrale.

Tourist Information

Pro Monza: Palazzo Comunale, Piazza Carducci, **t** 039 323 222, **e** *pro.monza@ tiscalinet.it*, **w** *www.monza.net/promonza* (*open Mon–Fri 9–12 and 3–6, Sat 9–12*).

Festivals and Markets

During the Grand Prix, in the first week of September, there is Monza Più, a series of events in the city's piazzas which includes market stands and shows.

There is an antiques market every second Sunday of the month in the centre of Via Bergamo.

Eating Out

Derby Grill, *Hôtel de la Ville, Viale Regina Margherita 15*, **t** *039 382 581*, **f** *039 367 647*. **Open** *daily exc Sat and Sun lunch, and Aug*. **Luxury**. Overlooking the park, this place has the town's finest food: try the ravioli with rocket and ricotta in pepper and pistachio sauce.

Antica Trattoria Dell'Uva, *Piazza Carrobiolo 2*, **t** *039 323 825*, **f** *039 383847*. **Moderate**. For somewhere less pricy to eat.

The Duomo

Duomo, **t** *039 323 404*. **Open** *daily 9–12 and 3–6.30. Museum* **open** *Tues–Sat 9–11.30 and 3–5.30, Sun 10.30–12.15 and 3–5.45*; **adm**. *Chapel of Theodolinda*; **adm**.

Back in the late 6th century Monza was the darling of the Lombard Queen Theodolinda, who founded its first cathedral after her conversion from Arianism by Pope Gregory the Great. Rebuilt in the 13th century, the Duomo on Via Napoleone bears a lovely green and white striped marble façade by the great Matteo da Campione (1396). The massive campanile dates from 1606, when the interior was given its Baroque facelift. To the left of the presbytery, **Theodolinda's chapel** has charming 1444 frescoes by the Zavattari brothers, depicting the life of the

queen who left Monza its most famous relic, preserved in the high altar: the gem-encrusted **Iron Crown of Italy**. The story goes that when his mother Helena unearthed the True Cross in Jerusalem, Emperor Constantine had one of its iron nails embedded in his crown. It became a tradition in the Middle Ages for every newly elected emperor to stop in Monza or Pavia to be crowned King of Italy before heading on to Rome to receive the Crown of Empire from the pope – a tradition Napoleon briefly revived when he had himself crowned in Milan's Duomo in 1805. The cathedral's museum contains Theodolinda's treasure: a processional cross given to her by Gregory he Great, the 5th-century ivory diptych of stilicho, her crown and the famous silver en and seven chicks symbolizing Lombardy and its provinces, as well a precious Syriac

cross belonging to her son Agilgulfo (it's not hard to see why Lombard names soon fell out of fashion) and Gian Galeazzo Visconti's goblet.

Just north of the Duomo, the 13th-century **Palazzo Comunale** or Arengario is the city's finest secular building.

Parco di Monza and Villa Reale

*Park **open** summer daily 7am–8.30pm, winter daily 7am–7pm. Villa **open** for visits by appointment through the tourist office (only the Teatrino di Carte, Cappella di Carte and Serrane can be visited); **adm.***

From the Arengario, Via C. Alberto leads north to the beautiful 800-hectare Parco di Monza, one of greater Milan's 'lungs', home to a horse-racing course, the 1922 Autodromo and site of the Italian Grand Prix. Until 1806, the park was the grounds of the neoclassical **Villa Reale**, built by Archduke Ferdinand of Austria and the favourite residence of Napoleon's Vicecroy Eugène de Beauharnais. The single sombre note is struck behind the 18th-century residence – an expiatory chapel built by Vittorio Emanuele III that marks the spot where his father Umberto was assassinated by an anarchist in 1900.

LAKE MAGGIORE

Italy's second-largest lake, Maggiore, winds majestically between Piemonte and Lombardy, its northern corner lost in the snow-capped Swiss Alps. In Roman times Maggiore was called Lacus Verbanus, for the verbena that still grows luxuriantly on its shores.

What really sets the lake apart, though, are the fabled Borromean Islands and their gardens, still the property of the Borromeo family of Milan, who also own all the lake's fishing rights – as they have since the 1500s. Unless you book well in advance, it is best to avoid July and August.

Stresa

Beautifully positioned on the lake, overlooking the Borromean Islands and under the majestic peak of Mottarone, Stresa is Maggiore's most beautiful town, bursting with flowers and sprinkled with fine old villas. A holiday resort since the last century, famous for its lush gardens and mild climate, it soared in popularity after the construction of the Simplon Tunnel in 1906; Hemingway used its **Grand Hôtel des Iles Borromées** as Frederick Henry's refuge from war in *A Farewell to Arms*. The little triangular **Piazza Cadorna** in the centre, shaded by age-old plane trees, is Stresa's social centre, the numbers of its habitués swollen by international congress participants and music lovers attending the **Settimane Musicali di Stresa**.

Two of Stresa's lakeside villas are open to the public: **Villa Pallavicino** on Strada Statale, No.33 (1850) and its colourful gardens; and the **Villa Ducale** on Corso Umberto 15 (1771), once the property of Catholic philosopher Antonio Rosmini (d. 1855).

Monte Mottarone

Stresa Lido, t 0323 30399. Cable leaves every 20mins, 9.20–12 and 1.40–5.30; adm.

From Stresa you can ascend Monte Mottarone (4,920ft/1,500m) via a cableway. The famous views take in all seven major

Getting There and Around

Trains from Milan's Stazione Centrale to Domodossola stop at Stresa.

Navigazione Lago Maggiore, t 0322 46651, **w** *www.navlaghi.it*, runs **steamers** to all corners of the lake; there are also frequent services by steamer or hydrofoil from Stresa, Baveno and Pallanza to the Borromean Islands.

Tourist Information

Lake Maggiore: e *infoturismo@ distrettolaghi.it*, **w** *www.lagomaggiore.it*.

Stresa: Via Canonica 3, **t** 0323 30150, **f** 0323 32561.

Eating Out

Stresa

Piemontese, *Via Mazzini 25,* **t** *0323 30235 Open Tues–Sun, exc Jan and half of Feb. Expensive.* Find a table in the garden to tuck into the divine spaghetti with melted onions, basil and pecorino and the excellent fish dishes.

Isole Borromei

Hotel Verbano, *Isola dei Pescatori, Via Ugo Ara 2,* **t** *0323 30408,* **f** *0323 33129,* **w** *www.hotelverbano.it.* **Expensive.** A restaurant where romantic views compensate for brusque service and average food.

Italian lakes; on a clear day, glacier-crested peaks from Monte Viso and Monte Rosa, over to the ranges of Ortles and Adamello, as well as much of the Lombard plain are also visible.

The Borromean Islands

Lake Maggiore became a private fief of the Borromei in the 1470s, and to this day they own some of the finest bits, including the sumptuous gardens and villas of the Isole Borromei. There are frequent boats from the mainland to the islands, or you can hire a boat and row there.

The closest island to Stresa is **Isola Bella**, a scattering of barren rocks until the 17th century, when Count Carlo III Borromeo decided to make it a garden in the form of a ship for his wife Isabella (hence the name Isola Bella), which was designed by Angelo Crivelli. The Borromei opened the delightful, larger **Isola Madre** to the public in 1978. Here they planted a luxuriant botanical garden, dominated by Europe's largest Kashmir cypress; its camellias begin to bloom in January. The 16th-century villa has a collection of 18th- and 19th-century puppet theatres, marionettes, portraits and furnishings. The third island, **Isola dei Pescatori**, also known as Superiore, is home to an almost too quaint and picturesque fishing village. A fourth islet called **San Giovanni**, just off the shore at Pallanza, is privately owned; its villa once belonged to Toscanini.

LAKE COMO

Sapphire Lake Como has been Italy's prestige romantic lake since the earliest days of the Roman Empire, when the Plinys wrote of the luxuriant beauty surrounding the several villas on its shores. It was just the sort of luxuriant beauty that enraptured the children of the romantic era, inspiring operas from Verdi, Rossini and Bellini. And it is still here, the Lake Como of the Shelleys and Wordsworths, the villas and lush gardens, the mountains and wooded promontories.

Como

Magnificently located at the southern tip of the lake's left leg, Como is a lively little city that has long had a bent for science, silk and architecture. In AD 23 it was the birthplace of Pliny the Elder, compiler of antiquity's greatest work of hearsay, the *Natural History*, and later it produced his nephew and heir Pliny the Younger, whose letters are one of our main sources of information on the cultured Roman life of the period. From c. 1050 to 1335, when Como enjoyed a period as an independent *comune*, it produced a school of master builders, known generally as the *Maestri Comacini*, rivals to Lugano's *Maestri Campionesi*.

Around Piazza Cavour

Como's historic centre, its street plan almost unchanged since Roman times, opens up to the lake at Piazza Cavour, with its cafés, hotels, steamer landing and pretty views. Two landmarks in the public gardens to the west offer an introduction to Como's more recent scientists and architects. The first, the circular **Tempio Voltiano** (*Viale Marconi, t 031 574705; open April–Sept Tues–Sun 10–12 and 3–6, Oct–Mar Tues–Sun 10–12 and 2–4; adm*), was built in 1927 to house the manuscripts, instruments and inventions of Como's self-taught physicist Alessandro Volta (1745–1827), who lent his name to volts in a hundred languages. A bit further on, the striking **Monumento ai Caduti** – a memorial to the fallen of the First World War – was designed by the young Futurist architect Antonio Sant'Elia of Como (1888–1916), who himself died in action on the Front. The monument was built by Giuseppe Terragni (1904–34), a Como native and the most inspired Italian architect to work during the Fascist period (ask the tourist office for a special Terragni town plan).

Piazza Duomo

From Piazza Cavour, Via Plinio leads back to Como's elegant salon, the Piazza Duomo. Unusually, the chief monuments are all attached: the **Torre del Comune** to the

Getting There

There are hourly Trenitalia **trains** from Milan's Centrale or Porta Garibaldi stations, taking you in some 40 minutes to Como's main San Giovanni station (**t** 147 888 088). Slower but more frequent trains run on the regional Milano-Nord line to the lakeside station of Como-Lago. From Como, trains to Lecco depart from San Giovanni.

Buses from Como run to nearly every town on the lake.

Tourist Information

Como: Piazza Cavour 16, **t** 031 269 712, **f** 031 240 111, **e** info@lakecomo.org, **w** www.lakecomo.com (open Mon–Sat 9–1 and 2.30–6).

Eating Out

Ristorante Teatro Sociale, near the cathedral at Via Maestri Comacini, **t** 031 264 042. **Open** Wed–Mon. **Cheap**. Traditional post-theatre inn, with a good fixed-price tourist menu that includes wine.

Terrazzo Perlasca, Piazza de' Gasperi 8, **t** 031 303 936. **Open** Tues–Sun. **Expensive**. Como is one of those towns where the restaurants tend to process clients with slipshod food and service, especially in summer. This is one that doesn't. The menu changes almost every day and features typical dishes like filetto di laverello (whitefish fillets) and fettuccine e funghi (pasta with local mushrooms), all accompanied by wonderful views over the lake.

charming white, grey and red marble striped town hall or **Broletto** (both built in 1215), one of the rare Romanesque (and not Gothic) symbols of civic might in the north; and this in turn to the magnificent **Duomo** (**t** 031 265244; open daily 8–12 and 3–7), looking spanking new thanks to a thorough 700th birthday cleaning. The Duomo is Italy's most harmonious example of transitional architecture, although Gothic dominates in the façade and lovely rose window and pinnacles. The sculpture and reliefs are mainly by the Rodari family (late 15th–early 16th century), who also sculpted the lateral doors.

Inside, the three Gothic aisles combine happily with a Renaissance choir and transept, crowned by a dome designed by the great late Baroque master Filippo Juvarra in 1744. Nine 16th-century tapestries hang along the nave, lending an air of palatial elegance; a pair of Romanesque lions near the entrance are survivors from the cathedral's 11th-century predecessor. But most of the art is from the Renaissance, with reliefs by Tommaso Rodari, and fine canvases by two of Leonardo's followers, Gaudenzio Ferrari and Bernardino Luini.

Piazza del Popolo

For a contrast, go behind the Duomo and across the train tracks to the Piazza del Popolo, where Giuseppe Terragni's ex-Casa del Fascio, now the **Palazzo Terragni**, stands out in all its functional, luminous beauty. Built in 1931 but completely unlike the typically ponderous travertine buildings constructed under Mussolini, it is 50 years ahead of its time, practically transparent, an essay in light and harmony, and the masterpiece of the only coherent architectural style Italy has produced in the 20th century. Its occupants, the Guardia di Finanza, allow visits to the ground floor.

Around Town

From the cathedral, main Via Vittorio Emanuele leads to Como's old cathedral, **San Fedele**, on this site since 914. It has a unique pentagonal apse and a doorway carved with chubby archaic figures and a griffon; the interior is lavishly decorated with 18th-century frescoes. Further up, in the Piazza Medaglie d'Oro Comasche, the **Museo Civico** (**t** 031 271343; open Tues–Sat 9.30–12.30 and 2–5, Sun 10–1; adm) is the city's attic of artefacts, from the Neolithic era until the Second World War, with interesting Roman frescoes along the way. From the piazza, down Via Giovio to the **Porta Vittoria**, is a striking skyscraper of a gate from 1192, its immaculate tiers of arches rising 72ft.

Near here, Como's small **Pinacoteca**, in Via Diaz 84, contains carved capitals and wonderful medieval paintings from the old monastery of Santa Margherita del Broletto. A short walk away from the Porta Vittoria, at the beginning of the Via della Regina (the road built by Lombard queen Theodolinda around Lake Como), is Como's Romanesque gem **Sant'Abbondio**, consecrated by Pope Urban II in 1095. The façade is discreet, and the twin campaniles are believed to be of Norman inspiration, while the interior, with its lofty vaults and forest of columns forming five aisles, offers a kind of preview of coming great events in Italian architecture. The elegant apse is decorated with 14th-century frescoes: note the knights in armour arresting Christ in Gethsemane.

On the east end of town, by the Villa Genio, is a **funicular** in Piazza de Gaspian 4, which takes you up to the nearby mountain village of Brunate. It offers spectacular views across the lake and Alps as far as Monte Rosa (**t** 031 303 608; *every 15–30 minutes; call for exact times; combined ferry/funicular ticket*).

BERGAMO

At the end of *A Midsummer Night's Dream*, Bottom and his mechanical pals, who played in 'Pyramus and Thisbe', dance a bergomask to celebrate the happy ending. Bergamo itself has the same stomping magnificent spirit as its great peasant dance, a city that mixes a rugged edge with the most delicate refinement: it has given the world not only a dance but the maestro of *bel canto*, Gaetano Donizetti; the Renaissance painter of beautiful women, Palma Vecchio; and the great master of the portrait, Gian Battista Moroni.

Piled on a promontory on the edge of the Alps, the city started out on a different foot, founded by mountain Celts who named it Bergheim or hill town. To this day the Bergamasques speak a dialect that puzzles

their fellow Lombards; their language, courage and blunt up-front character are all a part of the essential *bergheimidad* that sets them apart. Although old Bergamo owes many of its grace notes to the long rule of Venice (1428–1797), the culture traffic was by no means one-way: Bergamo contributed not only artists, but the Serenissima's most brilliant and honourable *condottiere*, Bartolomeo Colleoni (1400–75), as well as many of Venice's servants, porters and stock comic characters. Bergamo also contributed so many men to Garibaldi in its enthusiasm for the Risorgimento that it received the proud title 'City of the Thousand'.

There are two Bergamos: the Città Alta, the medieval and Renaissance centre up on the hill, and the Città Bassa, pleasant, newer and more spacious on the plain below, most of its streets laid out at the beginning of this century.

Città Bassa

The centre of the lower town is the large, oblong **Piazza Matteotti**, with the grand 18th-century Teatro Donizetti and, on the right, the church of **San Bartolomeo**, containing a fine 1516 altarpiece of the *Madonna col Bambino* by Lotto.

The Accademia Carrara
*Piazza G. Carrara 82, t 035 399 643. **Open** daily 9.30–1 and 2.30–5.45; **adm** (Sun free).*

This is one of the top provincial art museums in Italy, and certainly one of the oldest, founded in 1796 by Count Giacomo Carrara and housed in this neoclassical palace since 1810. It has exquisite portraits – Botticelli's haughty *Giuliano de' Medici*, Pisanello's *Lionello d'Este*, Gentile Bellini's *Portrait of a Man*, Lotto's *Portrait of Lucina Brembati* with a vicious weasel under her arm and a sickly moon overhead, and another strange painting of uncertain origin, believed to be of Cesare Borgia, with an uncannily desolate background.

Other portraits (especially the *Young Girl*, one of the most beautiful portraits of a child

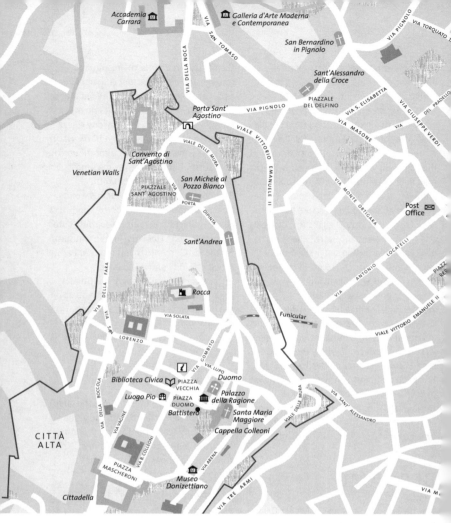

Accademia
Carrara

Galleria d'Arte Moderna
e Contemporanea

VIA PIGNOLO

VIA TORQUATO T...

VIA DELLA NOCA

VIA SAN TOMASO

San Bernardino
in Pignolo

Sant'Alessandro
della Croce

Porta Sant'
Agostino

VIA PIGNOLO

PIAZZALE
DEL DELFINO

VIA S. ELISABETTA

VIA GIUSEPPE VERDI

DEL PRADELLO

VIALE DELLE MURA

VIALE VITTORIO EMANUELE II

VIA MASONE

Convento di
Sant'Agostino

Venetian Walls

PIAZZALE
SANT'AGOSTINO

San Michele al
Pozzo Bianco

VIA MONTE ORTICARA

Post
Office

PORTA

VIA DIPINTA

VIA ANTONIO LOCATELLI

PIAZZ...
RES...

Sant'Andrea

VIA DELLA FARA

Rocca

VIA SOLATA

Funicular

VIALE VITTORIO EMANUELE II

VIALE VITTORIO EMANUELE II

VIA S. LORENZO

VIA GOMBITO

VIA VM. LUPO

Duomo

Biblioteca Civica

PIAZZA
VECCHIA

Luogo Pio

PIAZZA
DUOMO

Palazzo
della Ragione

VIA DELLA BOCCOLA

VIA VAGINE

Battistero

Santa Maria
Maggiore

VIALE DELLE MURA

VIA SANT'ALESSANDRO

CITTÀ
ALTA

VIA B. COLLEONI

Cappella Colleoni

PIAZZA
MASCHERONI

VIA ARENA

Museo
Donizettiano

VIA TRE ARMI

Cittadella

VIA ME...

ever painted) are by Bergamo's Giovan Battista Moroni (1520–78), the master to whom Titian sent the Rectors of Venice for their portrait, saying that only Moroni could 'make them natural'. There are beautiful *Madonnas*, three superlative ones by Giovanni Bellini, others by Mantegna (who couldn't do children), Fra Angelico, Landi and Crivelli (with his cucumber signature). The anti-plague Saint Sebastian is portrayed by three contemporaries in very different aspects – naked and pierced with arrows before a silent city, by Giovanni Bellini; well-dressed and sweetly contemplating an arrow, by Raphael; and sitting at a table, clad in a fur-trimmed coat, by Dürer. Other

paintings are by Bergognone, Cariani, Fra Galgario, Palma Vecchio and Prevetali (all from Bergamo); the Venetians Carpaccio, Vivarini, Titian, Veronese, Tintoretto, Tiepolo and Guardi; also Cosmè Tura, Foppa, Luini, Savoldo, Moretto, Clouet, Van Dyck and Brueghel.

Città Alta

On Viale Vittorio Emanuele II is the **funicular** up to the higher town (**t 035** *364222; open Mon–Sat 7am–midnight; adm*). Once you're at the top, Via Gombito leads from the upper station a short distance to beautiful Piazza Vecchia. Architects as

Getting There

Bergamo is an hour's **train** ride from Milan's Porta Garibaldi, and there are some trains from Centrale as well (freephone **t** 1478 88088). The station is at the end of Viale Papa Giovanni XXIII.

Tourist Information

Bergamo has two tourist offices (*www.apt.bergamo.it*): Viale Vittorio Emanuele 20, near the funicular station to the Città Alta, **t** 035 210204, **f** 035 280184; and Vicolo dell'Aquila Nera 2, in Città Alta, at **t** 035 242 226, **f** 035 242 994 (*both open Mon–Fri 9–12.30, 2–5.30*).

Eating Out

Bergamo prides itself on its cooking: look for *casoncelli* (ravioli filled with tangy sausage-meat, in a sauce of melted butter, bacon and sage), *polenta taragna* (with butter and cheese) and risotto with wild mushrooms. Many restaurants, surprisingly, feature seafood – Bergamo is a major inland fish market. In August, however, you might have to resort to a picnic.

Antica Hosteria del Buon Vino, *Piazza Mercato delle Scarpe, in Bergamo Alta, in front of the exit of the funicular*. **Open** *Tues–Sun*. A hearty cheap meal serving polenta (try the *tris*) and local hot and cold dishes.

Da Vittorio, *Viale Papa Giovanni XXIII 21, t/f 035 218 060*. **Open** *Thurs–Tues, exc three weeks in Aug*. **Expensive**. The classic for fish, specializing in seafood prepared in a number of exquisite ways, as well as a wide variety of meat dishes, polenta, risotto and pasta.

La Colombina, *Borgo Canale 12, t 035 261 402*. **Open** *Tues–Sun exc Aug and one week in Jan and June*. **Moderate**. Near Donizetti's birthplace, this almost perfect restaurant has stunning views from its dappled terrace, and a pretty Liberty-style dining room. Try the salad of local *taleggio* cheese with slivers of pear, a plate of cured meats, and the best *casoncelli* in town. Leave room for a slice of deep, dark, caramelized apple cake.

diverse as Frank Lloyd Wright and Le Corbusier have praised this square as one of Italy's finest for its magnificent ensemble of Renaissance and medieval buildings, all overlooking a low, dignified lion fountain.

At the lower end stands the **Biblioteca Civica** (1594), designed after Sansovino's famous library in Venice. Directly opposite, an ancient covered stair leads up to the 12th-century **Torre Civica**, with a 15th-century clock and curfew bell that still warns the Bergamasques to bed at 10pm; there is a **lift** to take visitors up for the fine views over Bergamo (*open April–Sept daily 9–12 and 2–8, Fri and Sat till 11pm, Sun 9–8pm, March daily 10–12 and 2 to 6, Oct weekends and holidays* only 10–12 and 2–6, Nov–Feb weekends and holidays only 10–12 and 2–4; adm). Next to the stair, set up on its large rounded arches, is the 12th-century **Palazzo della Ragione**, with a Lion of St Mark added recently to commemorate the city's golden days under Venice.

Through the dark, tunnel-like arches of the Palazzo della Ragione are glimpses of a second square resembling a jewel box. This is **Piazza del Duomo**, and the jewel box reveals itself as the sumptuous, colourful façade of the 1476 **Colleoni Chapel** (t 035 210061; open Tues–Sun 9–12.30 and 2.30–4.30, Nov–Mar until 5.30), designed for the old condottiere by Giovanni Antonio Amadeo while he worked on the Certosa at Pavia.

The Colleoni Chapel is even more ornate and out of temper with the times, disregarding all the fine proportions and serenity of the Tuscans for the Venetian love of flourish. Amadeo also sculpted the fine tombs within, a double decker for Colleoni and his wife; the golden equestrian statue on top by Sixus of Nuremberg makes him look like a wimp compared to Verrocchio's version in Venice.

His young daughter Medea's tomb is much calmer, and was brought here in the 19th century from another church. The ornate ceiling is by Tiepolo, and there's a painting of the Holy Family by Goethe's constant companion in Rome, the Swiss artist Angelica Kauffmann.

Flanking the chapel are two works by Giovanni, a 14th-century Campionese master: the octagonal **Baptistry** (t 035 278 111; open by appointment only) and the colourful porch and equestrian statue of St Alexander on the otherwise austere **Basilica of Santa Maria Maggiore** (1137).

The palatial interior with its sumptuous tapestries hits you like a gust of lilac perfume, but the 33 Old Testament scenes designed by Lorenzo Lotto and executed in intaglio by Capodiferro ('Ironhead') di Lovere are off limits. However four of the scenes can be seen on Sundays; their locked wooden covers, with unfathomable allegories, are food for thought. Donizetti's tomb, near the back of the church, has mourning putti and a keyboard. The third building on the square is an insipid neoclassical cathedral.

The rest of the Città Alta deserves a stroll; walk along the main artery, Via Colleoni (the condottiere lived at No.9) to the old fortress of the Cittadella, which houses the city's **Museo di Scienze Naturali** (open Tues–Sun 9–12.30 and 2.30–7.30, until 5.30 in winter) and **Museo Archeologico** (open Tues–Thurs 9–12.30 and 2.30–6, Fri–Sun 9–6).

Near the Cittadella is the bottom station of another funicular, up to **San Vigilio** where there is another fortress, the **Castello**, with superb views. Back at the Cittadella, quiet, medieval Via Arena leads around to the back of the cathedral, passing by way of the **Museo Donizettiano** (t 035 399269; open Tues–Sat 10–1 by appointment, Sun 10–1 and 2.30–5), with a collection of artefacts and instruments once owned by the great composer of bel canto, who died syphilitic and mad in 1848.

CITIES OF THE LOMBARD PLAIN

The three provincial capitals of the Lombard plain are among Italy's most rewarding art cities: Pavia, the capital of the ancient Lombards and the region's oldest centre of learning, embellished with Romanesque churches and its famous Renaissance Certosa; Cremona, the graceful city where the raw medieval fiddle was reincarnated as the lyrical violin; and Mantua, the dream shadow capital of the wealthy Gonzaga dukes and Isabella d'Este.

Pavia

Pavia is a serious no-monkey-business town. It is one of those rare cities that had its golden age in the three-digit years, that misty half-legendary time that historians have shrugged off as the Dark Ages. But these were bright days for Pavia, when it served as capital of the Goths and saw Odoacer proclaimed King of Italy after defeating Romulus Augustulus, the last Roman Emperor in the West. In the 6th century the heretical Lombards led by King Alboin captured Pavia from the Goths and formed a state the equal of Byzantine Ravenna and Rome, making Pavia the capital of their *Regnum Italicum*, a position the city maintained into the 11th century. Charlemagne came here to be crowned (774), as did the first King of Italy, Berengar (888), and Emperor Frederick Barbarossa (1155).

At the turn of the millennium the precursor of Pavia's modern university, the Studio, was founded; one of its first law students was the first Norman Archbishop of Canterbury, Lanfranc, born in Pavia in 1005. Pavia was the Ghibelline 'city of a hundred towers' and rival to Milan's, to whom it lost its independence in 1359. It was favoured by the Visconti, especially by Gian Galeazzo, who built the castle and founded the Certosa, and bears the mark of Pavia's great, half-demented sculptor-architect, Giovanni Antonio Amadeo.

The Duomo

Open daily 7.30–12 and 3–7.

Pavia's core retains its street plan from the days when it was Roman Ticinum. The *cardus* (Corso Cavour) and the *decumanus* (Corso Strada Nuova) intersect by the town hall or **Broletto**, begun in the 12th century, and the **Duomo**, a front-runner for the ugliest church

Getting There

There are **buses** roughly every 30 minutes between Milan and Pavia. They stop near the Certosa di Pavia, and arrive in, and depart from, Via Trieste. Bus information: SGEA, **t** 02 8954 6132, **w** www.infopoint.it.

Frequent **trains** link Pavia to Milan on the Genoa line (30mins). Eight trains a day from Milan's Centrale station stop at Certosa di Pavia. The train station is a 10-minute walk from the centre, at the end of Corso Cavour and Viale Vittorio Emanuele II.

Tourist Information

Via Filzi 2 (a couple of streets from the station), **t** 0382 22156, **f** 0382 32221, **w** www.apt.pv.it.

Eating Out

Pavia is well endowed with good restaurants. Specialities include frogs, salami from Varzi and *zuppa pavese* (a raw egg on toast drowned in hot broth). Good local wines to try are from the Oltrepò Pavese region, one of Lombardy's best. Cortese is a fresh dry white, Bonarda a meaty, dry red, Pinot a more fruity white.

Antica Osteria del Previ, *Via Milazzo 65*, **t** 0382 26203. **Open** Mon–Sat. **Moderate**. Situated on the banks of the Ticino, this is an old-fashioned place serving home-made salami, risotto with frog or radicchio and speck, and for *secondi* river-fish and snails.

Locanda Vecchia Pavia al Molino, *Via al Monumento 5*, **t** 0382 925 894. **Open** Tues–Sun, exc Wed lunch. **Expensive**. Located in the restored 16th-century mill of the Certosa. Brings former chic gourmet restaurant Locanda Vecchia Pavia and country inn Vecchio Mulino together under one roof. The restaurant maintains the tradition, style (and prices) of the former, with refined dishes such as truffle-filled home-made ravioli, or prawn with *lardo* of Colonnata and porcini mushrooms, and delicate desserts.

Osteria della Madonna del Peo, *Via Cardano 63, corner Via dei Liguri*, **t** 0382 302 833. **Cheap**. In the city centre, located in a homely vaulted inn. Serves typical Lombard dishes, such as risotti, roasted and braised meats, or stuffed guinea-fowl, which require lengthy cooking. Cheap menu at lunchtime and a good selection of Oltrepò wines.

in Italy. Begun in 1488, it owes its imposing design to Leonardo da Vinci, Bramante, Amadeo and a dozen others (proof that too many cooks spoil the broth), and its corrugated cardboard façade to an understandable lack of interest in finishing it. The last apses were added only in 1930. Next to the cathedral, a stump recalls the singularly unattractive 12th-century **Torre Civica**, whose sudden collapse in 1989 prompted serious attention to its famous Pisan relation.

Basilica di San Michele Maggiore

Open daily 7.30–12 and 3–7.

East of Strada Nuova, Via Capsoni leads to the Romanesque Basilica di San Michele Maggiore, founded in 661 but rebuilt in the 12th century after its destruction by lightning. Unlike the other churches of Pavia, San Michele is made of sandstone, mellowed into a fine golden hue, though the weather has been less kind to the intricate friezes that cross its front like comic strips, depicting a complete 'apocalyptic vision' with its medieval bestiary, monsters and human figures involved in the never-ending fight between Good and Evil. The solemn interior, where Frederick Barbarossa was crowned with the Iron Crown of Italy, contains more fine carvings on the capitals; the most curious, the fourth on the left, portrays the 'Death of the Righteous'. Along the top runs the women's gallery, while the chapel to the right of the main altar contains the church's most valuable treasure, a 7th-century silver crucifix.

The University

The yellow neoclassical quadrangles of the **University of Pavia**, famous for law and medicine, occupy the northeast quadrant of the ancient street plan along Strada Nuova. First a Studio, it was officially made a university in 1361. In the 18th century Maria Theresa worked hard to bring the university back to life after scholarship had hit the skids, and financed the construction of the main buildings. Three of Pavia's medieval skyscrapers or Torri survive in the middle of the university in

Piazza Leonardo da Vinci; the roof in the piazza shelters the crypt of the demolished 12th-century **Sant'Eusebio** church. You can meet some of the university's 17,000 students at the Bar Bordoni, on Via Mentana. In Piazza San Francesco d'Assisi, northeast of the main university, San Francesco d'Assisi (1228) was one of Italy's first churches dedicated to the saint; it has a façade adorned with lozenge patterns and a triple-mullioned window.

Castello Visconteo

Open Feb–Jun and Sept–Nov, Tues–Fri 10–1.30, Sat and Sun 10–7; Dec–Jan and July–Aug, Tues–Sun 9–1pm only.

At the top of Strada Nuova looms the Castello Visconteo, built in 1360 for Gian Galeazzo II, but partially destroyed in the Battle of Pavia on 24 February 1525 when Emperor Charles V captured Francis I of France, who succinctly described the outcome in a letter to his mother: 'Madame, all is lost save honour.' Three sides of the castle and its beautifully arcaded courtyard with terracotta decorations managed to survive, and now house Pavia's **Museo Civico**. The archaeological and medieval sections contain finds from Gaulish and Roman Pavia, robust Lombard carvings and colourful 12th-century mosaics. The picture gallery contains works by Giovanni Bellini, Correggio, Foppa, Van der Goes and others.

San Pietro in Ciel d'Oro

Behind the castle, Via Griziotti (off Viale Matteotti) leads to Pavia's second great Romanesque temple, San Pietro in Ciel d'Oro ('St Peter in the Golden Sky'), built in 1132 and named for its once-glorious gilded ceiling, mentioned by Dante in Canto X of the *Paradiso*. The single door in the façade is strangely off-centre; within, the main altar is one of the greatest works of the Campionese masters, the **Arca di Sant'Agostino**, a magnificent 14th-century monument built to shelter the bones of St Augustine, retrieved in the 8th century from Carthage by the Lombard king Luitprand (so the legend goes).

staunch ally of Pope Gregory II against the iconoclasts of Byzantium. Luitprand is buried in a humble tomb to the right, and in the crypt lies another Dark Age celebrity, the philosopher Boethius, slain by Emperor Theodoric of Ravenna in 524.

The Certosa di Pavia

Via del Monumento 5, t 0382 925613. Open Oct–Mar Tues–Sun 9–11.30 and 2.30–4.30; April Tues–Sun 9–11.30 and 2.30–5.30; May–Sept Tues–Sun 9–11.30 and 2.30–6.

The pinnacle of Renaissance architecture in Lombardy, and according to Jacob Burckhardt 'the greatest decorative masterpiece in all of Italy', the Certosa or Charterhouse of Pavia was built over a period of 200 years. Gian Galeazzo Visconti laid the cornerstone in 1396, with visions of the crown of Italy dancing in his head, and the desire to build a splendid pantheon for his hoped-for royal self and his heirs. Although many architects and artists worked on the project (beginning with the Campionese masters of Milan cathedral), the greatest imprint it bears is that of Giovanni Antonio Amadeo, who with his successor Bergognone worked on its sculptural programme for 30 years and contributed the design of the lavish façade.

Napoleon disbanded the monastery, but in 1968 a small group of Cistercians reoccupied the Certosa. The monks of today live the same style of contemplative life as the old Carthusians, maintaining vows of silence. A couple, however, are released to take visitors around the complex. If you arrive by the Milan–Pavia bus, the Certosa is a 1.5km walk from the nearest stop, a beckoning vision at the end of the straight, shaded land, surrounded by well-tended fields and rows of poplars once part of the vast game park of the Castello Visconteo in Pavia.

Once through the main gate and vestibule adorned with frescoes by Luini, a large grassy **court** opens up, lined with buildings that served as lodgings for visitors and stores for the monks. At the far side rises the sumptuous, detailed façade of the **church**, a marvel of polychromatic marbles, medallions, bas-reliefs, statues, and windows covered with marble embroidery from the chisel of Amadeo, who died before the upper, less elaborate level was begun. The interior plan is Gothic but the decoration is Renaissance, with later Baroque additions. Outstanding works of art include Bergognone's five statues of saints in the chapel of Sant'Ambrogio (sixth on the left); the tombs of Lodovico il Moro and his young bride Beatrice d'Este, a masterpiece by Cristoforo Solari; the beautiful inlaid stalls of the choir; and the tomb of Gian Galeazzo Visconti, all works of the 1490s and surrounded by fine frescoes. The sacristy contains a magnificent early *cinquecento* ivory altarpiece by the Florentine Baldassarre degli Embriachi.

Cremona

Cremona is famous for four things that have added to the sum total of human happiness: its Romanesque cathedral complex, Claudio Monteverdi, nougat and violins. It has been the capital of the violin industry since 1566, when Andrea Amati invented the modern violin from the old medieval fiddle. It quickly became fashionable, and demand across Europe initiated a golden age of fiddle-making, when Andrea's son Nicolò Amati, and his pupils Stradivarius and Giuseppe Guarneri, made the best violins ever. Walking around Cremona you can easily pick out the elegant curves and scrolls on the brick and terracotta palaces that inspired the instrument's Baroque form, while the sweetness of the violin's tone seems to have something of the city's culinary specialities in it, not only nougat but *mostarda di Cremona* – candied cherries, apricots and melons in a sweet or piquant mustard sauce, served with boiled meats. Today some 50 *liutai* (violinmakers) keep up the tradition, using similar methods and woods (poplar, spruce, pear, willow and maple); a school and research institute are devoted to the craft, and every third October (next in 2003) the city hosts a festival of stringed instruments. The city enjoyed

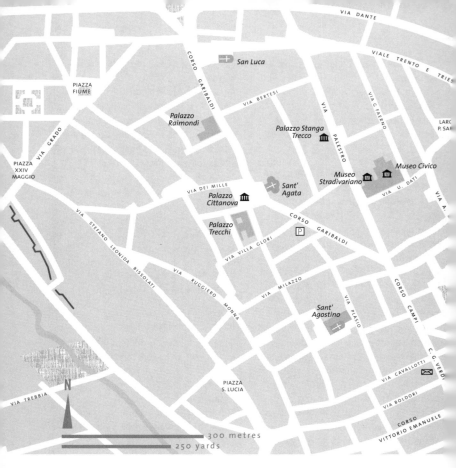

a happy, fruitful Renaissance, producing Monteverdi, the father of opera.

Via Palestro and Around

Cremona can be easily visited on foot, starting from the station and the Via Palestro. Here, behind a remodelled Baroque façade at Via Palestro 36, the **Palazzo Stanga** Trecco's 15th-century courtyard is an excellent introduction to the Cremonese fondness for elaborate terracotta ornament.

The **Museo Stradivariano** nearby at No.17 (*open Sept–July Tues–Sat 9–6, Sun and holidays 10–6; adm*) is an equally good introduction to the cream of Cremona's best-known industry, featuring casts, models, items from the master's workshop and drawings explaining how Stradivarius did it.

Along **Corso Mazzini** is Stradivarius' red marble tombstone, transferred from a demolished church. Corso Mazzini forks after a block; near the split, at Corso Matteotti 17, is Cremona's prettiest palace, the 1499 **Palazzo Fodri** (owned by Banca Cariplo; ask the guard to open the gate), with a courtyard adorned with frescoed battle scenes and terracottas.

The Torrazzo

*Piazza del Comune, t 0372 27633. **Open by appointment only; adm.***

Cremona's lovely medieval Piazza del Comune is seductive enough to compete in any urban beauty contest. By now you've probably caught at least a glimpse of its biggest feature, the curious pointed crown of the tallest belltower in Italy, the 370ft Torrazzo. Only slightly shorter than Milan cathedral, the Torrazzo was built in the 1260s has battlements as well as bells, and even tells the time thanks to a fine astronomical marble front. Built by the Comacini masters after an earthquake destroyed its predecessor in 1117, the main door or Porta Regia remains as it was originally, flanked by two nearly toothless lion telamones and four flat prophets, and crowned by a small portico known as the Rostrum, where 13th- and 14th-century statues of the Virgin and two saints silently but eloquently

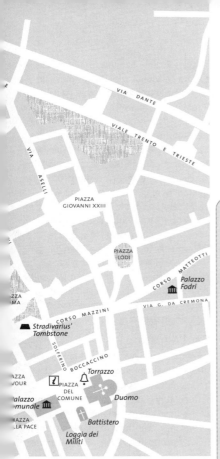

clock added in 1583 by Giovanni Battista Divizioli; the astronomical clock room can be visited. The stout-hearted can ascend 487 steps to the top for an eye-popping view; the less ambitious can purchase a famous Cremona TTT postcard (Torrazzo, *torrone* and *tette* – tits) to send home. The lower level houses a reproduction of a violinmaker's shop of Stradivarius' time.

The Duomo

Piazza del Comune, **t** *0372 22582.* **Open** *Mon–Sat 7.30–12 and 3.30–7, Sun 7.30–1 and 3.30–7.*

Linked to the Torrazzo in 1525 by a double loggia, the **Portico della Bertazzola**, the Duomo is the highest and one of the most exuberant expressions of Lombard Romanesque, with a trademark Cremonese flourish in the graceful scrolls added to the

Getting There

Cremona's railway station, north of the centre at the end of Via Palestro, is delightful: there are frequent **train** services from Milan's Centrale station, often changing at Codogno (fast trains 1hr 15mins, regional trains may be slower).

Or exchange your car for free use of a bicycle at the Via Villa Glori car park.

Tourist Information

Piazza del Comune 5, **t** 0372 23233, freephone from within Italy **t** 800 655 511, **f** 0372 534 080, **w** *www.cremonaturismo.com*.

Eating Out

Porta Mosa, *Via Santa Maria in Betlem 11,* **t** *0372 411 803.* **Open** *Tues–Sat mid-Sept–mid-Aug. Book ahead.* **Moderate**. A tiny family-run place serving delicious traditional dishes such as tortelli stuffed with squash and locally caught sturgeon steamed with herbs.

Ristorante Il Violino, *Via Sicardo 3,* **t** *0372 46101.* **Open** *Wed–Mon, exc Mon eve. Book in advance.* **Expensive**. Located just behind the Baptistry, this classy restaurant enjoys an enviable reputation for its regional dishes, starting with melt-in-your-mouth *antipasti*, and zesty *secondi* featuring meat or seafood.

Trattoria Mellini, *Via Bissolati 105,* **t** *0372 30535.* **Open** *Sept–July Tues–Sun, exc Sun eve.* **Moderate**. An older, rather more traditional restaurant on the west end of town, serving casseroled donkey and baby horse, or raw baby horse with truffle. Less controversial dishes include a kind of risotto with salami and savoy cabbage, and fresh pasta with sausage.

hold forth above a frieze of the months by the school of Antelami.

The cathedral was begun as a basilica, but when Gothic came into fashion the arms of a Latin cross were added; the new transepts, especially the north one, are almost as splendid from the outside as the main façade. Restoration of the interior has revealed primitive frescoes under the opulent 16th-century works by Romanino, Boccaccino and Pordenone (who painted the Crucifixion under the rose window); the right transept has some endearing sweet and simple paintings on the ceiling; the twin pulpits have nervous, delicate reliefs attributed to Amadeo or Pietro da Rho; the choir has exquisite stalls inlaid in 1490 by G.M. Platina – with secular scenes, still lifes and views of Cremona. In the crypt, with the tomb of Ombrono Tucenghi, patron saint of tailors (d. 1197), note the painting of old Cremona with its Manhattanesque skyline.

Battistero di San Giovanni

Piazza del Comune 8. Open Sat 3.30–7, Sun and hols 10.30–12.30 and 3.30–7.

Completing the sacred ensemble in Piazza del Comune is the octagonal **Battistero di San Giovanni** (1167, with another pair of lions supporting the portico, and two sides of marble facing to match the cathedral).

Loggia dei Militi

Piazza del Comune.

Across from the Duomo, the **Loggia dei Militi** (1292) was used as a rendezvous by the captains of the *comune's* citizen militia; the outdoor pulpit between two of the arches is a relic of the charismatic, itinerant preachers like San Bernadino of Siena, whose sermons were so popular they had to be held outside.

Palazzo del Comune

Piazza del Commune 8, t 0372 4071. Open Tues–Sat 8.30–6, Sun and hols 10–6; adm.

The Palazzo del Comune was begun in 1206 as the lavish seat of the Ghibelline party and now serves as Cremona's town hall. On show are paintings salvaged from churches, a superb marble fireplace of 1502 by Giovan

Gaspare Pedone, Baroque furniture – and the **Saletta dei Violini**, with the town's violin collection, starring Stradivarius' golden 'Cremonese 1715', which retains its original varnish – as mysterious as the embalming fluids of Ancient Egypt. Another of the master's secrets was in the woods he used for his instruments; like Michelangelo seeking just the right piece of marble in the mountains of Carrara, Stradivarius would visit the forests of the Dolomites looking for perfect trees that would one day sing. To hear the unique sound of such rare instruments, you can book a listening session, held in the Saletta (*t 0372 22138; free*). Once you are in the Palazzo, take some time to visit the Sala Rossa and Sala della Giunta (if there is not a plenary session) for their original décor.

Sant'Agostino

Cremona has several lofty churches with interiors that look like nothing as much as ancient Roman basilicas. One is the 14th-century church of Sant'Agostino, north of the Corso Vittorio Emanuele, on Via Plasio. Its striking red brick façade is adorned with fine terracotta decorations, and the centre nave is lined with statues of the virtues. There are good Renaissance frescoes in the right aisle by Bonifacio Bembo and a lovely pala of the *Madonna with Saints* (1494) by Perugino (*under restoration*).

Mantua (Mantova)

Mantua's setting hardly answers to one's great expectations of Italy, sitting in the midst of a table-flat plain, surrounded by three swampy, swollen lakes. Its climate is moody: soggy with heat and humidity in the summer and frosty under blankets of fog in the winter.

The local dialect is harsh, and the Mantuans, when they feel chipper, dine on braised donkey with macaroni. And yet this former capital of the art-loving, fast-living Gonzaga dukes is one of the most atmospheric old cities in the country –

Getting There and Around

Mantua is linked directly by **train** with Milan and Cremona from Milan Centrale.

You can rent a **bike** at the train station. For a **taxi**, ring **t** 0376 368 866.

Tourist Information

Piazza Mantegna 6, **t** 0376 328 253, **f** 0376 363 299, **w** www.aptmantova.it.

Eating Out

During the reign of the Gonzaga the Mantuans developed their own cuisine, which other Italians regard as a little peculiar. The notorious *stracotto di asino* (donkey stew) heads the list, but the Mantuans also have a predilection for adding Lambrusco to soup. Classic *primi* include *agnoli* stuffed with bacon, salami, chicken livers and cheese cooked in broth, *risotto alla pilota* (with onion, butter and grana cheese), or *tortelli di zucca* (pasta parcels stuffed with pumpkin, mustard and cheese, served with melted butter). Catfish, eel, crayfish, bass, pike (the delicious *luccio* in salsa, prepared with peppers and capers) and crispy-fried frog's legs are typical *secondi*. Mantua is also

the place to taste true Lambrusco; the foam should vanish instantly when poured. Another speciality is the *Sbrisoloni* (i.e. crumbling) cake made of flour, almonds and eggs – highly recommended.

Antica Osteria Fragoletta, *Piazza Arche 5*, *t 0376 323 300*. **Open** *Tues–Sun*. *Booking advisable*. **Cheap**. This former *trattoria* has become a trendier restaurant, with a nice atmosphere and good cuisine, appreciated by the local clientele.

Aquila Nigra, *Vicolo Bonacolsi 4*, *t 0376 327 180*, **w** *www.aquilanigra.net*. **Open** *Tues–Sun, exc Aug and Jan*. **Expensive**. A lovely place with its marble and traces of frescoes, serving exquisitely prepared regional dishes; the pasta courses such as ravioli filled with truffled duck are a joy, and there's a wide choice of seafood as well as meat dishes. A great wine list, cheeses and delicious desserts round off a special meal.

San Gervasio, *Vicolo San Gervasio 13*, *t 0376 323 873*. **Open** *Thurs–Tues Sept–July*. **Moderate**. Located in a superbly renovated 14th-century palace, this restaurant offers an excellent moderate menu *mantovano* and several fish dishes.

'a city in the form of a palace' as Castiglione called it. It's masculine, dark and handsome, with few of Cremona's sweet architectural arpeggios – poker-faced, but holding a royal flush of dazzling Renaissance art.

Basilica di Sant'Andrea

Rising above it all in Piazza Mantegna is the great basilica of Sant'Andrea, designed by Leon Battista Alberti in 1472 to house a precious relic: two ampoules of Christ's blood, said to have been given to St Andrew by St Longinus, the Roman centurion who pierced Christ's side. In Florence, Alberti was constrained by his patrons' tastes, but in Mantua he could experiment with the ancient forms he loved. Sant'Andrea is based on Vitruvius' idea of an Etruscan temple, with a single barrel-vaulted nave supported by side chapels, fronted with a unique façade combining a triumphal arch and a temple.

Duomo

Piazza Sordello. **Open** *daily 7–12 and 3–7*.

An archway leads into the grand cobbled **Piazza Sordello**, traditional seat of Mantua's bosses. On one side rise the sombre palaces of the Bonacolsi family, with their Torre della Gabbia, named for the iron cage they kept to suspend prisoners over the city. At the head of the piazza stands the **Duomo** with a silly 1756 façade that hides a lovely interior designed by Giulio Romano in 1545. Renaissance tapestries hang in the choir, and the enormous Trinity in the apse is by 17th-century Roman painter Domenico Fetti.

The Palazzo Ducale

Piazza Sordello, *t 0376 382150*. **Open** *Tues–Sun 9–6.30, Jun–Sept open Sat until 11pm; must book for the Camera degli Sposi*; *adm*.

Opposite the Bonacolsi palaces stands that of the Gonzaga, its unimpressive façade hiding one of Italy's most remarkable Renaissance abodes, both in sheer size and the magnificence of its art. The insatiable Gonzaga kept adding on until they had some 500 rooms in three main structures – the original Corte Vecchia, first built by the Bonacolsi in 1290, the 14th-century Castello, with its large towers overlooking the lake, and the Corte Nuova, designed by Giulio Romano. Throw in the Gonzaga's Basilica di Santa Barbara and you have a complex that occupies the entire northeast corner of Mantua, spreading 36,000 square metres. If you go in the winter, dress warmly – it's as cold as a dead duke.

One of the first rooms on the tour, the former **chapel**, has a dramatic, half-ruined 14th-century fresco of the Crucifixion, attributed by some to Tommaso da Modena, while another contains a painting of a battle between the Gonzaga and the Bonacolsi in the Piazza Sordello by Domenico Monore. Even more fascinating is the vivid **fresco of Arthurian knights** by Pisanello, Italy's International Gothic master. The fresco was believed lost until 1969, when layers of plaster were stripped away to reveal a remarkable work commissioned by Gianfrancesco Gonzaga in 1442. Beyond this are the remodelled **neoclassical rooms**, holding a set of 16th-century Flemish tapestries from Raphael's *Acts of the Apostles* cartoons (now in the V&A Museum, London). Beyond, the **Sala dello Zodiaco** has vivacious 1580 frescoes by Lorenzo Costa and the **Galleria degli Specchi** has mirrors and mythological frescoes, with a note, by the door, from Monteverdi, on the musical evenings he directed there in the 1600s.

The Gonzaga were mad about horses and dogs and had one room, the **Salone degli Arcieri**, painted with *trompe l'œil* frescoes of their favourite steeds. Sharing the room are works by Tintoretto and an enormous family portrait by Rubens. The duke's apartments hold a fine collection of classical statuary; the Sala di Troia has vivid 1536 frescoes by Giulio

Romano and his pupil, Rinaldo Mantovano; while another ducal chamber has a 17th-century labyrinth painted on the ceiling, each path inscribed in gold with 'Maybe Yes, Maybe No'.

In the 14th-century **Castello San Giorgio**, is the famous **Camera degli Sposi**, wherein lie the remarkable frescoes painted in 1474 by Mantegna, who like a genie captured the essence of the Gonzaga in this small bottle of a room. Restored to their brilliant original colours, the frescoes depict the life of Ludovico Gonzaga, with his wife Barbara of Brandenburg, his children, dwarves, servants, dogs and horses, and important events.

Palazzo d'Arco

Piazza d'Arco, t 0376 32 2242. **Open** *Nov–Feb Sat, Sun 10–12.30 and 2–5; Mar–Oct Tues–Sun 10–12.30 and 2.30–5.30;* **adm.**

The Palazzo d'Arco was rebuilt in 1784 over a 15th-century palace for the arty counts from Garda's north shore and has been left more or less as it was, with furnishings, paintings, instruments, a superb kitchen and, in a room preserved from the original palace, fascinating zodiac frescoes, attributed to Giovanni Maria Falconetto of Verona (*c.* 1515), painted in the period between Mantegna's death and Giulio Romano's arrival.

Palazzo Tè

Viale Te, t 0376 32 3266. **Open** *Tues–Sun 9–6, Mon 1–6; ticket office closes at 5.30;* **adm.**

At the end of Via Acerbi is Giulio Romano's masterpiece, the marvellous Palazzo Tè, its name derived not from tea, but from the rather less savoury *tejeto*, a local word for a drainage canal. On a former swamp, drained for a horsey Gonzaga pleasure ground, work began in 1527 when Federico II had Giulio Romano expand the stables to create a little palace for his mistress, Isabella Boschetti, of whom his mother, Isabella d'Este, disapproved. The project expanded over the decades to become a guest house suitable for the emperor Charles V, who visited twice.

Where to Stay

The Centre 154

Brera and the Northeast 155

University and the Southeast 160

Ticinese and Navigli 160

The West End 160

Youth Hostels 160

Milan has basically two types of accommodation: smart hotels for expense accounts; and seedy dives for new arrivals from the provinces. This bodes ill for the pleasure traveller, who has the choice of paying a lot of money for an up-to-date modern room with little atmosphere, or paying less for an uncomfortable, or worse, an unsafe place. Reserve in advance, because the exceptions to the rule are snapped up fast.

All accommodation in Italy is classified by the Provincial Tourist Boards. Price control, however, has been deregulated since 1992, leaving hotels to set their own rates, which means that in some places prices have rocketed. After a period of rapid and erratic price fluctuation, tariffs are at last settling down again to more predictable levels. In general, the quality of furnishings and facilities has improved in all categories in recent years. But you can still find plenty of older hotels and *pensioni* whose often charming eccentricities of character and architecture may frequently be at odds with modern standards.

Bear in mind also that in August much of Milan closes down, so that at this time it can be surprisingly easy to find a hotel. The following hotel associations provide a free reservation service:

Milan Hoteliers Association, *Corso Buenos Aires 77, t 02 674 8031, w www.traveleurope.it.*

Milano Hotels Central Booking, t *02 805 4242, w www. hotelbooking.com.*

During the trade fairs (especially the fashion shows in March and autumn, and the April Fair) it is busy, so book ahead.

Hotels and Guesthouses

Italian *alberghi* come in all shapes and sizes. They are rated from one to five stars, depending strictly on the facilities they offer. The star ratings are some indication of price levels, but for tax

reasons not all hotels choose to advertise themselves at the rating to which they are entitled, so you may find a two-star hotel just as comfortable as, or more so than, a four-star one. Conversely, you may find that a hotel offers few stars in hopes of attracting budget-conscious travellers, but charges just as much as a higher-rated neighbour. *Pensioni* are generally more modest establishments, though nowadays the distinction between these and hotels is becoming blurred. *Locande* used to be an even more basic form of hostelry, but these days the term may denote somewhere chic.

Price lists, by law, must be posted on the door of every room, along with meal prices and any extra charges (such as air conditioning, or even a shower in cheap places). Many hotels display two or three different rates; low-season rates may be about a third lower than peak-season tariffs. During high season you should always book ahead (a fax or phone reservation is less frustrating to organize than one by post). If you have paid a deposit your booking is valid under Italian law, but don't expect it to be refunded if you have to cancel.

If you arrive without a reservation, begin looking or phoning round for accommodation early in the day. If possible, inspect the room (and bathroom facilities) before you book, and check the tariff. Italian hoteliers may legally alter their rates twice during the year, so printed tariffs or lists (and prices quoted in this book!) may be out of date. Hoteliers who wilfully overcharge should be reported to the local tourist office. You will be asked for your passport for registration purposes.

Price Categories

Prices listed in this guide are for double rooms, with bath; you can expect to pay about two-thirds the rate for single occupancy, though in high season you may be

charged the full double rate. Extra beds are usually charged at about a third more than the room rate. Rooms without private bathrooms generally charge 20–30% less, and most offer discounts for children sharing parents' rooms, or children's meals. If you want a double bed, specify a *camera matrimoniale*. Breakfast is usually optional in hotels but obligatory in *pensioni*. You can usually get better value by eating breakfast in a bar, however.

luxury	over €300
very expensive	€200–300
expensive	€120–200
moderate	€80–120
cheap	up to €80

The Centre

Luxury

Grand Hotel Duomo F5
Via San Raffaele 1, t 02 8646 2027, f 02 864 50454; metro Duomo.
Decorated with the best and latest in Italian furniture design; this is an obvious but still classy address.

Star Hotel Rosa G5
Via Pattari 5, t 02 88 31, f 02 805 7964; metro Duomo.
Luxurious, decadent and sexy rooms to make you think twice about braving the outside world.

Very Expensive

Antica Locanda Dei Mercanti E4
Via San Tomaso 6, t 02 805 4080, f 02 805 4090, w www.locanda.it; metro Cordusio, tram 14, 24 or 27.
This discrete and charming inn has individually furnished rooms in classic style with fine, white fabrics. The top floor rooms have dramatic canopy beds and individual roof terraces.

De La Ville F4
Via Hoepli 6, t 02 867 651, f 02 866 609; metro Duomo, bus 61; wheelchair accessible.
Modern, with antique furnishings, courteous service,

and comfortable lounges, bar and excellent restaurant.

Giulio Cesare E4
Via Rovello 10, t 02 7200 3915, f 02 7200 2179; metro Cairoli.
On a quiet, central street; this hotel has air conditioning.

Grand Hotel Plaza F5
Piazza Diaz, t 02 85550, f 02 867 240; metro Duomo.
Ignore the ugly concrete façade and come inside to a luxury interior of plush red leather.

Hotel Ambasciatori G5
Galleria del Corso 3, off Piazza Beccaria, t 02 7602 0241, f 02 782 700; metro San Babila.
Luxuriate in this hotel's beautiful, refurbished period surroundings.

Hotel Brunelleschi F5
Via Baracchini 12, t 02 88431, f 02 804 924; metro Missori.
A monstrosity which, despite its exterior, is rather colourful and lively inside.

Hotel Galileo G5
Corso Europa 9, t 02 77431, f 02 7602 0584; metro San Babila.
Only stay in this modern, overpriced hotel if you have to.

Hotel Sir Edward F5
Via Mazzini 4, t 02 877 877, f 02 877 844; metro Duomo; wheelchair accessible.
Décor is 1980s-style mirrors and glitter.

Hotel Spadari F5
Via Spadari 11, t 02 7200 2371, f 02 861 184; metro Duomo.
Popular with models and foodies, this is modern Italian swank in one of Milan's true design hotels.

Expensive

Hotel Casa Svizzera F5
Via S. Raffaele 3, t 02 869 2246, f 02 7200 4690; metro Duomo.
A good value and friendly choice in a charming corner of the city.

Hotel Gritti E5
Piazza Santa Maria Beltrade 4, t 02 801 056, f 02 8901 0999; metro Duomo.
A friendly, central hotel on a charming little square, but with disappointing, small rooms.

London E4
Via Rovello 3, t 02 7202 0166, f 02 805 7037, e hotel.london@ traveleurope.it; metro Cairoli. Open Sept–July.
On a quiet street near the castle, with all the amenities. At the top of the expensive range.

Vecchio Milano E5
Via Borromei 4, t 02 875 042, f 02 8645 4292, e hotel -vecchiomilano@tiscadirect.it; metro Cordusio.
Small, elegant and charming hotel, with friendly staff.

Moderate

Hotel Rio F5
Via Mazzini 8, t 02 874 114, f 02 865 689; metro Duomo.
A small and well-priced, if slightly unremarkable, hotel.

Speronari F5
Via Speronari 4, t 02 8646 1125, f 02 7200 3178; metro Duomo.
Adequate and near the Duomo; rooms with bath cost a bit more.

Cheap

Hotel Nuovo G5
Piazza Beccaria 6, t 02 8646 4444, f 02 8646 0542; metro Duomo or San Babila.
A cheap and cheerful central option, with a flash exterior that belies its simple but clean rooms.

Brera and the Northeast

Luxury

Carlton Hotel Baglioni G3
Via Senato 5, t 02 77077, f 02 783 300; metro Montenapoleone.
Luxury for the minted and gilded, with designer doormen and predictably snooty staff.

Excelsior Gallia H1
Piazza Duca d'Aosta 9, t 02 67851, f 02 6671 3239, w www. excelsiorgallia.it; metro Centrale.
This hotel has hosted the likes of music composer Arturo Toscanini and Mikhail Gorbachev since it first opened in 1932. Spruced up

with briarwood furnishings and oriental rugs, it has spacious and elegant rooms and all amenities; the Health Centre offers Turkish baths and beauty treatments, and the Baboon Bar (it got its name during the war; ask how) is a mellow way to spend an evening.

Four Seasons G4
Via Gesù 8, t 02 77088, f 02 7708 5000, w www.fourseasons.com; metro Montenapoleone; wheelchair accessible.
Set in a 15th-century monastery, with enormous bathrooms, and plush sofas around the fire in the winter; with private garage.

Grand Hotel et de Milan F4
Via Manzoni 29, t 02 723 141, f 02 8646 0861, w www. grandhoteletdemilan.it; metro Montenapoleone.
Open since 1863 and once a favourite of Verdi and Hemingway, the Grand is now the fashion headquarters of Naomi Campbell and Kate Moss. Rooms are individ-ually furnished with antiques; the atmosphere is grand and gracious without being stuffy.

Principe di Savoia G2
Piazza della Repubblica 17, t 02 6230 5555, f 02 653 799; metro Repubblica; wheelchair accessible.
Stayed in by the likes of the Duke of Windsor and Maria Callas; the presidential suite is considered to be one of the world's most beautiful retreats. The hotel has its own airport bus, a divine restaurant (La Galleria, see 'Eating Out', p.164) and a private garage.

Very Expensive

Cavour G3
Via Fatebenefratelli 21, t 02 657 2051, f 02 659 2263, e hotel.cavour@ traveleurope.it, w www.hotelcavour.it; metro Montenapoleone or Turati.
An elegant hotel; note the public halls, the design of the spiral steps and the collection of drawings of La Scala costumes by Gio Ponti.

Map Key

24 Alba d'Oro
10 Albergo Nettuno
2   Antica Locanda Solferino
20 Carlton Hotel Baglioni
12 Casa Mia
19 Cavour
7   Excelsior Gallia
23 Four Seasons
22 Grand Hotel et de Milan
27 Hotel Ambasciatori
11 Hotel Brianza
1   Hotel Carlyle Brera
15 Hotel Cristoforo Colombo
14 Hotel Fenice
26 Hotel Galileo
9   Hotel Galles
5   Hotel Kennedy
28 Hotel Nuovo
17 Hotel Porta Venezia
13 Hotel Promessi Sposi
4   Hotel San Tomaso
8   Hotel del Sole
6   Hotel Verona
25 Hotel Vittoria
29 Jolly Hotel President
18 Manin
21 Manzoni
3   Principe di Savoia
16 Sheraton Diana Majestic

Gala Off maps
Viale Zara 89, **t** *02 6680 0891,*
f *02 6680 0463;* **metro** *Zara,*
tram *4 or 11.* **Open** *Sept–July.*
Set in a quiet garden, this is
a fine, moderate-sized hotel;
the rooms have beautiful
wrought-iron beds.

Manin G3
Via Manin 7, **t** *02 659 6511,*
f *02 655 2160,* **w** *www.*
hotel-manin.it; **metro** *Turati.*
This friendly hotel, with modern,
comfortable rooms, is one of the
city's quieter corners, facing the
Giardini Pubblici. It also has a nice
private garden.

Manzoni G4
Via Santo Spirito 20, **t** *02 7600*
5700, **f** *02 784 212,* **w** *www.hotel.*
manzoni@tin.it; **metro** *Monte-*
napoleone, **tram** *1 or 2.* **Open**
Sept–July. Book ahead.
A pleasant hotel on a quiet,
though central street, with private
garage and bright baths.

Sheraton Diana Majestic H3
Viale Piave 42, **t** *02 20581,*
f *02 2058 2058;* **metro** *Porta*
Venezia, **tram** *9 or 30.*
A fashionable, stylish, Liberty-style
hotel built at the turn of the
century, with garden views,
charming rooms, and a lovely
breakfast buffet.

Soperga Off maps
Via Soperga 24, **t** *02 669*
0541, **f** *02 6698 0352;*
metro *Centrale.*
Just east of the Stazione
Centrale, this hotel has
comfortable, soundproof
rooms, and serves big
breakfasts.

East Milan Hotels

Expensive

Antica Locanda Solferino F2
*Via Castelfidardo 2, t 02 657
0129, f 02 657 1361; metro
Moscova. Open Sept–July.
Book ahead.*
An atmospheric 19th-century
inn at the top of the expensive

range. All rooms are different,
and breakfast is brought to
your room.

Hotel Carlyle Brera E2
*Corso Garibaldi 84, t 02 2900
3888, f 02 2900 3993,
e citylights@brerahotel.com;
metro Moscova.*

This posh address has suitably
arty décor to match.

Valley Off maps
*Via Soperga 19, t 02 669 2777,
f 02 6698 7252; metro Centrale.*
Good budget hotel near
Stazione Centrale, with
comfortable rooms.

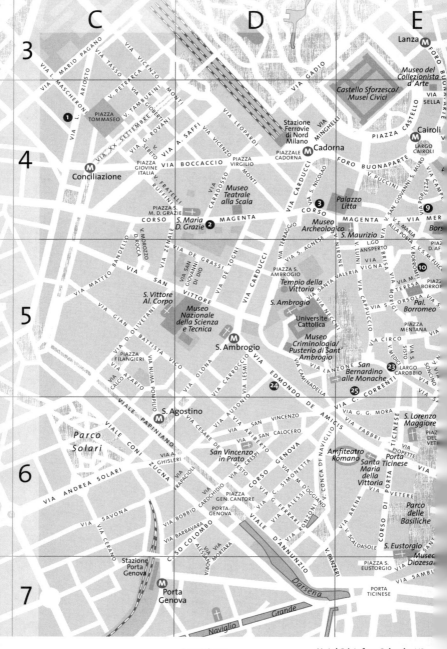

Moderate

Alba d'Oro H4
Viale Piave 5, **t** *02 7602 3880,*
f *02 7631 0371;* **metro** *Porta*
Venezia, **tram** *9 or 30.*
The 'Golden Dawn' is small and
safe, with baths down the hall.

Casa Mia G2
Viale Vittorio Veneto 30,
t *02 657 5249,* **f** *02 655 2228,*
e *hotelcasamia@libero.it;* **metro**
Repubblica or Porta Venezia.
A good-value hotel with all the
amenities and air conditioning in
some rooms.

Hotel Cristoforo Colombo H3
Corso Buenos Aires 3,
t *02 2940 6214,* **f** *02 2951 6096,*
e *info@hotelcristoforocolombo.*
com; **metro** *Porta Venezia.*
A three-star, central hotel giving
onto Milan's would-be Champs-
Elysées, with business facilities.

West Milan Hotels

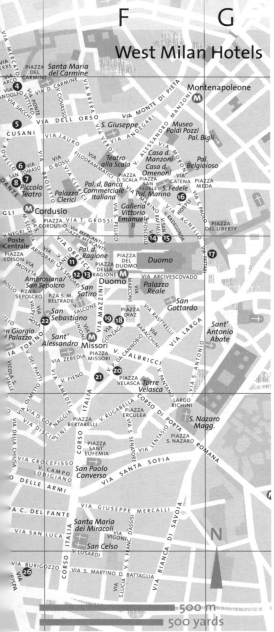

Map Key

4 Albergo Commercio
6 Antica Locanda dei Mercanti
1 Ariosto
23 Ariston
5 Bonaparte Hotel
16 De La Ville
14 Grand Hotel Duomo
18 Grand Hotel Plaza
8 Giulio Cesare
7 London
20 Hotel Brunelleschi
9 Hotel Cairoli
15 Hotel Casa Svizzera
22 Hotel Gritti
3 Hotel King
25 Hotel Regina
19 Hotel Rio
13 Hotel Sir Edward
11 Hotel Spadari
21 Hotel Ullrich
26 La Cordata
2 Palazzo delle Stelline
24 Pierre Milano
12 Speronari
17 Star Hotel Rosa
10 Vecchio Milano

Hotel Promessi Sposi H3
Bastioni di Porta Venezia,
t 02 2951 3661, f 02 2940 4182;
metro *Porta Venezia.*
A romantic hotel with all the
amenities.

San Francisco Off maps
Viale Lombardia 55, t 02 236 1009,
*f 02 2668 0377; **metro** Piola.*
A safe and acceptable choice.

Cheap

Albergo Nettuno H2
Via Alessandro Tadino 27,
t 02 2940 4481, f 02 2952 3819;
metro *Porta Venezia.*
An economical, though
slightly seedy, option near
Centrale Stazione.

Hotel Brasil Off maps
Via Modena 20, t/f 02 749 2482,
*e hotelbrasil@libeno.it; **tram** 5,*
bus *92.*
Clean and functional rooms.

Hotel Brianza H2
Via Panfilo Castaldi 16,
t 02 2940 4819, f 02 2953 1145;
metro *Repubblica.*
Uninspiring, but clean rooms.

Hotel Fenice H3
Corso Buenos Aires 2,
02 2952 5541, f 02 2952 3942;
metro *Porta Venezia.*
warm welcome awaits you in
this small, modern and functional
hotel, which is also very close to
the station and shops.

Hotel Galles I2
Via Ozanam 1, t 02 204 841,
f 02 204 8462, w www.galles.it;
metro *Lima.*
A refurbished hotel off lively Corso
Buenos Aires, with soundproofed
rooms and a terrace with massage
facilities.

Hotel Kennedy G2
Viale Tunisia 6, *t 02 2940 0934,*
f 02 2940 1253; *metro Repubblica.*
No-frills rooms on the sixth floor
of a modern building.

Hotel Porta Venezia H3
Piazza di Porta Venezia,
t 02 2941 4227, *f 02 2024 9397;*
metro Porta Venezia.
Another cheap option, but with a
more lively atmosphere.

Hotel San Tomaso G2
Viale Tunisia 6, *t/f 02 2951 4747;*
metro Repubblica.
On the third floor of the same
building as the Kennedy, above,
with similarly dour rooms but
friendly multi-lingual staff.

Hotel del Sole I1
Via Gaspare Spontini 6, *t 02 2951*
2971, *f 02 2951 3689;* *metro Lima.*
Comfortable but unspectacular,
with ensuite rooms.

Hotel Verona H2
Via Carlo Tenca 12, *t 02 6698 3091,*
f 02 6698 7236; *metro Repubblica.*
A sparse, bargain option – some
rooms have Italian television.

University and the Southeast

Very Expensive

Jolly Hotel President G5
Largo Augusto 10, *t 02 77461,*
f 02 783 449; *metro Duomo.*
A pricey chain hotel, very
convenient for shopping.

Moderate

Hotel Vittoria I5
Via Pietro Calvi 32, *t 02 545 6520,*
f 02 5519 0246, *e hotelvittoria@*
interfree.it; *tram 27,* *bus 60.*
A small, friendly and romantic
hotel with comfortable rooms.

Cheap

Hotel Ullrich F5
Corso Italia 6, *t 02 8645 9156,*
f 02 804 535; *metro Missori.*
More of a *pensione* with the
family touch; a pleasant place on
the 6th floor of an old *palazzo*.

Ticinese and Navigli

Expensive

Pierre Milano D5
Via de Amicis 32, *t 02 7200 0581,*
f 02 805 2157, *e info@hotelpierre*
milano.it; *tram 2 or 14,* *bus 94;*
wheelchair accessible.
Friendly hotel with well-designed
rooms, with all the amenities.

The West End

Very Expensive

Ariosto C4
Via Ariosto 22, *t 02 481 7844,*
f 02 498 0516, *w www.brerahotel.*
com; *metro Conciliazione.*
This early 20th-century
characterful mansion has nice
rooms overlooking a lovely little
courtyard. Special weekend and
children's rates; Internet access.

Ariston E5
Largo Carrobbio 2, *t 02 7200 0556,*
f 02 7200 0914, *w www.brerahotel.*
com; *metro Sant'Ambrogio.* **Open**
Sept–July.
An environmentalist's dream,
with 100% cotton futons,
hydro-massage showers, recycled
everything and ion-emitting
machines. There's a no-smoking
floor and bicycles to borrow; with
Internet access, and special
weekend and children's rates.

Bonaparte Hotel E4
Via Cusani 13, *t 02 85601,*
f 02 869 3601; *metro Cairoli.*
A Radisson SAS hotel, but highly
recommended for its character.

Expensive

Hotel Cairoli E4
Via Porlezza 4, *t 02 801371,*
f 02 7200 2243; *metro Cairoli.*
A quiet, comfortable hotel,
popular with business travellers.

Hotel King D4
Corso Magenta 19, *t 02 874 432;*
metro Cadorna.
Comfortable though bland hotel,
but with all the amenities.

Hotel Regency Off maps
Via Giovanni Arimondi 12, *t 02 3921*
6021, *f 02 3921 7734;* *tram 12.*
A must for Italian Art Nouveau
fans, with rhapsodic floral
wallpaper and vases; convenient
for Fiera trade fairs.

Moderate

Hotel Regina E5
Via Cesare Correnti 13, *t 02 5810*
6913, *f 02 5810 7033,* *e info@*
hotelregina.it; *metro Sant'*
Ambrogio; wheelchair accessible.
Stylish, yet well-priced hotel.

Cheap

Albergo Commercio E4
Via Mercato 1, entrance on Via
Erbe, *t/f 02 8646 3880;* *metro*
Lanza. Book ahead.
A clean but busy, good-value hotel.

Hotel Montebianco Off maps
Viale Montebianco 90,
t 02 4801 2130, *f 02 4800 0658,*
w www.hotelmontebianco.com;
metro Lotto.
Outside the city centre, this hotel
has well-thought-out design and
well-appointed rooms.

Palazzo delle Stelline D4
Corso Magenta 61, *t 02 481 8431,*
f 02 4851 9097, *w www.hotel*
palazzodellestelline.it; *metro*
Cadorna; wheelchair accessible.
A *palazzo*, now a hotel and
conference centre, where Da Vinci
is said to have grown vines while
painting the *Last Supper*.

Youth Hostels

La Cordata (Casa Scout) E7
Via Burigozzo 11, *t 02 5831 4675;*
metro Missori.
Private hostel where you can also
use the kitchen facilities.

Ostello Piero Rotta Off maps
Via Salmoiraghi 2, *t 02 3926 7095,*
f 02 3300 0191; *metro Lotto.* **Open**
7–9.30am and 3.30pm–12am;
max stay is 3 days.
Milan's modern youth hostel, near
San Siro stadium. An IYHF card is
required (can be bought there).

Eating Out

The Centre 164

Brera and the Northeast 164

University and the Southeast 168

Ticinese and Navigli 169

The West End 172

In moneyed Milan you'll find some of Italy's finest restaurants and the widest range of international cuisine; on the down side, an average meal will cost you considerably more than it would almost anywhere else in Italy. That said, you will still pay less than you would in comparable London restaurants. Presume unless otherwise stated that all are closed in August; so few restaurants remain open that their names are printed in the paper. At other times, the best places to find a selection of cheaper restaurants are in the Brera, Ticinese and Navigli districts.

Eating Habits

There are those who eat to live and those who live to eat, and then there are the Italians, for whom food has an almost religious significance, unfathomably linked with love, *La Mamma* and tradition. In this singular country, where millions of otherwise sane people spend many of their waking hours worrying about their digestion, standards both at home and in the restaurants are understandably high. Few Italians are gluttons, but all are experts in the kitchen; to serve a meal that is not properly prepared is tantamount to an insult.

Breakfast (*colazione*) in Italy is no lingering affair, but an early-morning wake-up shot to the brain: a cappuccino (first thing in the morning is the only time of day at which any self-respecting Italian will touch the stuff), a *caffè latte* or a *caffè lungo* (espresso with hot water), accompanied by a croissant-type roll, called a *cornetto* or *briosce*, or a fancy pastry. This repast can be consumed in any bar and repeated throughout the morning. Breakfast in Italian hotels seldom represents very good value, although larger buffets are becoming popular.

Lunch (*pranzo*), generally served around 1pm, is the most important meal of the day for the Italians (except for many office workers in Milan who get by on a rapid snack). This consists of, at the bare minimum, a first course (*primo piatto* – any kind of pasta dish, broth or soup, rice dish or pizza), a second course (*secondo piatto* – a meat dish, accompanied by a *contorno* or side dish, usually a vegetable, salad, or potatoes), followed by fruit or dessert and coffee. You can, however, begin with the *antipasti* – the appetizers Italians do so brilliantly, ranging from warm seafood delicacies to raw ham (*prosciutto crudo*), salami in a hundred varieties, lovely vegetables, savoury toasts, olives, pâté and many, many more. There are restaurants that specialize in *antipasti*, and they usually don't take it amiss if you decide to forget the pasta and meat and just nibble on these scrumptious *hors-d'œuvres* (though in the end it will probably cost more than a full meal). Most Italians accompany their meal with wine and mineral water – *acqua minerale*, with or without bubbles (*con* or *senza gas*), which supposedly aids digestion – concluding their meals with a *digestivo* liqueur.

Cena, or supper, is usually eaten around 8pm. This is much the same as *pranzo* although lighter, without the pasta (the Italians believe it lies too heavily on the stomach at night): a pizza, eggs or a fish dish and salad are common. In restaurants, however, they offer all the courses, so if you eat a light lunch you can still go for the works in the evening. For a list of Italian specialities, *see* 'Language', p.199 and box, opposite.

Eating Out

In Italy the various terms for types of restaurants – *ristorante*, *trattoria* or *osteria* – have been confused. A *trattoria* or *osteria* can be just as elaborate as a restaurant, though rarely is a *ristorante* as informal as a traditional *trattoria*. Unfortunately, the old habit of posting menus and

Saffron

Saffron is Milan's fetish spice, and appears in most dishes *alla milanese*. The origins of its use go back to a Belgian stained-glass maker, working on the Duomo in 1574, who was called 'Saffron' by his fellows because he always sprinkled a bit of the stuff in his mixes to make the glass colours deeper and richer. The other glass-workers laughed and joked that he loved saffron so much that he would soon be adding it to his food. During the wedding of Saffron's daughter, his apprentice, meaning to play a prank, actually had the chef put saffron in the rice; everyone was astonished at the yellow concoction, but it was delicious, and the Milanese have been making their saffron *risotto alla milanese* ever since.

prices in the windows has fallen from fashion, so it's often difficult to judge variety or cost. Invariably the least expensive type of restaurant is the *vino e cucina*, simple places serving simple cuisine for simple everyday prices. If you're uncertain, do as you would at home – look for lots of locals. When you eat out, mentally add to the bill (*conto*) the bread and cover charge (*pane e coperto*) and a 15% service charge. This is often included in the bill (*servizio compreso*); if not, it will say *servizio non compreso* and you'll have to do your own arithmetic. Additional tipping is at your own discretion.

People who haven't visited Italy for years and have fond memories of eating full meals for under a pound will be amazed at how much prices have risen; though in some respects eating out in Italy is still a bargain, especially when you figure out how much all that wine would have cost you at home. In many places you'll often find restaurants offering a menu *turistico* – full, set meals of usually meagre inspiration. More imaginative chefs often offer a menu *degustazione* – a set-price

Milanese Specialities

The Milanese like their food and they like it to be fairly substantial; they tend to use butter instead of olive oil, and there's a great fondness for cheese and frying in breadcrumbs. Some Milanese dishes, like the *cotoletta alla milanese*, are devoured with relish across Italy, while others are so quirky (the sweet tortellini of Crema, for instance) that you can only find them in one place. Favourite *antipasti* include meats (*salame di Milano, carpaccio, prosciutto* and *bresaola* – dried salt beef served with lemon, oil and *rucola*), *carciofi alla milanese* (artichokes with butter and cheese), mozzarella fried in breadcrumbs, *peperonata* (red pimentos, onions and tomatoes cooked in butter and olive oil).

First and often second courses are often based on *polenta* (yellow cornmeal, a bit like American cornmush), boiled until thick and served with butter and cheese, or cut in slices, or shaped and fried, baked or grilled. Lombard classics are *polenta e osei* (polenta slices topped with roast birds), *polenta alla Lodigiana* (round slices of polenta fried in breadcrumbs), *polenta pasticciata* (baked with cheese, meat and mushroom sauces) and Lake Iseo's baked *polenta* with tench.

As Europe's major producer of rice, Lombardy is also famous for its *risotti*, which are typically served as a first course. Look for traditional saffron-tinted *risotto alla milanese, risotto alla Monzese* (with sausage meat, tomato and Marsala) and Mantuan *risotto alla pilota*, with butter and onions, or more seasonal concoctions with porcini mushrooms or asparagus, or even fruit and raisins in some *cucina nuova* restaurants. Lombardy's pasta specialities may be served with gorgonzola, or stuffed with pumpkin and cheese, meat, fish, or spinach in melted butter and sage. If served *alla mantovana* the sauce includes meat, walnuts, white wine and cream. Another dish is *Pizzoccheri*, buckwheat noodles from the Valtellina, served with butter and cheese. Donkey meat appears with alarming frequency on menus from Lake Orta to Mantua; even King Kong would balk before *stu'a'd'asnin cünt la pulenta* (stewed donkey with polenta).

But don't despair – other meat courses include classics such as *ossobuco alla milanese* (veal knuckle braised with white wine and tomatoes, properly served with risotto), *cotoletta alla milanese* (breaded cutlet), duckling (excellent in Nedar, with macaroni), *fritto misto* (veal slices, calves' liver, artichokes and zucchini, fried in breadcrumbs), *busseca* (tripe stew, with eggs, cheese and cream), *fritto alla lombardo* (rabbit pieces fried in breadcrumbs) and the hearty regional pork and cabbage stew, *cazzoela* or *cassuoela* (two of 25 different spellings).

Gorgonzola, Bel Paese and *grana padana* (like parmesan) are the region's most famous cheeses, and soft, creamy mascarpone is also a Lombard product. *Bitto*, made of goat's and sheep's milk in the Valtellina, is well worth a try. *Polenta* is also in desserts, but *torta di tagliatelle* (a cake with egg pasta and almonds) is perhaps more appealing. Each province has its own highly individual sweets, although the Milanese cake *panettone*, a light fruit cake, has become an Italian Christmas tradition.

gourmet meal that allows you to taste their daily specialities and seasonal dishes. Both of these are cheaper than if you had ordered the same food à la carte. When you leave a restaurant you will be given a receipt (*scontrino* or *ricevuta fiscale*) which according to Italian law you must take with you out of the door and carry for at least 60 metres. If you aren't given one, it means the restaurant is probably fudging on its taxes and thus offering you lower prices. There is a slim chance that the tax police may have their eye on you and the restaurant, and if you don't have a receipt they could slap you with a heavy fine.

There are several alternatives to sit-down meals. The 'hot table' (*tavola calda*) is a stand-up buffet where you can choose a simple prepared dish or a whole meal, depending on your appetite. The food in these can be impressive; many offer only a few hot dishes, pizza and sandwiches, though in every fair-sized town there will be at least one *tavola calda* with seats where you can contrive a complete dinner outside the usual hours. Little shops that sell pizza by the slice or weight are common in resorts and city centres. At any grocer's (*alimentari*) or market (*mercato*) you can buy the materials for countryside or hotel-room picnics. For really elegant picnics, have a *tavola calda* pack up something nice. And if everywhere else is closed, there's always the railway station – bars will at least have sandwiches and drinks, and perhaps some surprisingly good snacks you've never heard of before. Some of the station bars also prepare *cestini da viaggio*, full-course meals in a basket to help you through long train trips. Common snacks you'll encounter include *panini* of *prosciutto*, cheese and tomatoes, or other meats; *tramezzini*, little sandwiches of plain, square white bread that are much better than they look; and pizza, of course.

Hard-working Milan has been slower than Italy's more southern cities such as Bologna, Florence and Rome in adopting the habit of brunch, and happy hour, known as *aperitivo*, is also only just coming into vogue. With this less stringent attitude to eating times, many *caffès* in Milan now stay open from the early hours of the morning for cappuccinos and brunch, through to the night, when they double as jazz and live music lounges (*see* 'Nightlife and Entertainment', p.173).

Most restaurants will be open 12–3 and 8–11.30, unless otherwise stated. Milan is also well endowed with American and Italian fast-food places, the best being self-service chain **Brek**, and **Pastarito**.

Price Categories

The categories are for a three-course meal without wine.

very expensive	over €50
expensive	€30–50
moderate	€20–30
cheap	below €20

The Centre

Restaurants

Very Expensive

Peck F5
Via Victor Hugo 4/Via Cantu,
t *02 876 774;* **metro** *Duomo.* **Open** *Aug–June Mon 3–7.30, Tues–Sat 8.45am–7.30pm.*
A name that has meant the best in Milan for over a hundred years, with its epicurean delicatessen and shop (*see* 'Shopping', p.183), or in its tantalizing modern cellar restaurant; their unctuous *risotto alla milanese* is hard to beat.

Savini F4
Galleria Vittorio Emanuele II,
t *02 7200 3433;* **metro** *Duomo.* **Open** *Mon–Fri, and Sat eve.*
A bastion of Milanese tradition (since 1867), where you can try Lombard classics at the pinnacle of perfection – especially the *secondi*. The often-abused *cotoletta* and *risotto* retain their primordial freshness, as do the earthy *cassoeula* and *osso buco.*

Moderate

Coco's E4
Via San Prospero 4, **t** *02 4548 3253;* **metro** *Cordusio.* **Open** *daily 11am–11pm.*
Self-service counter with great veggie-burgers and inexpensive eco-'soul food'.

Trattoria Milanese E5
Via Santa Marta 11, **t** *02 8645 1991;*
metro *Duomo or Cordusio.*
Open *Wed–Mon.*
A family-run *trattoria* which offers true Milanese dishes in a sober, yet charming ambience.

Cheap

Govinda E5
Via Valpetrosa, 3/5, **t** *02 862 417;*
metro *Duomo.* **Open** *Tues–Sat, and Mon eves.*
Good, well-priced vegetarian food.

Ristorante San Tomaso E4
Via San Tomaso 5, **t** *02 874 510;*
metro *Cairoli.* **Open** *Mon–Fri, and Sat eves.*
This place is popular with the working Milanese for its lunchtime self-service buffet; moderately priced in the evening.

Trattoria da Pino G5
Via Cerva 14, **t** *02 7602 1911;*
metro *Duomo or Cordusio.*
Open *Mon–Sat.*
Central, with a fixed €9 menu.

Caffès

Antica Gelateria del Corso G5
Galleria del Corso 4, **metro** *Duomo.*
Open *Mon–Fri 9am–1pm, Sat and Sun brunch 12–4pm.*
Three floors of saccharine paradise, including delicious ice creams, sandwiches, pastries and salads, as well as cocktails.

Caffè Sant'Ambroeus G4
Corso Matteotti 7, **metro**
Montenapoleone or San Babila.
Open *Tues–Sun 7.45am–8.15pm.*
Founded in 1936, this bar, with its wonderful period décor, is a favourite with Milanese.

Panino del Conte F4
Via dei Bossi 7; **metro** *Duomo.*
Open *Mon–Sat 7am–2am.*
Try the famous *Piadina del Conte* in this noble sandwich shop.

Panino Giusto G5
Piazza Beccaria 4; **metro** *Duomo.*
Open *daily 8am–6pm.*
One of the nicest and oldest *caffès* with branches in the Navigli, Garibaldi and city centre areas.

Brera and the Northeast

Restaurants

Very Expensive

Don Lisander F4
Via Manzoni 12, **t** *02 7602 0130;*
metro *Duomo or Montenapoleone.*
Open *Sept–June Mon–Sat.*
This restaurant has a creative menu serving international dishes; with a summer garden.

La Galleria G2
Piazza della Repubblica 17,
t *02 6230 2026;* **metro** *Repubblica.*
Open *daily 12–3 and 8–11.30.*
The restaurant of the Hotel Principe di Savoia serves excellent gourmet Paduan food in luxury surroundings of polychrome marble, crystal and *trompe l'œil.*

Nino Arnaldo I4
Via Carlo Poerio 3, **t** *02 7600 5981;*
metro *Porta Venezia.* **Open** *Mon–Fri, and Sat eves.*
One of Milan's most elegant restaurants and most creative chefs; he offers original pasta dishes, with choice desserts such as exquisite cinnamon ice cream, and *zabaione.*

Nobu F4
Via Manzoni 31, **t** *02 7231 8645;*
metro *Montenapoleone.* **Open** *daily for lunch, and Mon eves.*
Part of the Armani flagship store and sister to the London Nobu, this is a super-stylish and accordingly expensive place to be seen. Sushi downstairs, with an ultra-chic New York-style restaurant upstairs; with great wines.

Ran G1
Via Bordoni 8, **t** *02 669 6997;*
metro *Gioia.* **Open** *Mon–Sat.*
If you need a break from Italian cuisine, try this elegant sushi bar.

Sogo F5
Via Fiori Oscuri, **t** *02 8646 5367;*
metro *Montenapoleone.* **Open** *Tues–Sat.*
An equally stylish sushi bar, but with a more creative touch.

Expensive

13 Giugno I4
Via Carlo Goldoni 44, t 02 719 654;
metro *Porta Venezia.* **Open**
Mon–Sat.
Sicilian seafood recipes in 1930s
ambience, with a piano bar every
evening and a pleasant garden to
dine out in the summer.

Bice G4
*Via Borgospesso 12, t 02 7600
2572; metro Montenapoleone.*
Open *Tues–Sun.*
Sophisticated, traditional cuisine
and impeccable service; a
favourite of local VIPs.

Centro Ittico Off maps
*Via Aporti 35, t 02 614 3774; metro
Loreto.* **Open** *Tues–Sat, Mon eves.*
Fish comes directly from the
market counter to your plate here.
Expect lemon sorbet for dessert.

Chandelier I2
*Via Broggi 17, t 02 2024 0458;
metro Lima.* **Open** *Tues–Sat, and
brunch on Sun.*
Mediterranean fusion cuisine
with eclectic ethnic décor.

Hong Kong Off maps
*Via Schiaparelli 5, t 02 670 1992;
metro Centrale.* **Open** *Tues–Sun.*
This secluded place combines
Chinese *haute cuisine* with
elegant and refined décor.

La Terrazza I2
*Via Ozanam 1, t 02 204 8433; metro
Lima.* **Open** *daily exc Mon eves.*
On the top floor of the
Hotel Galles (*see* p.159). Offers
al fresco traditional dining, with a
view over the Duomo's spires.

La Terrazza di Via Palestro G3
*Via Palestro 4, 4th floor, t 02 7600
2186; metro Palestro.* **Open** *Mon–
Fri, and Sat eves.*
Innovative seafood dishes, with a
view onto the gardens around
Porta Venezia.

La Volpe e l'Uva G4
*Via Senato 45, t 02 7602 2167;
metro Montenapoleone.* **Open**
*Tues, Thurs and Fri, for lunch and
eves, Wed and Sat, for lunch only.*
Owned by two imaginative
sisters – great cooking in
intimate surroundings.

Piccolo Sogno I3
Via Stoppani 5, t 02 2024 1210;
metro *Porta Venezia.* **Open**
Mon–Fri, and Sat eve.
From the proprietor of the
famous former 'Ami Berton' –
traditional and regional cuisine
prepared to perfection.

Vini e Cucina G2
*Via P. Castaldi 38, t 02 2951
9840; metro Repubblica.* **Open**
daily exc Mon eve.
An internationally acclaimed
New York-style restaurant
specializing in fish and
seafood dishes.

Moderate

Al Sodo Off maps
*Via Paisiello 22, t 02 7063 0400;
metro Loreto or Lima.* **Open** *daily
exc Mon eve.*
Classical Italian hospitality with a
wide range of traditional and
regional dishes.

Armani Caffè F4
*Via Croce Rossa 2, t 02 7231 8680;
metro Montenapoleone.* **Open**
*daily, lunch only. In summer,
an outside bar opens in the
evenings. Non-smoking.*
Expensive, Mediterranean
dishes – but it's more about
style than economy here – right
down to the designer saltcellars
and chairs.

Endo G1
*Via Fabio Filzi 8, t 02 6698
6688, metro Loreto.* **Open**
Tues–Sun.
Opened in 1970, this is Milan's
oldest Japanese restaurant.
Cheap lunch menu, with
takeaway.

Geppo I2
*Via G. Morgagni 37, t 02 2951
4862; metro Loreto.* **Open**
Mon–Sat. Cash only.
Another name in Milanese
pizza lore, with 50 kinds to
choose from.

I Malavoglia H3
*Via Lecco 4, t 02 2953 1387;
metro Porta Venezia.* **Open**
Tues–Sun.
Superlative Sicilian cuisine. The
speciality here is raw tuna.

Il Patio I3
*Via Rosolino Pilo 14, t 02 2940
0327; metro Porta Venezia.*
Open *Mon–Sat.*
With an attractive garden
setting, this place specializes in
oysters, fish and delicious
meat dishes.

Latteria San Marco F3
*Via San Marco 24, t 02 659 7653;
metro Moscova.* **Open** *Mon–Fri.
Cash only. No booking possible,
arrive early.*
Favoured by media types,
this busy inn still retains its
family-run status, with the
father in the kitchen, mother
and two daughters serving.
Excellent puddings.

San Fermo F3
*Via San Fermo della Battaglia 1,
t 02 2900 0901; metro Moscova or
Turati.* **Open** *Mon–Sat.*
One of business Milan's secrets –
serves light, tasty economic
lunches and affordable, full
dinners. Often busy, but service is
fast and efficient.

Tipica Osteria Pugliese H2
*Via Tadino 5, t 02 2952 2574;
metro Lima or Porta Venezia.*
Open *Mon–Sat.*
You can fill your dish with
antipasti cheaply here, from a
selection of 40 specialities,
including special *burrata*
(mozzarella with creamy core) and
nodini (hard knots of mozzarella)
from Apulia (the heel of Italy). Also
worth trying is pasta, meat and
fish cooked in a wood oven.
Friendly atmosphere and service,
appreciated by a host of actors,
singers and football players, grin-
ning from pictures on the walls.

Tre Pini Off maps
*Via Tullio Morgagni 19,
t 02 6680 5413; bus 42 or 43.* **Open**
Sun–Mon.
Near Central Stazione, this is
the place to go for roasted
meat and fish. Cooking takes
place in a chimney which
burns olive wood in the
middle of the conservatory in
winter, and in the garden pergola
in summer.

Cheap

Da Rino Vecchia Napoli
Off maps
*Via Chavez 4 (between Stazione
Centrale and Parco Lambro)*, *t 02
261 9056*; *metro Pasteur*, *tram 33*,
bus 55 or 62. *Open Tues–Sat, and
Sun eves. Booking advisable.*
This pizzeria offers a vast selection
of prize-winning, championship
pizzas; they also do good *antipasti*,
gnocchi, and fish dishes.

Joya G2
Via P. Castaldi 18, *t 02 2952 2124*;
metro Porta Venezia. *Open
Mon–Fri, and Sat eves.*
Considered one of Italy's best
vegetarian restaurants, with
cheap lunch menus and
moderately-priced evening meals.

Osteria del Treno H2
Via S. Gregorio 46, *t 02 669 1706*;
metro Porta Venezia. *Open Sun–Fr*
This atmospheric former railway
workers' club has a well-priced
self-service counter at lunch, and
excellent sit-down dinners.

Trattoria Brianza Off maps
Via Aporti 22, *t 02 613 663*; *metro
Centrale*. *Open Tues–Sun. Cash onl*

Map labels (North Milan):

G | H | I

Stazione Centrale
Pirellone
PIAZZA DUCA D'AOSTA
Alba di Milano
Caiazzo Ⓜ

V. DEL GRILLO
BORROMEO
VIA
VIA G. GENERALE FARA
VIA EMILIO CORNALIA
VIA G. B. PIRELLI
Centrale Ⓜ
VIA F. FILZI
VIA VITTOR PISANI
VIA FABIO
VIA NAPO
VIA VITRUVIO
VIA LEPETIT
VIA MAURO MACCHI
VIA SETTEMBRINI
VIA SETTALA
VIA DOMENICO SCARLATTI
VIA PETRELLA
VIA GOMES
VIA MERCADANTE
VIA BUENOS AIRES
VIA MONTEVERDI

12
13
VIA EMILIO ADDA
VIVIANI
IBERAZIONE
PIAZZA SAN GIOACHINO
VIA CAPPELLINI
VIA CARLO
VIA CARLO TENCA
VIA BOSCOVICH
VIA TORRIANI
LUIGI SETTEMBRINI
VIAL. SETTALA
VIA BENEDETTO MARCELLO
VIA TADINO
CORSO BUENOS AIRES
VIA SPONTINI
VIA PONCHIELLI

VIA F. FINOCCHIARO
VIA F. CASATI
PIAZZA CINCINNATO
14
15
GREGORIO
VIA TADINO
VIA F. CASATI
BOSCOVICH
Lima Ⓜ
VIA OZANAM
23
PIAZZALE BACONE
VIA PLINIO
EUSTACHI

PIAZZA DELLA REPUBBLICA
Repubblica Ⓜ
17 16
VIALE TUNISIA
VIA D'ANNUNZIO
VIALE LAZZARETTO
VIA LECCO
VIA L. PALAZZI
VIA MASERA ALDROVANDI
VIA GIORGIO JAN
22
VIA MOSCAGNI
24

18
VIA TAICHETTI
VIALE VITTORIO VENETO
VIALE PANFILO CASTALDI
VIA SETTALA
CORSO BUENOS AIRES
VIA OMBONI
VIA JAN BROGGI
PIAZZALE LAVATER
VIA DE FILIPPI
VIA F. REDI
VIA BARTOLOMEO

sposizione manente Belle Arti
BASTIONI DI PORTA VENEZIA
20
PIAZZA CADAMOSTO
PIAZZA ROMANA
VIA PANCALDO
VIA RAMAZZINI
VIA V. ZAMBELETTI
VIA ANTONIO STOPPANI
25

VIA MANIN
Giardini
19
Porta Venezia
21
V. SPALLANZANI
VIALE REGINA GIOVANNA
VIA FRISI
PIAZZA VII NOV 1917
VIA ROSARNO PILO
26

Pubblici
Palazzo Dugnani
useo del Cinema
Planetarium
PIAZZA OBERDAN
PORTA VENEZIA
VIA MALPIGHI
VIA MASCAGNI
VIA G. SIRTORI
VIA LAMBRO
VIA MEZZO
PIAZZA MARIA ADELAIDE DI SAVOIA

VIA PALESTRO
29
Villa Reale / Galleria d'Arte Moderna
Museo di Storia Naturale
VIA BORGHETTO
VIA NINO BIXIO
VIA POERIO
VIA PISACANE
VIA ABAMONTI
VIA RISTORI

VIA D. VECCHIO
OLITECNICO
AZZA
OUR
P.LE MORANDI
Palazzo Castiglioni
VIA SALVINI
VENEZIA
Palazzo Rocca-Saporiti
PIAZZE DUSE
VIALE
VIALE
VIA F. BELLOTTI
PZA F.LLI BANDIERA
VIA CIRO MENOTTI
VIA G. MODENA
CASTEL MORRONE
VIA G. UBERTI

30
Palazzo Senato
CORSO VENEZIA
Palestro Ⓜ
VIA CAPPUCCINI
VIA SERBELLONI
VIA BAROZZI
VIA MOZART
VIA ROSSINI
LUIGI MAINO
PIAVE
KRAMER
27

ELLA SPIGA
ANDREA
Palazzo Serbelloni
VIA S. DAMIANO
VIA RIVAIO
VIA MAGGIOLINI
Palazzo Isimbardi
PORTA MONFORTE
28
VIA CARLO GOLDONI

Museo di Milano
Seminario Arcivescovile
Casa Fontana-Silvestri
CORSO MONFORTE
PIAZZA D. TRICOLORE
CORSO CONCORDIA
PIAZZA RISORGIMENTO
CORSO INDIPENDENZA
N

BAGUTTA
EOTTI
PIAZZA SAN BABILA
arlo
San Babila Ⓜ
VIA MASCAGNI
VIA MAYR
GUICCIARDINI
VIA MACEDONIO MELLONI

500 m
500 yards

---

his old-style *trattoria* still has
ts own bowling green, with a
well-priced lunch menu.

Caffès

10 Corso Como Caffè F1
Corso Como 10; metro Garibaldi.
Open *10am–1am exc Mon lunch.*
or classy brunch; Mediterranean
ushi, truffle omelettes and other

---

delicacies. Or stay until late and
sip cocktails surrounded by its
Zen-like atmosphere.

Art & Soul Café F2
Porta Garibaldi; metro Garibaldi.
Open *Mon–Sat 11am–11pm, Sun
11am–4pm.*
New age, well-priced vegetarian
food, served in the foyer of the
Smeraldo theatre (*see p.179*).

Atomic Bar H2
Via F. Casati 24; metro Repubblica.
Open *Wed–Mon, happy hour
6–8pm, DJ after 10pm.*
Avant-garde disco bar, popular
for after-concert parties.

Caffè Cova G4
*Via Monte Napoleone 8; metro
Montenapoleone; tram 2 or 20.*
Open *Mon–Sat 9am–2.30am.*

Map Key

6	10 Corso Como Caffè	13	Endo	28	Nino Arnaldo	
27	13 Giugno	24	Geppo	33	Nobu	
4	Al Panino	19	I Malavoglia	15	Osteria del Treno	
1	Al Vecchio Porco	35	Ice.it&Dreams	25	Piccolo Sogno	
5	Antica Trattoria della Pesa	26	Il Patio	3	Radestky	
		17	Joya	12	Ran	
33	Armani Caffè	2	L'Altra Farmacia	11	San Fermo	
7	Art & Soul Café	38	La Felicità	36	Sogo	
14	Atomic Bar	18	La Galleria	10	Speakeasy	
31	Bice	23	La Terrazza	20	Tipica Osteria Pugliese	
32	Caffè Cova	29	La Terrazza di Via Palestro	21	Viel	
22	Chandelier	30	La Volpe e l'Uva	8	Viel	
34	Don Lisander	9	Latteria San Marco	37	Viel	
				16	Vini e Cucina	

A Milanese institution famous for its pastries; open since 1837.

Ice.it&Dreams F4
Via Brera 26; metro Montenapoleone. Open daily 9–2 and 6–11.
Feast on creamy *gelati* and *aperitivos*, surrounded by local art.

Radetsky E2
Corso Garibaldi 105; metro Moscova. Open daily 7.30am–1am, brunch 10am–3pm.
The brunches and *aperitivos* here are popular among city managers.

Rossi Off maps
Viale Romagna 23, metro Piola. Open Wed–Mon.
Some of the best ice cream in Milan is scooped out here at this minuscule place. Exquisite chocolates and tiramisu.

Speakeasy F2
Via Castelfidardo 7; metro Moscova. Open Tues–Sun, Sun brunch 12–4pm, happy hour 7–9pm.
US-style 1930s bar, with a vast selection of US dailies.

Trendy Milan
Some of the city's latest places to be seen, eating or otherwise:
10 Corso Como Caffé, (metro Garibaldi; *see* p.167), **L'Altra Farmacia** (bus 57; *see* p.172), **La Brisa** (metro Cordusio; *see* p.172), **Latteria San Marco** (metro Moscova; *see* p.165), **New World** (tram 14; *see* p.172), **Nobu**, (metro Montenapoleone; *see* p.164), **Officina 12** (metro Porta Genova; *see* p.169), **Quattrocento** (tram 79; *see* p.169), **Vini e Cucina** (metro Repubblica; *see* p.165).

Viel E3
Foro Buonaparte; metro Cairoli. Other branches: Viale Abruzzi 23; metro Loreto. Via Solferino 12; metro Moscova. Corso Buenos Aires 15; metro Porta Venezia. Via Cannobio; metro Missori. Open Thurs–Tues.
Milan's most surprising ice cream flavours; try the fresh fruit *gelati*.

University and the Southeast

Restaurants

Expensive

Il Giardino dei Segreti I4
Via P. Sottocorno 17, t 02 7600 8376; tram 9, 20 or 23. Open Wed eve–Mons. Booking advisable.
One half 'Hanging Gardens of Babylon', the other half airy and simple, with tasty delicacies and traditional, wholesome fare.

La Piola Off maps
Via Perugino 18, t 02 5519 5945; tram 27, bus 45 or 73. Open Mon–Fri, and Sat eves.
Delicious and unusual cuisine from Puglia (southern Italy), with a strong leaning towards fresh seafood.

Moderate

Al Merluzzo Felice H7
Via L. Papi 6, t 02 545 4711; metro Porta Romana. Open Mon–Sat.
Very welcoming Sicilian inn serving excellent and distinctive seafood and fish dishes.

Al Penny F7
Viale Bligny 42, t 02 583 21230; tram 15. Open daily exc Mon eves.
Rustic Tuscan cuisine served in a cheerful and friendly atmosphere.

Jucker Zupperia I4
Via Pasquale Sottocorno 50, t 02 700 9813; tram 9, 20 or 23. Open daily exc Mon eves.
A superb kitchen, with its various soups all made from natural ingredients. Take away, or snuggle up on the single diner bar.

Taverna Calabiana Off maps
Via Calabiana 3, t 02 5521 3075; Metro Lodi T.I.B.B.; tram 24. Open Tues–Sat.
Interesting Italian recipes inspired by the Piemontese region: meats, sauces, with sumptuous desserts.

Trattoria del Pescatore Off maps
Via Vannucci 5, t 02 5832 0452; metro Porta Romana. Open Mon–Sat. Book ahead.
A popular fisherman's inn, with good-value and wholesome seafood dishes.

Cheap

Trattoria del Nuovo Macello Off maps
Via C. Lombroso, t 02 5990 2122; tram 27, bus 45 or 73. Open daily exc Mon eves. Major cards only.
Creative, good value cuisine at this eternal of the Milan gastro scene.

Caffès

Acerba 2 G6
*Via Orti 4; **metro** Crocetta or Porta Romana. **Open** Tues–Sun.*
Daily brunch in an old carriage garage. Excellent choice of cakes.

Bar della Crocetta G6
*Corso di Porta Romana 67; **metro** Crocetta. **Open** Tues–Sun 8am–2am.*
After the theatre, come here for a *panino augusto*.

Bar Quadronno F6
*Via Quadronno 34; **metro** Crocetta. **Open** Tues–Sun 7am–2pm.*
The city's oldest sandwich maker, with a loyal clientele.

Martinique Café F5
*Via Cannobio 37; **metro** Missori. **Open** Tues–Sun, happy hour 6–9pm.*
Longstanding jazz and soul bar with over 100 distilled labels, and sushi.

Ticinese and Navigli

Restaurants

Very Expensive

Aimo e Nadia Off maps
*Via Montecuccoli 6, **t** 02 416 886; **metro** Bande Nere. **Open** Mon–Sat, exc Sat lunch. Book ahead.*
Aimio and his wife Nadia have earned themselves an unparalleled reputation for high quality Lombard and national cuisine, made from stringently selected fresh, local ingredients. Famous throughout Milan and extremely popular.

Antica Osteria del Ponte
Off maps
*Along the Naviglio Grande in Cassinetta di Lugagnano, **t** 02 981 8663. **Open** Tues–Sat.*
Although it's 20km from Milan, this holy temple of Italian cuisine should not be missed by any serious gourmet, with heavenly dishes such as ravioli filled with lobster and zucchini, marvellously prepared fish, and perfect pastries – nearly every dish is based on Italian traditions. The beautiful décor is intimate and elegant.

La Scaletta C6
*Piazzale Stazione Porta Genova 3, **t** 02 5810 0290; **metro** Porta Genova. **Open** Tues–Sat, and Mon eves. Booking advised.*
A culinary bastion, with exquisite pasta and risotto, fish and rabbit, all beautifully presented. Excellent desserts and wines; a truly memorable meal.

Sadler Osteria di Porta Cicca
Off maps
*Via Troilo 14, off Via Conchetta, **t** 02 5810 4451; **tram** 3 or 15. **Open** Mon–Sat. Major cards only.*
A moveable feast of new combinations and ingredients, created by one of Milan's most experimental chefs, all served up in a small, refined setting. Personal service and excellent wines.

Expensive

Al Porto D6
*Piazzale General Cantore, **t** 02 832 1481; **metro** Porta Genova. **Open** Tues–Sat, and Sun and Mon eves.*
A fish restaurant in a 19th-century toll house near the Darsena, with a beautiful winter garden.

Aurora C6
*Via Savona 23, **t** 02 8940 4978; **metro** Porta Genova. **Open** Tues–Sun.*
Belle Epoque dining rooms and lovely Piemontese cuisine, with an emphasis on mushrooms and truffles, as well as a bewildering array of cheeses, and a superb *tarte tatin*. Great value, and lovely on summer evenings.

Quattrocento Off maps
*Via Campazzino 14, **t** 02 895 1777, **w** www.4cento.com; **tram** 79. **Open** Tues–Sun. Must book.*
Considered by many to be the best place to eat in Milan. Set in a converted 15th-century monastery by a stream – now transformed

into a mellow, wood-filled minimalist Zen shrine with great food, and of course beautiful people.

Moderate

Al Pont de Ferr D7
*Ripa di Porta Ticinese 55, **t** 02 8940 6277; **metro** Porta Genova. **Open** Mon–Sat, eves only. Arrive early to avoid the queues.*
Try dishes such as pigeon with mushrooms and *polenta* in this busy restaurant; with delicious wines.

La Compagnia dei Naviganti e Viaggiatori I7
*Via Cuccagna 4, **t** 02 551 6154; **metro** Lodi or Porta Romana. **Open** Tues–Sun, eves only.*
Try this Japanese restaurant managed by Italians and Brazilians in an old *cascina* (country house), which also hosts exhibitions and cultural events; the result is convincing.

Officina 12 D7
*Alzaia Naviglio Grande 12, **t** 02 8942 2261; **metro** Porta Genova. **Open** Tues–Sun.*
In an enormous hi-tech loft – traditional pizzeria meets urban regeneration.

Osteria delle Vigne D7
*Ripa di Porta Ticinese 61, **t** 02 857 5617; **metro** Porta Genova. **Open** Tues–Fri, eves only.*
A chilled out, good value, delicious and friendly restaurant; the pick of many in this buzzing district.

Pasto di Conversazione D7

Alzaia Naviglio Grande 6,
t 02 5810 6646; metro Porta
Genova. Open Tues–Sun, eves only.
Major cards only.
Simple but wholesome meals,
with a wide choice of wines.

Ponte Rosso D7

Ripa di Porta Ticinese 23, t 02 837
3132; metro Porta Genova. Open
Mon–Sat, exc Wed eves.
Romantic old-world bistro atmosphere, with excellent cuisine,

including traditional dishes from
Trieste, and Lombard specialities.

Trattoria all'Antica C6

Via Montevideo 4, t 02 5810 4360;
metro Sant'Agostino. Open
Mon–Fri, Sat eves.
Serves simple, fresh and
abundant Lombard fare.

Trattoria Toscana E6

Corso di Porta Ticinese 58,
t 02 8940 6292; tram 3 or 20.
Open Mon–Sat, eves only,
until 3am (kitchen closes
at 1am).

A jolly place, with music and
drinks in the garden, and dishes
like gnocchi filled with ricotta, and
swordfish with thyme.

Cheap

Il Naviglio C7

Via Casale 5, t 02 8940 0768;
metro Porta Genova. Open
Wed–Sun, and Tues lunch.
Try this place for very good
vegetarian and macrobiotic
food and takeaway for
around €13.

Central and South Milan Restaurants

Map Key

Acerba 2
Al Penny
Al Pont de Ferr
Al Porto
Antica Gelateria del Corso
Aurora
Bar della Crocetta
Bar Quadronno
Berlin Café
Blues Canal
Caffè Sant'Ambroeus

3 Coco's
16 Ecologica
14 Govinda
25 Il Naviglio
1 Kota Radja
2 La Brisa
23 La Scaletta
19 Le Biciclette
12 Martinique Café
29 Officina 12
27 Osteria delle Vigne
5 Panino del Conte

10 Panino Giusto
31 Panino Guisto
30 Pasto di Conversazione
11 Peck
28 Ponte Rosso
4 Ristorante San Tomaso
6 Savini
21 Trattoria all'Antica
8 Trattoria da Pino
15 Trattoria Milanese
18 Trattoria Toscana
13 Viel

Osteria Tagiura Off maps
*Via Tagiura 5, t 02 4895 0613; bus
50, 90 or 91. Open Mon–Sat lunch
only, Thurs and Fri eve only. Must
book. Cash only.*
This friendly and affordable
family-run *osteria* has *antipasti* or
full meals on offer, with fish on
Fridays, daily home-made pasta,
and unparalled *testaroli al pesto*.

Caffès

Berlin Café E6
*Via G. Mora 7; metro Porta Genova;
tram 2 or 14. Open daily 8am–7pm.*
Sunday brunches are well worth
the visit here, set in a historical
bar of teutonic inspiration.

Blues Canal D7
*Via Casale 7; metro Porta
Genova. Open daily, Sun brunch,
12–4pm.*
Live classical music for Sunday
brunch, and live jazz in the
evenings in this Irish-American
style place; spot Louis Armstrong's
trumpet amongst those hanging
on the wall.

Ecologica E5–6
*Corso di Porta Ticinese 40; tram 3
or 20. Open Thurs–Tues.*
Milan's first completely
ecological café, and a trendy
place for brunch; all its dishes
are made with natural
ingredients, including its delicious
ice cream treats.

Le Biciclette D6
*Via Torti and Conca di Naviglio 10;
tram 2 or 14. Open Mon–Sat
6pm–2am, Sun 12.30–4.30 and
6pm–2am.*
Trendy café, in an old bicycle shed.

The West End

Restaurants

Very Expensive

Alfredo Gran San Bernardo
Off maps
*Via Borgese 14, t 02 331 9000;
tram 12 or 14. Open Mon–Sat.
Major cards only.*
Has famous vanilla mousse, and
fabulous risottos and *cassoeula*.

Franca Paolo e Lele Off maps
*Viale Certosa 235, t 02 3800 6238;
tram 14. Open Mon–Fri. Major
cards only.*
A broad menu of impressive
regional specialities, served with a
great choice of wines.

Expensive

Al Vecchio Porco D1
*Via Messina 8, t 02 313 862; tram 12
or 14, bus 94. Open Mon–Sat,
eves only.*
A trendy pizzeria.

Antica Trattoria della Pesa E2
*Viale Pasubio 10, t 02 655 5741;
metro Garibaldi or Moscova.
Open Mon–Sat.*
This 19th-century *trattoria* has
traditional cooking to the point
where you can eat an original
Italian cuisine academy *risotto
alla milanese*, *ossobuco*, *cassoeula*
with *polenta* as well as 'new'
dishes such as home-made
cappelletti in capon broth and
tagliolini with butter and truffle.

Arrow's C1
*Via Mantegna 17, t 02 341 533; tram
1 or 29, bus 94 Open Mon–Sat.*
One of the best places for top
quality seafood dishes, especially
the scampi gnocchi with peas.

La Brisa E5
*Via Brisa 15, t 02 8645 0521;
metro Cordusio or Sant'Ambrogio.
Open Tues–Sat, and Mon eves.*
A favourite with celebs, with great
and abundant classic regional
dishes and a menu geared
towards seasonal specialities.

Moderate

Innocenti Evasioni Off maps
*Via Bindellina, t 02 3300 1882;
tram 14. Open Tues–Sat, eves only.*
True to its name, this place offers
an escape from the city, with its
country-style rooms overlooking a
garden, and an eclectic and
constantly changing menu.

Kota Radja C4
*Piazzale Baracca 6, t 02 468
850; metro Conciliazione.
Open Tues–Sun.*
Be prepared for less familiar but
very tasty Chinese dishes, served
in an elegant environment.

L'Altra Farmacia D2
*Via Rosmini 3, t 02 3451 300; bus 57
or 94. Open Mon–Sat 9am–2am.*
This place is a favourite with
journos and VIPs, with plenty of
ambience and a wide range of
wines and *grappas*.

La Felicità E4
*Via Rovello 3, t 02 865 235; metro
Cairoli. Open daily exc Mon eves.*
Chinese restaurant for a romantic,
cheaper meal.

New World Off maps
*Viale Certosa 15, t 02 3921 6132;
tram 14. Open Tues–Sun.*
One of the latest trendy places to
be seen 'munching the crust'; the
atmosphere is cosmopolitan and
multi-ethnic.

Sadler Wine & Food Off maps
*Via Montebianco 2/a, t 02 481
4677; metro Lotto or Amendola
Fiera. Open Mon–Sat.*
An offspring of the famous Sadler
of the Navigli (see p.169); has over
350 wine labels with creatively
elaborate traditional dishes.

Tomoyoshi Off maps
*Via Sacco 4, t 02 466 330;
metro De Angeli. Open Tues–Sun.*
A sushi bar with cold dishes only
and a fixed lunch menu. Takeaway
also available.

Caffès

Al Panino E2
*Viale Crispi 5; metro Garibaldi.
Open Tues–Sun 8–6.*
The latest sandwich shop to open;
there are 80 types to choose from,
as well as warm focaccias, cold
dishes and fries.

Cremeria Buonarroti B3
*Via Buonarroti 9; metro
Buonarroti. Open Tues–Sun
7am–1pm.*
Crème de la crème – literally,
especially the strawberries bathed
in *gianduja* chocolate.

Nightlife and Entertainment

Nightlife 174

Bars 174

Clubs 177

Entertainment 177

Opera 178

Live Music 178

Theatre 179

Film 179

Nightlife

Milan's nightlife, live music and theatre venues are one of the city's biggest draws, a natural extension of Italian creative flair and appetite for design. In fact, bars and clubs are springing up in ever more surprising forms in the city, from disused churches to the currently *di tendenza* (in vogue) hybrid, the disco-restaurant.

It was not always thus in Milan though, for while nightclubs took care of themselves, the *aperitivo* and brunch cultures have only just infiltrated a previously workaholic population. Food and drink fashions to have hit town recently are an appetite for sushi, cranberry juice and a paradoxical retro appetite for Nescafé. And much newfound inspiration comes from London, Paris and New York, reflected in the themes of the city's bars.

The trouble with all this attention to design and detail however, is that you sometimes walk away feeling that the Italians never really let their hair down. The trendiest areas for bars and clubs is around Corso Garibaldi, and towards the Navigli district, where the pursuit of hedonistic leisure is alive and well.

Bars

Bars and cafes are usually open 7pm–1am. For bars with live music, *see* p.179.

The Centre

Café de Paris G4
Galleria de Cristoforis 2, t 02 795 239; metro Duomo. Open Mon–Sat 7pm–1pm.
Pure retro-French style, mixed with a taste of Belle Epoque *alla Milanese*. Very popular for breakfast, *aperitivos* and cocktails.

La Banque F4
Via Porrone 6, t 02 8699 6565; metro Cordusio. Open Tues–Sun 6pm–2am.
Set in luxurious, coloured-marble surrounds bathed in soft light, this

sumptuous resto-bar becomes a dance-mecca in the basement.

Max G4
Via Durini 23, t 02 7625 59623; metro San Babila, bus 54 or 62. Open 11am–2am.
Mythical in the city for its sushi, this restaurant-bar in the upscale boutique shop BCBG is for foodies keen to be seen in the latest ethno-chic resto. After 10pm the music gears up for dancing.

Brera and the Northeast

Aliya I4
Piazza Risorgimento 20, t 02 39 597 7424; metro San Babila. Open daily 8pm–1am.
Once you are ensconced in this venue's cushioned garden it will be hard to find a reason to leave. Sit back and enjoy a Pina Colada while supping on sushi.

Art Deco Café I3
Via Lambro 7, t 02 2952 4760; metro Porta Venezia. Open daily 8pm–2am.
A hi-tech-style bar with original, innovative décor. Very popular at *aperitivo* time before becoming a lively disco-bar, with loud music from local DJs.

Bar Basso Off maps
Via Plinio 39, (Città Studi area), t 02 2940 0580; metro Lima, bus 60 or 92. Open Wed–Mon 10am–1.30am.
The place to go for happy hour: over 500 cocktails and home-made ice creams, in a venue with a 19th-century *salotto* and a country-style section.

Casablanca F1
Corso Como 14, t 02 626 0186; metro Garibaldi. Open Tues–Sun 12–3pm, 8pm–3am.
This cocktail bar-restaurant is one of the new trendy places to be seen. Live music evenings alternate with DJs; in summer, people dance in the garden.

Diana Garden H3
Viale Piave 42, t 02 20581; metro Porta Venezia; tram 29. Open daily 6pm–12am.
Set in the garden of the Diana hotel, this bar is currently one

of the fashionable *aperitivo* destinations. Liberty-style with an illuminated 'tropical' garden outside. A marquee in summer comes complete with an enormous stuffed lion.

Dixieland E1
Via Quadrio 9, t 02 659 8513; metro Garibaldi, bus 51. Open Tues–Sun 8pm–3am.
A slightly kitsch western-style restaurant-bar, complete with effigies of Apaches with Native Indian feathers. The DJ music clashes amusingly. Popular with showbiz types and models.

Jamaica F4
Via Brera 26, t 02 876 723; metro Lanza, bus 61. Open Mon–Sat 9pm–2am.
The old rendezvous of artists and intellectuals in the twenties and thirties, this used to be the meeting place of the Scapigliati painters (the 'Wild-Haired Ones').

Lollapaloosa F1
Corso Como 15, t 02 655 5693; metro Garibaldi. Open 8pm–2am.
Loud and Irish.

MacDuff's Pub E2
Via Volta, t 02 2900 2574; metro Moscova. Open Mon–Sat 11am–1am.
Despite the touristy name, this place serves up an authentic Scottish atmosphere together with a broad range of whiskies, and delicious salmon snacks.

Matricola Pub Off maps
Viale Romagna 43; bus 91, tram 23. Open Mon–Sat 7pm–1am.
Homesick Brits will find relief at this Guinness-owned place; pub lunches and 'English' breakfasts.

Orient Express F3
Via Fiori Chiari 8, t 02 805 6227; tram 3 or 12. Open daily for brunch 10–4, and Mon–Sat 8pm–2am.
Retro-bar evokes the famous train

Reve G4
Via della Spiga 42, t 02 7600 1505; metro Montenapoleone. Open Mon–Sat 9.30am–9pm.
An early evening bar, also a favourite with shoppers. Famous for its *aperitivos*, cakes and rolls.

Wine

Italy is a place where everyday wine is cheaper than Coca-Cola or milk, and where nearly every family owns some vineyards or has relatives who supply their daily needs – which are not great. Even though they live in one of the world's largest wine-growing countries, Italians imbibe relatively little; shockingly, teetotallers number in the millions.

To accompany its infinite variety of regional dishes, Italy produces an equally bewildering array of regional wines, many of which are rarely exported and best drunk young. Unless you're dining at a restaurant with an exceptional cellar, do as the Italians do and order a carafe of the local wine (*vino locale* or *vino della casa*). It's inexpensive, and you won't often be disappointed.

Most wines are named after the grape and the district they come from. If the label says DOC (Denominazione di Origine Controllata) it means that the

wine comes from a specially defined area and was made according to a certain method.

Lombardy produces many commendable wines which are comparable with the more illustrious vintages of Piedmont and Tuscany, although its residents often snobbily prefer to drink wine from other regions, leaving the enterprising Swiss (many of whom own local vineyards) to snap up the most interesting vintages and whistle them over the border in their Mercedes car boots.

Lombardy's noblest wines come from the Valtellina, where the vines grow on steep walled terraces, and cables are used to transfer the harvested grapes to the valleys below. Delicious light sparkling wines, fresh white wines and mellow reds hail from the Franciacorta region, and are often found in restaurant carafes around the Lakes. Southwest Lombardy's Po Valley produces a large quantity of wine, in a huge zone known as DOC Oltrepò

Pavese, much sold through cooperatives; the three potent reds with funny names, Buttafuoco, Barbacarlo and Sangue di Giuda, go down especially well. Lake Garda is surrounded by vineyards, from the well known Bardolino and Bianco di Custoza to the elegant dry white Lugano.

Italians are fond of post-prandial digestives – the famous Stock or Vecchia Romagna brandies are always good. *Grappa* (*acquavitae*) is usually stronger, and often drunk in black coffee (a *caffè corretto*).

Fernet Branca, Cynar and Averna are well-known *aperitivo* digestives. Other popular choices are: potent liqueurs like Strega from Benevento; apricot-flavoured Amaretto; lemon-flavoured Limoncello; cherry Maraschino; aniseed Sambuca; and any number of locally brewed elixirs such as Braulio (Valtellina) and San Giacomo (Val Vigezzo), which are often made by monks.

That's Amore G2
Via Monte Santo 8, t 02 2906 0626; metro Repubblica.
Open *daily 12pm–3pm and 6pm–2am.*
A stylish new pizzeria and cocktail bar, with 1950s American décor. Great for brunch.

Transilvania Off maps
Via Bruschetti 11, t 02 669 1971; metro Centrale. **Open** *8pm–3am.*
A horror bar created by Italian horror cinema director Dario Argento; DJ music, trademarked cocktails and excellent beer.

Xe Mauri Off maps
Via Confalonieri 28, t 02 3360 697; metro Garibaldi. **Open** *Tues–Sun 11am–3pm and 7pm–midnight.*
Venetian meets Indonesian cuisine in this laguna-bar ideal for early evening drinks. The *baccala* (cod) is mythical among Milanese.

University and the Southeast

Fresco Art H6
Viale Montenero 23, t 02 5412 4675; tram 29, 9 or 30. **Open** *Tues–Sun 7.30pm–2am.*
This relatively tranquil bar is inspired by Zen and Feng Shui. It has a buffet and bar, and holds occasional exhibitions by young artists for a suitably contemplative backdrop.

Havana F7
Viale Bligny 50, t 02 669 1971; bus 92. **Open** *Tues–Sun.*
Another Cuban venue with live music, salsa and merengue dancers every night.

Hop H5
Viale Regina Margherita, corner of Via Fratelli Campi, t 02 5412 2690; tram 27 or 29. **Open** *daily 7pm–2am.*
This place serves some of the best beer in Milan, from Weiss beer to double malts; the

choice and service are excellent, as are the intimate and elegant surroundings.

Pogue Mahones H7
Via Salmini 3, t 02 5830 9726; metro Porta Romana. **Open** *7pm–2am.*
Another lively pub. Hosts occasional live Irish bands.

Ragno d'Oro F7
Piazza Medaglie d'Oro 2, t 02 5518 4699; metro Crocetta. **Open** *daily 7.30pm–1am.*
Once a horse-drawn tram depot, but now an enormous dance-expo-restaurant-type venue, set in the lee of the old Spanish city walls. With marquees in summer.

Shambala G7
Via Ripamonti 337, t 02 552 0194; metro Porta Romana. **Open** *8pm–1am.*
Atmospheric resto-bar that serves fusion cuisine inspired by Southeast Asia; with a garden illuminated in soft light. Seating

is Eastern-style, legs crossed on cushions.

Volo F7
Viale Beatrice d'Este, t 02 5832 5543; metro Crocetta. **Open** *Tues–Sun. 8pm–12am.*
With a beautiful outdoor space open between spring and autumn, this ball-games themed bar-restaurant has become popular for its sushi-hour, offering seafood, rice and a cocktail for €12.

Ticinese and Navigli

Cantine Isola Off maps
Via P. Scarpi 30, t 02 331 5249; bus 94. **Open** *Tues–Sun 9am–9pm.*
This is one of Milan's historic wineries for nostalgic wine-lovers. Over 400 labels are on offer, which can be tried at the bar accompanied by tasty snacks.

Cocquetel E6
Via Vetere 14, t 02 836 0688; tram 2, 3 or 8. **Open** *8am–2am.*
Popular, and ideal for happy hour, with hundreds of cocktails.

Grand Café Fashion E6
Corso di Porta Ticinese, t 02 8940 29971; metro Porta Genova. **Open** *12–3.30pm and 7pm–1am.*
In the Navigli area, one of the most popular bars.

Guggenheim D6
Via Conca del Naviglio 5, t 02 832 2988; bus 94. **Open** *daily 7pm–3am.*
The long bar with red walls is the centrepiece of this busy bar, with creative décor and internet facilities.

Julep's Off maps
Via Torricelli 21, to2 8940 9029; tram 15, bus 59 or 86. **Open** *Sun–Fri 12–3pm and 7pm–2am.*
For fajitas and New York-style cuisine, with jazz music in the background, and a big counter where you can eat.

L'Exploit E6
Via Piopette 3, t 02 8940 8675; tram 3, bus 94. **Open** *Tues–Sun 6pm–2am.*
Set against the ancient Roman columns of the basilica

of San Lorenzo, this is the meeting point for all Milan's affluent, trendy youth at the beginning of every evening as they spill out onto the square, munching the abundant appetizers and sipping cocktails.

La Bodeguita del Medio E7
Via Col di Lana, t 02 8940 0560; tram 9 or 15. **Open** *7pm–2.30am.*
A popular cigar bar, with Cuban music, food and atmosphere.

Metal Bar – Trattoria Toscana E6
Corso di Porta Ticinese 58, t 02 8940 6292; tram 3. **Open** *Mon–Sat 6.30pm–3am.*
A classic pub-bar, known for its abundant portions of food and *aperitivo* cocktails, set in a beautiful illuminated garden.

Yguana E6
Via Papa Gregorio XIV 16, behind Piazza della Vetra, t 02 8940 4195; tram 2, 3 or 8. **Open** *Wed–Mon 11am–3pm and 6pm-3am.*
This tropical bar, decorated like a Henri Rousseau canvas, is a favourite for after-dinner drinks in a mellow atmosphere.

The West End

Atiemme E2
Bastioni di Porta Volta 15, t 02 655 2365; metro Moscova. **Open** *11am–3pm and 8pm–3am.*
This fashionable former train station has great cocktails and music.

Dizzy Café E2
Piazza Lega Lombarda 1, t 02 345 1605; tram 3 or 12. **Open** *Tues–Sun 12–3pm and 6.30pm–2am.*
A cocktail bar that aims to be a taste of old America; with a great range of cocktails and snacks. Also good for Sunday brunch.

Frescobar E1
Via Bramante 9, t 02 349 4576; metro Moscova, tram 3 or 12. **Open** *Tues–Sun 7.30pm–2am.*
Original, informal and elegant, this bar has an eclectic décor of

mirrors, lamps and kitsch. Great for Sunday brunch or early evening cocktails, or a stop-off during a day's shopping.

Light E1
Via Maroncelli 8, t 02 6269 0631; metro Garibaldi. **Open** *daily 8pm–2.30am.*
This is the definitive late lounge, a perfect place to end an evening in mellow surrounds, calmed by billowing white drapes, cushions and soft white lighting. Earlier on, it also serves fashionable but expensive food.

Magenta D4
Via Carducci 13, t 02 805 3808; bus 94, tram 19 or 24. **Open** *Tues–Sun 8am–3am.*
A historical Art Nouveau café, bar and beer house.

Makia C2
Corso Sempione 28, t 02 3360 4012; tram 1, 29 or 33. **Open** *daily 8pm–2am.*
Ice, white and transparency are the themes that greet you when you enter this fashionable American-style bar, popular for its buffet at *aperitivo* time.

Moscatelli E2
Corso Garibaldi 93, t 02 655 4602; metro Moscova. **Open** *Tues–Sun 12.30–7.30pm, 9pm–1.30am.*
A beloved Milanese oasis for the fashion-weary. At 150 years old, it is the city's oldest *bottiglieria* (wine bar).

Roialto C1
Via Piero della Francesca 55, t 02 3493 6616, bus 57 or 94. **Open** *daily 6pm–2am.*
One of the coolest bars in town. This former garage was turned into a vast eclectic hangar of Russian armchairs and French 1930s tables, with 1950s American lamps, Turkish carpets and English bookcases for décor. The centre-piece is the 1930s wooden bar. Friendly service makes this an inspirational place either for a quiet drink or a noisier few.

The English Football Pub F3
*Via Meravigli 3, t 02 8005
5125; metro Cordusio,
tram 24. Open daily 7pm–1am.*
As expected, this pub is the
place to go to watch English,
or in fact any football in the
company of compatriots and
ample beers.

Clubs

The club scene in Milan, as in
the rest of Italy, is often concerned
more with appearance than
dancing and having a good time.
If you search it out, however,
it is possible to discover some
places where the emphasis
is reversed.

Generally, clubs open every day
until 3am (though this is often
extended at weekends), and the
pricey admission fee entitles you
to one free drink.

13 Tocqueville E1
*Via Alexis de Tocqueville,
t 02 2900 2973; metro Garibaldi
Open Tues–Sun 10pm–4am.*
This recently opened rest-disco is
set underground in a maze of
mirrors and neon lights. Popular
with students.

Alcatraz Off maps
*Via Valtellina 25, t 02 6901 6352;
metro Garibaldi. Open Sat and Sun
10pm–3.30am.*
This is one of the regular live
music and pop concert venues in
the city, with 3,000 square metres
to strut your stuff in. Recorded
and live music is divided by two
enormous walls.

Gasoline E1
*Via Bonnet 11, t 02 2900 3678;
metro Garibaldi. Open Thurs
11pm–4am, Fri and Sat 12pm–4am,
Sun 5–10pm.*
An underground though
very popular club, with slightly
eccentric patrons and a 'Gay Tea
Dance' on Sundays.

Gattopardo C1
*Via Piero della Francesca 47,
02 345 7699; bus 94. Open daily
30pm–2am.*
Inspired by the Visconti film
The Leopard, this is a sumptuous

club-bar, a favourite with Milan's
dot-com rich, set in an atmospheric former church.

Hollywood F1
*Corso Como 15, t 02 659
8996; metro Garibaldi. Open
Tues–Sun.*
A disco popular with models,
fashion victims and designers.

Karma Off maps
*Via Fabio Massimo 36,
t 02 569 4755; metro Corvetto.
Open 8pm–1am.*
Modelled on Paris' Buddha Bar,
this corner of Parco delle Rose is
one of the trendiest dance venues
of the moment, with three bars
and two dance floors.

Magazzini Generali Off maps
*Via Pietrasanta 14, t 02 5521 1313;
metro Lodi T.I.B.B. Open Wed–Sun
10pm–3am.*
The city's most popular dance
venue, in converted warehouses
and featuring house, jungle and
international DJs. Occasional live
music and concerts.

Modus Vivendi D1
*Via Lomazzo 12; bus 57. Open
Mon–Sat 6pm–1am.*
Set in an 18th-century church,
this is one of Milan's most
unmissable and intimate venues,
hidden in a small courtyard, with
great cocktails.

Plastic Off maps
*Viale Umbria 120, t 02 733 996;
metro Porta Romana. Open
Thurs–Sat 11pm–4am.*
A wonderful, bizarre and very chic
club with fussy doormen. Small
and shiny, with a very eclectic
clientele and drag-queen shows;
Thursday is gay night.

Propaganda Off maps
*Via Castelbarco 11, t 02 5831 0682;
metro Porta Genova. Open
Fri–Wed 7pm–1am. Wed eve free
for students.*
Alternates disco and live concerts.

Shocking F1
*Via Bastioni di Porta Nuova 12,
t 02 659 5407; metro Repubblica.
Open Tues–Sat 10.30pm–3am.*
Another fashionable choice of
models and would-be models.

The Base Off maps
*Viale Forlanini, t 02 7611
8495; tram 12. Open daily
7pm–1am.*
House music in a 1980s-style club.

Tropicana Club Latino F7
*Viale Bligny 52, t 02 5831 8232;
metro Porta Romana. Open Tues,
and Thurs–Sat.*
The place to go for Latin
American dancing.

Zenith De Sade Off maps
*Via Valtellina 21, t 02 688 8898;
tram 12. Open Tues–Sat 10pm–3am.*
With red walls and sofas the
length of the walls, this is a
favourite student rendezvous.

Entertainment

As you might expect from the
home of one of the world's great
opera houses, Milan's arts scene is
alive and well, fuelled by the city's
wealth and the legacy the opera
house has pulled in its wake. But
art and performance in Milan is
not just about La Scala. Equally
fine and moving musical performances of a more understated
nature can be enjoyed in the city's
abundant churches and there is
much experimental theatre being
performed on the fringes of the
city's drama scene.

For detailed listings of these,
check in the daily *Corriere della
Sera* and *La Repubblica*'s
Wednesday *Tutto Milano*
magazine. For clubs with live
music, check under the heading
'Ritrovi'. Other sources include: the
free paper, *Milano Mese*, available
at the main tourist office; *Hello
Milan*, with information on Milan
in English (available from the
tourist office); *City Milano* and
Metro, two free local newspapers
with listings and events at the
back; and URBAN, a free arts
newspaper with listings and
information on Milan.

The local edition of the *Herald
Tribune* also has a daily Italian
supplement in English, including
listings for events in Milan. Finally,
brochures from the various

theatre and orchestra companies prove very useful, in particular the *Teatro Mese* (Theatre Monthly).

Opera

La Scala F4
Piazza della Scala, t 02 860 775 (24hrs), w www.teatroallascala. org; metro Duomo or Cordusio. Season runs 7 Dec–mid-July, and mid-Sept–mid-Nov. **Closed** *for renovation until December 2004 (see p.75).*

For many, an evening at La Scala is in itself the reason for visiting Milan. Finding a good seat at a moment's notice is all but impossible; you could try through your hotel's concierge, or just show up at the box office an hour or so before the performance starts to see what's available. Chances are it will be a vertiginous gallery seat, or you may be squeezed in under the ceiling; standing tickets were recently abolished because of security concerns, but comparatively cheap tickets can be bought for the upper galleries.

Meanwhile, La Scala theatre and opera company has moved to a temporary location at the **Teatro Arcimboldi** (*see* below).

As opera is not everyone's cup of tea, it is worth noting that La Scala, when it is back up and running, also hosts ballets, concerts and recitals. It has its own orchestra, the **Orchestra e Coro del Teatro alla Scala** and ballet company, the **Corpo di Ballo**. The building is also the residence of the city's **Orchestra Filarmonica** (*see* below).

Ticket Information
Box Ticket, Largo Cairoli (metro Cairoli); **La Biglietteria**, Via Molino delle Armi 3 (tram 15, bus 94); **Ricordi**, in the Galleria Vittorio Emanuele II at Corso Buenos Aires 33 (metro Duomo); **Stazione Cadorna kiosk** (metro Cadorna); **Virgin Megastore**, Piazza Duomo 8 (metro Duomo).

Teatro Arcimboldi Off maps
Viale dell'Innovazione, (in the city's Bicocca district, 5km northeast), t 02 7602 4314, or t 02 647 0926 (bookings or info, Mon–Fri 9–1 and 2–6), w www.teatroallascala.org.

This theatre was built in the industrial suburbs as a temporary home for La Scala. Larger than La Scala, with 2,400 seats compared to 1,800, the Teatro Arcimboldi was half financed by Signor Pirelli of the tyre company fame and built in a record and rather controversial 27 months. After La Scala reopens, the Arcimboldi will be used for travelling opera companies, theatre, and special events.

It's the opposite of the ornate La Scala, with simple hardwood walls and moveable glass panels along the auditorium's walls and ceilings, which are meant to improve the acoustics (the critics, however, complain that this makes the orchestra too dominant). They also proved to be a bit dangerous – not long after the theatre's debut in January 2002, 100 of these panels came crashing 40ft down into the seats during a dance recital. Fortunately they emitted alarming creaking noises in advance, and the audience was evacuated in time.

Live Music

Classical Music

Auditorium di Milano Off maps
Corso San Gottardo 42A (box office), t 02 8942 2090, w www. orchestrasinfonica.milano.it or www.auditoriumdimilano.org; tram 3 or 15, bus 59.

A new musical venue in a 1940s building, which holds concerts by the Symphonic Conservatory Giuseppe Verdi, as well as jazz, choral and chamber music.

Conservatorio di Musica Giuseppe Verdi H4
Via del Conservatorio 12, t 02 762 1101 or t 02 7600 1854. **Open** *mid-Sept–June.*

Classical music is performed here for the public and for broadcast.

Orchestra Filarmonica
Off maps
In the Teatro degli Arcimboldi, Viale dell'Innovazione (tickets available at ticket office at Piazza Diaz 6), t 02 647 0926.
Milan's main orchestra, normally at home in La Scala, now moved with the opera company while La Scala is being renovated.

L'Orchestra Milano Classica Off maps
Palazzina Liberty, on Largo Marinai d'Italia, t 02 472595 or t 02 2851 0173; tram 27.
Performs classical outdoor concerts.

Spazio Oberdan G2
Viale Vittorio Veneto 2, t 02 7740 6372; metro Repubblica.
For a more contemporary ear, this place hosts performances of modern classical music.

Teatro dal Verme E4
Via San Giovanni sul Muro 2, t 02 7600 1900, w www.ipomeriggi.org; metro Cairoli. **Open** *Tues–Sun for 9pm performance.*
Hosts concerts by the Orchestra da Camera della Lombardia chamber orchestra and light chamber music in the form of *I Pomeriggi Musicali* (musical afternoons) beginning at 4pm daily.

Jazz

Blues House Off maps
Via S. Uguzzone 26, off Viale Monza (in Sesto San Giovanni, northeast of the city), t 02 2700 3621. **Open** *Tues–Sun.*
Plays exclusively blues.

Gimmies H5
Via Cellini 2, t 02 5518 8069; metro San Babila. **Open** *daily 7.30pm–1am.*
Exclusive piano bar favoured by Italian media celebs and theatre types.

Grilloparlante D7
Alzaia Naviglio Grande 36, t 02 8940 9321; metro Porta Genova. **Open** *daily 7pm–1am.*
Enter an old Navigli house, cross the courtyard and you'll find

Concerts in Churches

For those who want to enjoy classical music in more reverential surrounds, Milan sponsors a series of Renaissance and Baroque concerts of music and poems in the city's churches:

For information on concerts held in **San Simpliciano** (see p.87), **Sant'Alessandro** (see p.102) and **San Satiro** (see p.79), ring **t** 02 7600 5500, or see **w** www.quartettomilano.it for further details.

Concerts are also held in **San Maurizio** (see p.119) and **San Marco** (see p.87) throughout the year; admission is often free.

For something a little different, **Santa Maria della Passione** (see p.101) often puts on organ recitals for two and four hands. See local lisings or contact **t** 02 7631 7176.

this place, which alternates between live jazz and blues, both by amateurs and professionals. Country, rock and even classical music is sometimes featured.

Le Trottoir E3
Corso Garibaldi 1, corner of Via Tivoli, **t** 02 801 002; **metro** Garibaldi or Lanza, **tram** 4 or 12. **Open** 7pm–1am.
An artists bar in Brera with live music and a good restaurant on the upper floor with well-priced menus. In the summer it is quite usual for people to play chess on the pavement (the 'trottoir', hence the name).

Scimmie D7
Via Ascanio Sforza 49, **t** 02 8940 2874; **metro** Porta Genova, **tram** 3. **Open** Wed–Mon 8pm–3am.
Diverse but high-quality jazz offerings, from Dixieland to fusion; in the summer the action moves to a canal barge.

Tangram Off maps
Via Pezzotti 52, **t** 02 8950 1007; **metro** Famagosta. **Open** Mon–Sat.
Schedules a mix of jazz, funk, rythm and blues.

Pop Concerts

Milan is a certain stop for major international artists or groups touring Italy. Though often held at the San Siro stadium (see pp.124 and 186), concerts may also be at:

Alcatraz Off maps
Via Valtellina 25, **t** 02 6901 6352; **metro** Garibaldi.
See 'Clubs', p177.

Filaforum Off maps
Via di Vittorio, **t** 02 488 571, **w** www.fillaforum.it; **tram** 3 or 15.

Other Live Music

For bars with occasional live music, see pp.174-6.

Black Friars E6
Corso di Porta Ticinese 16, **t** 02 5810 6130; **bus** 94, **tram** 3. **Open** Mon–Sat 6pm–3am.
Set in a 17th-century building, this Irish pub has a genuinely monastic atmosphere, complete with mosaics and shadows and an illuminated sacristy. Live music and modern DJs alternate with Gregorian chants to make for a heady mix, accompanied by superb Guinness and seafood dishes.

Dynamo Off maps
Piazza Greco 5, **t** 02 670 4353, **w** www.dynamo.it; **metro** Turro. **Open** daily 8pm–2am.
A mellow venue with two floors: jazz in the basement and other live music on the ground floor.

Tunnel Off maps
Via Sammartini 30, **t** 02 6671 1370; **metro** Centrale. **Open** Oct–May 10pm–3am.
Italian and international acts play at this, one of Milan's historic live rock, folk and blues music venues, for small intimate audiences.

Zythum Off maps
Via Rutilia 16, **t** 02 569 1616; **metro** Porta Romana. **Open** daily 8pm–2am.
A brewery-cum-fusion restaurant with a sushi corner. The ware-house hosts live music and events.

Theatre

Milan has an abundance of theatres hosting a wide range of performances and plays.

Ciak Off maps
Via Sangallo 33, **t** 02 7611 0093, **w** www.teatrociak.com; **tram** 5.
Lovers of cabaret will be entertained here.

Piccolo Teatro E4
Via Rovello 2, **t** 02 7233 3222; **w** www.piccoloteatro.org; **metro** Cordusio. Central booking, reserve as far in advance as possible. Performances also at Teatro Giorgio Strehler, Largo Greppi and Teatro Studio, Via Rivoli 6, (and sometimes at Teatro Lirico, near the Duomo at Via Larga 14, **t** 02 809 665).
Founded after the Second World War and run for years by brilliant director Giorgio Strehler, the Piccolo has a repertory ranging from commedia dell'arte to the avant-garde. Tickets are priced low, so anyone can go.

Smeraldo Theatre F2
Piazza XXV Aprile 10 (Porta Garibaldi), **t** 02 2900 6767, **w** www.smeraldo.it; **metro** Garibaldi or Moscova.
A plush theatre which holds the Art and Soul Café (see p.168) and hosts famous musicals.

Teatro Nazionale A4
Piazza Piemonte 12, **t** 02 4800 7700, **w** www.teatronazionale. com; **metro** Wagner.
Puts on both plays and musicals.

Film

Milan is well-stocked with multiplex cinemas that play the latest blockbusters, but it also has a number of art-house picture houses. In the main cinemas, which are mostly located around Piazza Duomo, most 'English-language' films are dubbed into Italian, although some are still subtitled for budget reasons. The voices of the dubbers are almost as famous in Italy as the actors, and are sometimes preferred, even to the likes of Clint Eastwood. Monday is Italy's most popular cinema night, when everyone tends to go out as a pick-me-up after the end of the weekend. Certain cinemas have reductions on Wednesdays, and as a general rule expect your neighbours to give a running commentary to their cinema partner – silence not being an Italian *forte*. The following cinemas offer English-language films or subtitles. If you want to see a film in English, make sure it says *versione originale*.

Ambasciatori G5
*Corso Vittorio Emanuele II 30,
t 02 7600 3306; **metro** Duomo.*

Anteo F2
*Via Milazzo 9, **t** 02 659 7732
metro Repubblica. **Open** Sept–July.*
Films in English are shown regularly here, and it has a nice Osteria del Cinema where you can dine well, cheaply and quickly, before and after screenings.

Arcobaleno H2
*Viale Tunisia, **t** 02 2940 6054;
metro Repubblica.*

Brera Multisala E2
*Corso Garibaldi 99, **t** 02 2900 1890;
metro Moscova.*

Centrale F5
*Via Torino 30, **t** 02 87 4826;
metro Duomo.*

Mediolanum G5
*Corso Vittorio Emanuele II 24,
t 02 7602 0818; **metro** Duomo.*

Mexico C6
*Via Savona 57, **t** 02 4895 1802;
metro Porta Genova.*

Shopping

Books and Music 182

Clothes and Accessories 182

Department Stores 183

Food 183

Household Goods and Antiques 184

Jewellery 184

Late Shopping 184

Markets 184

Perfumeries 184

'Made in Italy' has become a byword for style and quality, especially in fashion and leather, but also in household goods, jewellery, sports cars, coffee machines, gastronomic specialities, and antiques (both reproductions and the real thing). And where more so than in glossy Milan, Italy's major shopping city, the cynosure of innovative style and fashion throughout the world? Surprisingly in this Aladdin's cave, big-city competition keeps prices lower than most Italian cities and usually much lower than you'll find in posh resort boutiques. Yet after an hour of window-shopping, only a die-hard fashion slave would disagree with Walter Benjamin's theory that 'Monotony is nourished by the new'.

Most shops are closed all day Sunday and Monday mornings (except during the Christmas period), and in August. Food stores close on Monday afternoons. The big sales begin in mid-January and around 10 July.

Books and Music

The English Bookshop C3–4
*Via Mascheroni 12, t 02 469 4468;
metro Conciliazione.*
An excellent selection of English books.

The American Bookstore E4
*Via Camperio 16, t 02 878 920;
metro Cairoli.*
Another English bookshop.

Feltrinelli F5
*Piazza Duomo, t 02 8699 6903;
metro Duomo.*
A classic Italian bookshop, with foreign language magazines.

Franco Maria Ricci G5
*Via Durini 19, t 02 798 444;
metro Duomo.*
For beautiful art editions.

Messaggerie Musicali G5
*Galleria del Corso, t 02 7605 5431;
metro Duomo.*
One of the best shops in town for musical scores and recordings.

Mondadori Multicenter A4
*Via Marghera 29, t 02 480 471;
metro Wagner.*
A megastore with the latest-generation software, hardware, games, e-books and portable phones, as well as an online travel agent, ticket booking office, auditorium and internet café.

Ricordi Mediastore F4
*Galleria Vittorio Emanuele II,
t 02 8646 0272; metro Duomo.*
A Milanese music megastore (also sells tickets for events).

Rizzoli F4
*Galleria Vittorio Emanuele II 79,
t 02 8646 1071; metro Duomo.*
One of the city's best-stocked bookshops (with many English titles), owned by the family that founded the *Corriere della Sera*, Milan's newspaper.

Virgin Megastore F4
*Piazza Duomo 8, t 02 7200 1370;
metro Duomo.*
This chain has a huge selection of music and videos.

Clothes and Accessories

Milan's artsy displays of clothing and accessories are a window-shopper's paradise. And though prices are on the whole up to 20% cheaper, there are still greater bargains to be had in Milan. In recent years, a number of outlets are sprouting up in and around the city selling genuine designer-label clothes at knock-down prices, sometimes up to 70% off. The clothes are usually the surplus from the end of a collection or seasonal line, so don't expect the latest catwalk designs. If you're like most people though, this won't matter.

Most of the big names in fashion have their boutique headquarters in the **Quadrilatero d'Oro**, defined by Via Monte Napoleone, Via della Spiga, Via S. Andrea and Via Borgospesso (*see* 'Brera and the Northeast', p.81, and 'A Shopping Trip', p.130). Via della Spiga is chock-a-block with top designers,

such as Bottega Veneta, Byblos, Krizia, Luciano Soprani and Dolce e Gabbana. Via Monte Napoleone also has its share: Alberta Ferretti, Roccobarocco, Ferragamo, Prada, Ungaro, Versace, Fratelli Rossetti and Nazareno Gabrielli. Also, on Via S. Andrea are Chanel, Prada (again, and Via della Spiga as well), Helmut Lang, Fendi, Ferré and Trussardi.

A bit further afield, there are several minor galleries which branch off the **Corso Vittorio Emanuele II**, each with good quality and reasonably priced shops. The shops on busy **Via Torino** also have some of Milan's more affordable prices, especially in clothes and footwear. Another shopping street with excellent merchandise and reasonable prices is **Via Paolo Sarpi** (*metro Moscova*). For quirkier, smaller designer shops, head for **Via Brera** or **Corso di Porta Ticinese**. For children's clothes, *see* 'Children's and Teenagers' Milan', p.190.

Armani F4
Via Durini 23–25 and Via Manzoni 31, t 02 7231 8600; metro Montenapoleone.
Armani's Megastore on Via Manzoni has three floors dedicated to the maestro's new home collection as well as his Emporio lines. A sushi bar, café and restaurant are added pleasures (*see* 'Eating Out', p.165).

D Magazine G4
*Via Montenapoleone 26, t 02 7600 6027; w www.d.magazine.it;
metro Montenapoleone.*
Gigli and Armani, up to 50% off.

Decathlon Off maps
*Via Milano, Baranzate di Bolate,
t 02 3830 9510; metro Piola.*
For the latest sportswear.

Dibiemme Fashion G6
*Corso di Porta Romana 121,
t 02 546 9776; metro Crocetta.*
A label gold-mine, set back from the street.

Diffusione Tessile G5
Galleria San Carlo 6, t 02 7600 0829; metro Duomo.
Specializes in MaxMara clothes.

Dolce & Gabbana Industria H4
Via Rossini 70, Legnano, t 0331 545 888, w www.dolcegabbana.it;
metro Palestro.
A bit of a trek, but worth it.

Fendi G4
Via Sant'Andrea 16, t 02 7602 1617;
metro Montenapoleone.
The stalwart of Italian fashion.

Giuliana Cella G3–4
Via Borgospesso 12, t 02 2906 2582;
metro Montenapoleone.
Ethno-chic showroom with exclusive wools from Central Asia and refined embroidery.

Gucci G4
Via Monte Napoleone 5, t 02 771 271; metro Montenapoleone.
The famous name in leather.

Il Salvagente Off maps
Via Fratelli Bronzetti 16, t 02 7611 0328; tram 27.
Stocks surplus exclusive labels.

Laura Biagiotti G3–4
Via Borgospesso 19, t 02 783 308;
metro Montenapoleone.
A worthwhile designer boutique.

Mercatino Michela G3–4
Via della Spiga 33 and Corso Venezia 8, t 02 799 748; metro Montenapoleone.
Second-hand designer fashions.

Missoni G4
Via Sant'Andrea, corner of Via Bagutta, t 02 7600 3555;
metro Montenapoleone.
Ravishing knits for men and women.

Moschino F4
Via Durini 14, t 02 7600 4320;
metro Duomo.
Milan's bad boy of fashion.

Surplus E–F2
Corso Garibaldi 7, t 02 869 3693;
metro Moscova.
With a marvellous array of second-hand garments.

Valentino G4
Via Santo Spirito 3, t 02 7600 6182;
metro Montenapoleone.
Classic designer wear.

Versace G4
Via Monte Napoleone 11, t 02 7600 528; metro Montenapoleone.
Glitzy Italian designs.

Lingerie, Shoes and Accessories

Al Guanto Perfetto F5
Via Mazzini 18, t 02 875 894;
metro Duomo.
Milan's most famous glove shop for over a hundred years.

Franzi E3
Via Palermo 5, t 02 801 436;
metro Moscova.
Established in 1864, this is a chic outlet for elegant leather.

Guenzati F5
Via Mercanti 1, t 02 8646 0423;
metro Duomo.
Goods that will make a velvet-lover's heart flutter; they also do made-to-order.

La Bonnetterie C4–5
Via San Michele del Carso 18, t 02 469 1297; metro Conciliazione.
A sexy shop of undergarments.

Lorenzi G4
Via Monte Napoleone 9, t 02 7602 2848; metro Montenapoleone.
The city's most refined pipe and male accessories shop, with a remarkable shaving museum.

Pollini G4
Corso Vittorio Emanuele II 30, t 02 794 912; metro Duomo.
For designer shoes.

Rosy F4
Via Manzoni 42, t 02 7600 2070;
metro Montenapoleone.
Elegant and very sensual designer underwear for designer bottoms.

Department Stores

COIN H5
Piazza 5 Giornate 1/a, t 02 5519 2083; metro San Babila.
A department store that is a good bet for reasonably priced fashions.

La Rinascente F5
Piazza del Duomo, t 02 88521;
metro Duomo.
A monument almost as well known as the Duomo next door

(see 'The Centre', p.70), this is Milan's biggest and oldest department store; it's also the only one to have been christened by Gabriele D'Annunzio. Its six floors of merchandise have especially good clothing and domestic sections, and offer an array of kitchen gear dear to the heart of the Italian cook. The top-floor café has great views of the cathedral.

Food

Cova G4
Via Monte Napoleone 8, t 02 7600 0578; metro Montenapoleone.
For elegant confectionery dating back to 1817 amid crystal surroundings. Try the famous sacher torte or their Christmas *panettone.*

Il Salumaio G4
Via Monte Napoleone 12, t 02 7600 1123; metro Montenapoleone.
Offers an infinite array of nearly every gourmet item you can imagine, with a recently opened restaurant.

Peck F5
Via Spadari 9. t 02 802 3161;
metro Duomo.
Home of Milanese gastronomy, with a wide choice of Italian and foreign delicacies. Peck extended the original **Casa del Formaggio** on nearby Via Speronari (selling the city's best cheeses since 1894) and **Bottega del Maiale** (cheese and pork shops) to include exotic delicacies, a wine cellar with over 40,000 labels, and an exclusive restaurant on nearby Via Victor Hugo (*see* 'Eating Out', p.164). Peck Rosticceria, where you can have lunch, has opened in nearby Via Cantù.

Sadler Wine & Food
Off maps
Via Conchetta, t 02 481 4677;
tram 79.
Famous and well-stocked deli in the Navigli area.

Household Goods and Antiques

If you are looking for antiques, be sure to demand a certificate of authenticity – reproductions can be very, very good. To get your antique or modern art purchases home, you will have to apply to the export department of the Italian Ministry of Education and pay an export tax; your seller should know the details. Be sure to save receipts for Customs.

Milan also has several well-known furniture shops, including: **Artemide** and **Flos** on Corso Monforte, **De Padova** on Corso Venezia, **Dilmos** in Piazza San Marco and **Alias** on Via V. Monti.

Cassini G5
Via Durini 18, t 02 780 698; metro San Babila.
For designer sofas and chairs.

Fontana Arte F4
Via Santa Margherita 4, t 02 8646 451; metro Cordusio.
For designer lamps.

Le Mani d'Oro I1
Via Gaffurio 5; metro Loreto.
This shop specializes in *trompe l'œil* objects and decorations.

Romani Adami G4
Via Bagutta 3; metro Montenapoleone.
Specialists in antique jewellery.

Jewellery

Milan's jewellers were actually the first to set up shop in the fashion headquarters that is the Quadrilatero d'Oro in the 1930s. Other fine jewellers now on Via Monte Napoleone in the Quadrilatero d'Oro include: **Faraone**, **Cartier**, **Martignetti**, **Damiani** and **Cusi**, as well as:

Buccellati G4
Via Monte Napoleone 4, t 02 780 903; metro Montenapoleone.
Considered by many to be the best jewellery designer in Italy, this shop features exquisitely delicate gold work and jewels, each piece individually crafted.

Bulgari G3–4
Via della Spiga 6, t 02 798 832; metro Montenapoleone.
The world-famous jewellers.

Calderoni G4
Via Monte Napoleone 23, t 02 7600 1293; metro Montenapoleone.
This is the city's oldest jeweller.

Late Shopping

Autogrill Duomo F5
Piazza Duomo, t 02 8633 1922; metro Duomo. **Open** 6.30pm– midnight.
A small market.

Supercentrale G1
Stazione Centrale; metro Centrale. **Open** daily until midnight, shops until 9pm.
Late-night supermarket.

Markets

The tourist office has a list of markets; most of them are open 9am–1pm, and nearly all markets close in August.

Fiera di Senigallia D6
Viale D'Annunzio (along the banks of the Darsena); metro Porta Genova, tram 20. **Open** Sat 8.30– 5.
Flea market with clothing, records and handicrafts.

Mercato dell'Antiquariato di Brera F3
Via Fiori Chiari; metro Lanza. **Open** Aug–June, third Saturday of each month.
For antiques, books, postcards and jewellery.

Mercato della Darsena D6–7
Along the banks of the Darsena; metro Porta Genova, tram 20. **Open** daily.
This is one of the best food markets in Milan, selling cheeses, meats, fruit and veg.

Mercato del Sabato C–D6
Viale Papiniano; metro S. Agostino, tram 20. **Open** Tues and Sat morns.
Huge Saturday clothes market, sometimes featuring cast-offs from the fashion shows.

Mercato di Piazza Wagner B4
Piazza Wagner; metro Wagner. **Open** daily 8.30–1 and 4–7.30 exc Mon afternoons.
This lovely, old covered market is a veritable hanging garden of sausages, fish, fruit and cheeses.

Mercatone dell' Antiquariato D7
Naviglio Grande; metro Porta Genova. **Open** last Sunday of every month exc July.
This increasingly popular (and expensive) antiques market has anything from 18th-century tables to Liberty lamps.

Plant, Flower and Pet Market F4
Piazzetta Reale, or in Piazzetta Mercanti; metro Duomo. **Open** Sun morn Mar–June, Sept–Dec.
An understandably lively affair.

San Donato Market Off maps
Metro San Donato (suburb south of Milan). **Open** Sun mornings.
Flea market.

Stamp and Coin Market F5
Piazza Duomo; metro Duomo. **Open** Sunday morn.
For collectors – postcards too.

Perfumeries

Boutique Guerlain D4
Corso Magenta 5, t 02 867 000; metro Cadorna.
An outlet for Guerlain's entire range of women's perfumes.

Profumerie Brambilla F2
Corso di Porta Nuova 48, t 02 659 8602; metro Repubblica.
A beloved health and beauty centre, perfumerie and costume jewellery shop all in one.

Yrama C3
Largo Quinto Alpini 7, t 02 4800 5052; w www.yrama.it; metro Conciliazione.
Exotic and exclusive niche fragrances, made exclusively by and for designers.

Sports and
Green Spaces

Spectator Sports 186

Activities 187

Green Spaces 188

Spectator Sports

With its citizens utterly obsessed by Doric and Corinthian stereotypes of beauty, if not health, Milan is one of the best-equipped cities in Italy for sport.

Basketball

Aside from football, another high-profile sport in Italy is basketball. For the public and minor teams, Milan also hosts an American-style championship called 'Streetball' every September in Piazza Castello.

Olimpia Milano Off maps
Via Caltanissetta 3, t 02 2700 01657; bus 54 or 61.
Scarpette Rosse (Little Red Shoes) is the nickname of Olimpia Milano, the city's league team founded in 1933. Tickets for their games can be bought at the Banca Commerciale Italiana.

Cycling

The **Giro d'Italia**, the Italian equivalent of the Tour de France, is the big national race, of which Milan hosts the final stage in June. In March, there is also the **Milano–San Remo** race, while in winter the city hosts an indoor cycling championship over six days, innovatively called **Sei Giorni di Ciclismo** (or, six days of cycling).

Football

There is no doubting which sport comes first in the hierarchy of the Milanese consciousness and that is the national sport of *il calcio* – football. The city has 80 public football pitches ranging from suburban scrubland to the temple of the San Siro stadium (*see* below).

Affiliation to one or other of these two clubs has continually divided the Milanese, if not the whole population of Italy, for the last century; the twice-yearly

derby is often the source of violence as the city is draped in the opposing uniforms of the two teams.

Playing in red and black and known as the *Rossoneri*, **AC Milan** was founded in 1899 by an Englishman named Alfred Edward, who lived in Milan. The club was originally called the Milan Cricket and Football Club but cricket, not really suiting the short Italian concentration span, never quite caught on.

The club is now owned by Silvio Berlusconi's vast media empire, another reason for the vitriol aimed at it by opposing fans. The club was certainly a symbol of national pride in the early 1990s however, when they seemed invincible, in both their home league of Serie A and in the European Champions League.

Inter was founded in 1908 and enjoyed its heyday in the 1960s although they are usually fairly high up in the Italian league and European competition. Most football fans will be familiar with the image of their greatest asset, Ronaldo (now moved on to another team), known locally as *il fenomeno*, wearing the clubs black and blue, *Nerazzurri* strip.

Tickets for games can be obtained from the stadium ticket offices (*see* below). Inter tickets can also be bought in the Banca Popolare di Milano, Banca Briante, Banca Agricola Milanese and Milano Ticket agencies. Tickets for AC Milan can be bought at the Cariplo Bank and Milan Point.

AC Milan G2
Via Turati 3, t 02 62281,
w www.acmilan.com;
metro Turati.
The team trains every day at Milanello, a citadel to football near Varese (Carnago) but fans are not usually allowed to watch.

Inter Milan G5
Via Durini 24, t 02 77151,
w www.inter.it; metro
San Babila.
The club trains in Appiano Gentile, near Como, to which visitors are allowed. Ring the office for training times.

Museo Inter e Milan Off maps
Via Piccolomini 5, gate 4, t 02 404 2432/02; metro Lotto, tram 24.
Open daily 10–6; adm €10.
Traces the club's history, with a tour of the stadium.

San Siro (Meazza) Stadium Off maps
Via Piccolomini 5, t 02 400 92175; metro Lotto, tram 24.
Milan's Giuseppe Meazza stadium, known internationally as San Siro, is sometimes referred to by the Milanese as the *la scala del calcio*, signifying the supposed perfection of football, if not the drama played out on the pitch. The stadium (which has an uneven pitch since it doesn't get enough light due to the closing roof) is home to two of the great Italian club sides: AC Milan, known as il Milan (with the accent on the first syllable) and Internazionale, known as l'Inter (*see* above).

Horse-racing

Ippodromo del Galoppo Off maps
Piazzale sello Sport 15, t 02 482 161; metro Lotto, tram 24. Open weekends March– Nov 9–6.30.
Founded in 1920, *Ippica* is the nickname given to this race-course next to the San Siro football stadium, the Ippodromo di San Siro. One ticket grants entry to both circuits.

Trotter Off maps
Piazzale dello Sport 15, corner of Vicolo Piccolimini, t 02 404 2646; tram 24. Open weekends, and summer eves.
Founded in 1925, this course's summer evening races are particularly fun.

Motor-racing

Every year in September the nearby city of Monza is draped in the red of Ferrari as the Formula One Grand-Prix circus rides into town. On Grand-Prix day there is a shuttle bus from Monza station to the circuit.

Autodromo Nazionale di Monza Off maps
Parco di Monza, t 039 24821 (t 2482 1212 for tickets), w www.monzanet.it
Tickets for the Grand-Prix can be obtained from the Autodromo ticket office (above) or from: **Automobile Club Milano**, Corso Venezia 43, **t** 02 77451; **Acitour Lombardia**, Corso Venezia 43, **t** 02 76006350; or **AC Promotion**, Piazza Eleanora Duse 1, **t** 02 7600 2574.

Rugby

The Italians do play rugby, although their performances in the Six Nations suggest they have a way to go. The real heartland of rugby in Italy is in the north-east, but you can still watch a match in Milan at **Centro Sportivo Giuriati**, (*see* 'Sports Centres', below).

Milan has two teams, **Asr Milano** and **Cus Milano**, both playing in the nation's B league.

Activities

Every year over two million Milanese flood into the city's gyms, and one million into its public baths. With this in mind, most visitors should find enough choice to practise most forms of physical exercise.

Athletics

If you want to pound the track yourself, this is possible at any one of the following centres: **Centro Sportivo XXV Aprile**, Via Cimabue 4, **t** 02 3926 2162; **Centro Sportivo Saini**, Via Corelli 136, **t** 02 756 1280; **Centro Sportivo Giuriati**, (*see* 'Sports Centres', below).

Basketball

For a casual game, you can go to the **Filaforum Milanofiori** (*see* 'Sports Centres', below).

Boating

Amici dei Navigli Tours F5
Via Marconi 1, t 02 6702 0280, w www.naviganavigli.it/ itinerarioing.htm; metro Duomo.
This environmental organization also does boat tours along the Naviglio Grande.

Associazione Naviglio Grande D7
Alzaia Naviglio Grande 4, t 02 8940 9971, w www.naviglio grande.mi.it; metro Porta Genova. Open Tues–Sat 9.30–6.
An organization which devotes itself to protecting and promoting the canal heritage.

Climbing

Obviously there are no mountains in Milan but you can practise for the real thing on the face of the Dolomites or Alps, or simply go to a gym: **Golden Gym Sporting Club**, Via Broschi 26, **t** 02 839 4233; **PalaUno**, Via Carriera 8, **t** 02 423 5315 (min 2 people).

Cycling

Cycling is a popular sport in Italy, and at weekends the parks and country roads can be busy with streamlined, cat-suited, fast-moving cyclists taking their two wheels very seriously.

If you're not into spectating and want to have a go yourself, either for leisure or as a means of transport, you will find that many Milanesi cycle unequipped with 'unfashionable' helmets. Also, watch out for that infamous Italian driving, and mind the cobbles and the tramlines!

For a leisurely ride, try the full length of the **Naviglio Grande**, which stretches southwest of the city centre, passing villas and the medieval centre of

Vigevano, heading towards the town of Abbiategrasso. (*See* 'A Walk Through the Navigli', p.126, and 'Ticinese and Navigli', p.110).

Aws Off maps
Via Ponte Seveso 73, t 02 6707 2145; metro Centrale.
Bicycles can be hired from here, but don't expect the latest mountain bike or racer.

Ciclobby D2
Via Cesariano 11, t 02 331 3664; metro Moscova. Open Tues-Fri 5–7pm.
For more information on urban bike journeys.

Football

If you want to play yourself there are plenty of football pitches in the city, the best of which are at the **Lido, Filaforum** and **Saini** sports centres, (*see* 'Sports Centres', below). Alternatively, you will usually find amateurs trying to recreate free-kicks from the preceding Sunday in the city's numerous parks.

There are also pubs where people meet to watch football and get together 5-a-side teams. Try one of the following: **Osteria del Calcetto**, Corso Garibaldi 46, **t** 02 805 1865. **Osteria del Pallone**, Viale Gorizia 30, **t** 02 5810 5641.

Ice-skating

If you want to practise your ice-skating moves, you can do so either at the **Filaforum** (*see* 'Sports Centres', below) or at one of the following bespoke ice-rinks: **Palazzo del Ghiaccio**, Via Piranesi 14, **t** 02 73981. **PalAgora**, Via dei Ciclamini 23, **t** 02 4830 0946.

Motor-racing

Even if you've got a Fiat 500 instead of a Ferrari, you can test the revolver-shaped bends of Monza's **Grand Prix Autodromo** (*see* above), when it opens itself up to private vehicles *open Sunday afternoons Nov–Feb*).

Running

In April, Milan hosts the annual **StraMilano**, supposedly the city's marathon, but in reality a sponsored 15-kilometre *sortie* around the city centre, departing at the Piazza Duomo and finishing in the Arena Civica in Parco Sempione.

Skiing

Every Sunday in winter, the *tangenziale* motorway is blocked with people returning from St Moritz, which, on a traffic-free day, is only an hour and a half away. Many of the Milanese take a house or apartment there for the season, to ski and to swan around in the latest ski gear. Other favourite resorts are further afield, in such places as Cortina, beloved haven of film stars and celebrities.

Sports Centres

Centro Sportivo Giuriati
Off maps
Viale Pascal 6, t 02 7060 0358; bus 93.
For Rugby matches and athetics.

Centro Sportivo Saini Off maps
Via Corelli 136, t 02 756 1280; bus 54.
Milan's most completely equipped sports complex; no membership is necessary.

Filaforum Milanofiori Off maps
Via Di Vittorio 6, Assago (7km from city centre), t 02 4570 0466/9808; metro Famagosta.
Offers bowling, basketball, roller skating, squash and swimming.

Lido di Milano Off maps
Piazzale Lotto 15, t 02 3926 6100; metro Lotto.
Built in 1930; you can windsurf here, play tennis and football.

Vigorelli B1
Via Arona 15, t 02 331 1513; tram 19.
Near the Fiera di Milano, this complex is central to the history of sport in Milan. Recently refurbished, it was named after cyclist, Giuseppe Vigorelli. It is also the venue of the only concert ever performed by the Beatles in Italy.

Sports Reading

If you prefer armchair sport or want to read up on the background of your favourite sport or club, try **Libreria dello Sport**, Via Carducci 9, t 02 805 5355. This is an unmissable stop-off for lovers of books on sport, many of which are available in many different languages.

Swimming

There are any number of pools accessible to the public in Milan, including the **Lido di Milano**, **Saini** and **Filaforum** (*see* 'Sports Centres', above). Other public pools are at **Cozzi**, Viale Tunisia 35, t 02 2900 1247; and **Samuele**, Via Mecenate 76, t 02 506 1347, or at the places below.

Idroscalo Off maps
Via Circonvallazione Idroscale – Segrate, t 02 756 0393; bus 73.
Near Linate airport, this artificial lake is perfect for swimming, windsurfing, canoeing, jet-skiing and water-skiing.

Piscina Cozzi H2
Viale Tunisia 35, t 02 659 9703; metro Repubblica, tram 1 or 30.
A popular, Olympic-sized public pool, with a Fascist-era exterior.

Piscina Solari C6
Parco Solari, Via Montevideo 20, t 02 469 5278; metro San Agostino, tram 20.
A pool with floor-to-roof windows overlooking the park.

Tennis

There are public tennis courts at the following sports centres (call in advance to make a booking): **Centro Sportivo Saini**, **Filaforum**, **Milanofiori** and **Lido di Milano** (*see* 'Sports Centres', above).

Green Spaces

Giardino della Guastella G5
Via Francesco Sforza and Via San Barnaba; tram 12, 23 or 27, bus 37, 60, 73, 77, 84 or 95. Open daily 8–5.
Milan's oldest public park; an understated and pleasing spot in the city (*see* p.100).

Giardinni Pubblici G3
Bastioni di Porta Venezia, Corso Venezia, Via Manin; metro Turati, Palestro or Porta Venezia.
The city's main municipal gardens, with a zoo, swans, playgrounds and a Natural History Museum (*see* p.91).

Parco delle Basiliche
Piazza della Vetra; tram 3, 15 or 20.
Milan's third largest park (*see* p.108).

Parco Forlanini Off maps
Via Corelli – near Linate airport; tram 12, bus 45 or 73.
A flat park for a leisurely cycle ride.

Parco Monte Stella Off maps
Via Cimabue; metro QT8.
Laid out on an artificial mountain created from the rubble from the Allied bombings. It is certainly the only park that will provide any challenging inclines for cyclists.

Parco Nord Off maps
Via Clerici 150, Sesto San Giovanni; metro Gessate, then take bus 920, 921 or 922 to Cassano d'Adda or Trezzo sull'Adda.
Has marked cycle paths along the scenic banks of the river Adda.

Parco Sempione D3
Foro Buonaporte, Corso Sempione; metro Cadorna, Cairoli or Lanza. Open daily 6.30am–8pm, until 11.30pm in mid-summer.
Milan's largest park, surrounding the Castello Sforzesco. It was originally the garden of the ducal palace in the Middle Ages and was once a hunting reserve (*see* p.115).

Parco Solari C6
Via Andrea Solari and Via Montevideo; metro San Agostino.
One of the few green spaces to the southwest of the city, with a pool (*see* 'Swimming').

Children's and Teenagers' Milan

Babysitting 189

Books 189

Cinema 189

Clothes 189

Cookery 190

Eating 190

Entertainment 191

Hotels 191

Parks 191

Sights and Museums 191

Sport 191

Theatre 191

Toys 192

Even though the declining birth rate and the recent legalization of abortion may hint otherwise, children are still the royalty of Italy. They are pampered, often obscenely spoiled, probably more fashionably dressed than you are, and never allowed to get dirty. In spite of it all, most of them somehow manage to be well-mannered little charmers. If you're bringing your own *bambini* to Italy they'll receive a warm welcome everywhere. Many **hotels** offer advantageous rates for children and have play areas, and if a **circus** visits town you're in for a treat; it will either be a sparkling showcase of daredevil skill or a poignant, family-run, modern version of Fellini's *La Strada*.

Despite Milan's more obvious attraction for adult activities, there is still plenty to stimulate the young mind in the city, be it in the parks, or at a number of the more child-friendly museums and exhibitions. Milan's **Natural History Museum** has not only stuffed rhinos, but also a good playground in the gardens nearby. Other good bets are **canal tours** or a trip to the top of the **Duomo**.

Babysitting

Milan has a number of crèche and babysitting services, several of which will offer your child bilingual care while you are away:

Agency Tate & Nanny G1
Via M. Gioia 41, t 02 6698 4030; metro Gioia.

Baby Sitter Center Off maps
Via Vittadini 3, t 02 826 3845; metro Porta Romana.

La Duga Off maps
Via Giambellino 32, t 02 425 094; tram 2. (Also open Sundays).

La Lampada di Aladino
Off maps
Via Sebanico 9, t 02 6884325/6; metro Garibaldi.
For foreign au-pair girls.

Milano Work Service Off maps
Via F.lli Bronzetti 3, t 02 7010 9757; tram 27. (Also open Sundays).

Books

Most of Milan's bookshops only sell books in the Italian language. The Feltrinelli chain of book stores (*see* 'Shopping', p.182) is the most likely to have English language books. Otherwise, the city has many shops where, for those who concentrate on the pictures, cartoons, comics and picture books for children are a speciality:

La Bottega delle Fiabe Off maps
Viale Piceno 35, t 02 717 394; tram 27. Open 8am–7pm.
A laboratory-cum-bookshop that can actually personalize comic-strips and illustrated books, substituting the real protagonists with the name of your child and their friends.

Libreria dei Ragazzi F5
Via Unione, t 02 7200 4166; metro Missori.
The first bookshop in the city to specialize in children's books.

Cinema

The following cinemas screen children's films (dubbed or sometimes subtitled into the Italian language). Call ahead for details.

Cinecircolo Asteria Off maps
Via G. da Cermenate 2, t 02 846 0919; tram 15, bus 95.

Nuovo Arti H4
Via Mascagni 8, t 02 7602 0048; metro San Babila, bus 94.

Clothes

Combine the Italian obsession for clothes with its obsession for children and you have a veritable mania. Milan is choc-a-block with sartorial suggestions for tomorrow's models. Sadly, although the cloth is cut smaller, the bill seems to stay the same.

Chicco F5
Piazza Diaz 2, t 02 8699 8597; metro Duomo.
Everything for the world of children. One of many branches in the city.

Giorgio Armani Junior G5
Via Durini 3, t 02 794 248; metro San Babila.
To really spoil them.

Il Pinco Pallino G4
Via della Spiga 42, t 02 781 931; metro Montenapoleone.
Elegance and cuteness for little ones.

L'Angelo E4
Via Dante 18, t 02 866 151; metro Cordusio or Cairoli.
Here you will find elegance for young masters and madams.

La Luna e B–C2
Via F Ferruccio 16, t 02 349 4960; metro Buonarroti.
A small boutique, popular with fashion-conscious mums.

Meroni Si' E3
Via Madonnina 10, t 02 805 7406; metro Lanza.
In the heart of the Brera, this designer-owned shop sells very smart and cute clothes.

Prenatal E4
Via Dante 7, t 02 869 2535; metro Cairoli.
One of eight branches of this well-known chain store for children's clothes and accessories.

Cookery

La Nostra Cucina Off maps
Corso Indipendenza 5, t 02 738 5110 tram 27.
If you want to start them young in the art of Italian cooking, take your children here, where they can learn the first secrets of Italian cuisine and playfully cover themselves in flour at the same time.

Eating

Italian children are often taken out to dinner, where they are allowed to stay up late and are generally exhibited around the table. As a result, save perhaps for the more sophisticated restaurants, children are always welcome and spoilt in restaurants, and especially in the more popular pizzerias and *trattorias*.

Entertainment

Aquatica Off maps
Via G. Airaghi 61, **t** *02 4820 0134*, **w** *www.parcoacquatica.com*; **tram** *24.* **Open** *Jun–Sept.*
A summer paradise for aquatic children; a waterworld of slides, pools and waterjets.

Idroscalo Off maps
Rivoltana 64, Segrate, **t** *02 756 0393*, **bus** *36.* **Open** *all year.*
This is Milan's nearest Luna Park, with all manner of rides.

Play Planet Off maps
Via Veglia 59, **t** *02 668 8838*; *Via Copernico 9*, **t** *02 4840 9408*; **metro** *Zara*, **tram** *2*, **bus** *42.* **Open** *daily 8am–6pm.*
An America-style recreation centre with slides, pools, games and fun of all sorts for all the family.

Hotels

Most of Milan's hotels are oriented towards the business traveller and not travelling families. However, children are always welcome and, though cots may not be available in some of the cheaper hotels, most establishments will be only too happy to set up an extra bed or two in your room for an extra cost.

Parks

Though not blessed with open spaces, Milan's parks offer plenty of room for parents to relax while their children charge around letting off steam. The **Giardini Pubblici** are probably a better bet than the **Parco Sempione**, where there may be too much going on by way of dog walking and outdoor events. For green spaces, *see* p.188.

Sights and Museums

While churches and art galleries will have most children sulking and dragging their heels, there are a number of sights which children might find take their fancy.

Acquario Civico E3
Parco Sempione, Via Gadio, **t** *02 8646 2051*; **metro** *Lanza.* **Open** *Tues–Sun 9.30–5.30*; **adm** *free.*
The aquariums here should fascinate little ones; there are 35 tanks of exotic and Mediterranean fish (*see* p.115).

Duomo F5
Piazza del Duomo; **metro** *Duomo.* **Open** *Tues–Sun 9.45–5.45*; **adm** *free; baptistry* **adm** *€1.50 (tickets at the bookshop, closed 1–3pm); treasury and crypt* **adm** *€1. Cathedral roof,* **open** *daily Nov–Feb 9–4.45, Mar–Oct 9–5.45*; **adm** *€3.30 for steps or €5 for the lift from outside the cathedral). Note that the façade will be covered for restoration work until late 2004.*
Milan's enormous cathedral will probably look to most children like something out of one of their fairytales. A trip up to see the view from the top is bound to take their breath away (*see* p.70).

Museo Civico di Storia Naturale H3
Giardini Pubblici, **t** *02 8846 3280*; **metro** *Palestro.* **Open** *Tues–Fri 9–6 and Sat–Sun 9–6.30*; **adm** *free.*
Complete with stuffed animals and stories from prehistory (*see* p.92).

Museo del Giocattolo e del Bambino Off maps
Palazzo Martinitt, Via Petteri 56, **t** *02 2641 1585*; **metro** *Lambrate.* **Open** *Tues–Sun 9.30am–12.30pm, 3–6pm*; **adm** *€4.10, or free for under-14s on Sundays.*
This is one of the largest museums of its type and subject-matter in Europe, offering a

journey through the history of play and playthings. With a beautiful display of over 2,000 toys dating back to 1700, this is another great place to bring the kids; the museum has dolls, teddies and figurines, as well as antique toy soldiers, model railways and dolls' houses.

Museo della Scienza e della Tecnica C–D5
Via S. Vittora 21, **t** *02 4855 5330*; **metro** *Sant'Ambrogio.* **Open** *Tues–Fri 9.30–5 and Sat–Sun 9.30–6.30*; **adm** *€6.20.*
With lots of buttons to push and things to touch, this should make a very satisfactory interactive visit for children (*see* p.122).

Planetarium H3
Corso Venezia 57, **t** *02 2953 1181*, **w** *www.brera.mi.astro.it/~planet*; **metro** *Porta Venezia or Palestro*, **tram** *9, 29 or 30.* **Open** *Mon–Fri 9–12.30 and 2–5.30*; **adm** *free.*
This fascinating place will have children wondering at the stars (*see* p.92).

Sport

For more information on skating rinks and leisure centres, as well as spectator sports, *see* 'Sports and Green Spaces', p.185. The following swimming pools have classes that teach children how to swim:

Piscina Lampugnano Off maps
Via Lampugnano 76, northwest of the city, **t** *02 308 8390*; **metro** *Bonola.*

Swim Education Club Off maps
Via Isimbardi 22, **t** *02 846 5152*; **metro** *Famagosta; and Via Brocchi 7*, **t** *02 7063 5457*; **metro** *Lambrate.*

Theatre

Teatro delle Marionette C5
Via degli Olivetani 3, **t** *02 469 4440*; **metro** *Sant'Ambrogio.*
This is a puppet theatre performing Italian variations on the Punch and Judy theme.

Toys

Avalon H1–2
*Via Settembrini 20, **t** 02 2940 0410;*
***metro** Centrale.*
All the latest merchandizing and
trendy toys in the field of fantasy,
sci-fi and horror.

Imaginarium G5
*Largo Augusto 10, **t** 02 7601 1992;*
***metro** Duomo.*
A branch of the Spanish chain
offering alternative toys from
natural materials.

La Citta 'del Sole F5
*Via Orefici 13, **t** 02 8646 1683;*
***metro** Duomo.*
Traditional toys for bringing
children into touch with nature,
from young ornithology to early
astronomy.

Gay and
Lesbian Milan

Information and Organizations 194

Activities 194

Events 194

Bars and Clubs 194

As would be expected in any city pertaining to be modern and cosmopolitan, Milan is open to homosexuality, even if it is not quite as progressive in this regard as Bologna. Italians are generally a pretty tactile lot; suffice it to say that open declarations of affection, homosexual or heterosexual, are commonplace and accepted.

Over the years Milan has developed a well-known gay scene, with pubs, clubs and bars opening up all over the city, though many of them are concentrated in the streets between the Stazione Centrale and the Stazione di Porta Garibaldi area. These range from ordinary gay meeting points to funky lounge bars and clubs, to hardcore leather joints and gay meeting centres with saunas and swimming pools.

Information and Organizations

The most useful website is the national Italian gay website: *www.gay.it/guida*, which provides city-by-city and regional listings of bars, clubs, festivals, magazines and local organizations.

Italy has two gay organizations, ARCIGay and ARCILesbica. Membership provides access to its associated venues around the country and costs around €30 a year. It can be obtained on the door of one of the clubs, or from the local ARCI offices (*see* below).

Milan also has an association for transsexuals, **ARCI Trans**, contact Deborah Lambillotte on **t** 0335 560 7316.

For further information or assistance:

ARCIGay I5
*Centro d'Iniziativa Gay ArciGay,
Via Bezzecca 3, t 02 541 22 225,
e cigmilano@libero.it, w www.
arcigay.it; metro Porta Romana.*

For information on gay events, and for membership cards (to be allowed entry to most gay clubs

and bars; on the premises is a gay and lesbian interest book and video library.

ArciLesbica E2
*Corso Garibaldi 91, t 02 6311
8654, w http://women.it/arciles;
metro Moscova, bus 41 or 94.
Open for events only. Helpline
(same number, above) open Thurs
7–9pm.*
Italy's main political organisation for lesbians.

Telefono Amico
*t 02 5412 2227. Open Tues
10pm–1am, Wed 9pm–11.30pm,
Thurs 10pm–11pm.*
Gay chat and information lines.

Events

In June every year Milan hosts the five-day **International Gay and Lesbian Film Festival**, which is tied in with Bologna's. Details of the event can be found at **w** *www.cinemagaylesbico.com*, or contact **e** *info@cinemagaylesbico. com*, or the ARCI-Gay Milan office (*see* above).

Activities

For sports, **GATE, t** 0347 263 1440 is a gay volleyball association, and **ATO, t** 0338 366 4921 is a gay tennis association.

Bars and Clubs

Below are listed a number of specifically gay bars and clubs, many of which will only allow you in with an ARCIGay or ARCILesbica pass.

Many other clubs, such as Gasoline, Hollywood and Plastic (*see* 'Nightlife and Entertainment', p.177), put on gay and lesbian nights. It's best, however, to phone ahead for details.

Note that in Italy there is often no real distinction between a bar and a club; most places, apart from normal pubs, are a hybrid of both, serving food, drink and then turning into a place for late-night dancing. Contact ARCI-Gay (*see* above) for an update on the latest venues.

After Line Off maps
*Via Sammartini 25, t 02 669 2130;
metro Centrale, tram 2. Open
9pm–3am.*
Milan's main gay men's disco-bar.

Alexander Cabaret D6
*Via Ronzoni 2, t 02 8940
2330; metro Porta Genova. Ring
ahead for details.*
Gay and straight shows.

Argo's Club Off maps
*Via Resegone 1, t 02 607 2249;
bus 91. Open Sun–Thurs
10pm–3am, Fri–Sat 10pm–6am.*
Gay music, video, drinks and strip shows.

Birreria Uno Alternativa F1
*Via Borsieri 14, off Via de Castillia,
t 02 6900 3271; metro Gioia.
Open Mon–Sat 5pm–3am.*
Gay pub-restaurant.

Cafeole Club Off maps
*Via Chiesa Rossa 69, t 02 846
3041; metro Famagosta. Open
daily 7pm–3am.*
Favourite gay meeting place.

Cicip e Ciciap E5
*Via Gorani 9, t 02 867 202;
metro Missori, tram 9. Open
Wed–Sun 8.30pm–2am.*
Gay club for women only.

Cocksucker Off maps
*Via Derna; metro Cimiano.
Open daily 8pm–2am.*
No words minced, and only leather worn.

Company Bar Off maps
*Via Benadir 14, t 02 282 9481;
metro Cimiano. Open daily
8pm–2am.*
For gays only, with a dark room. ARCI pass needed.

H.D. Off maps
*Via Tajani 11, t 02 718 990; metro
Piola. Open daily 8pm–2am.*
Monday is gay night, with striptease.

Metropolis Off maps
*Via Broni 10, t 02 5681 5570;
tram 24. Open 8.30pm–2am.*
Gay bar with darkroom.

Next Groove Off maps
*Via Sammartini 23 (next to After
Line), t 02 6698 0450; metro
Centrale. Open daily 8pm–2am.*
A gay- and lesbian-only venue.

No Ties Off maps
*Via Giacosa 58, t 02 261 9089;
metro Rovereto. Open daily
8pm–2am.*
ARCI pass only. Gays only.

Nuova Idea F1
*Via de Castilla 30, t 02 6900 7859;
metro Garibaldi. Open daily
8pm–3am.*
Bar-cum-club with live shows on
Thursdays.

One Way Club G5
*Via F. Cavallotti 204, Sesto San
Giovane, t 02 2421341; metro
San Babila. Open 8pm–4am.*
Out of town club for men
only, with dark room. ARCI
pass only.

Querelle F1
*Via de Castillia 8, t 02 683
900; metro Garibaldi. Open
6pm–3am.*
This is one of Milan's oldest
gay and lesbian meeting places.

Recycle 'Mister Sister' Off maps
*Via Calabria 5, t 02 376 1531; bus 90
or 91. Open Wed–Sun 9pm–2am.
Call for details.*
Private club for women only.

Segreta E4
*Piazza Castello 1, t 02 860
3307; metro Cairoli. Open
daily 6pm–2am.*
A bar-club for a younger
gay crowd.

Sottomarino Giallo Off maps
*Via Donatello 2, t 02 2940 104;
metro Loreto. Open 7.30–2am.*
Meaning 'Yellow Submarine';
a venue for women only, with
mixed entry allowed on
Wednesdays and Fridays.

Towanda! Off maps
*Via Imbonati 3, t 02 6900 8868;
bus 41 or 52. Open Tues–Sun
exc Thurs 9pm–1am.*
Gay club.

Transfer Off maps
*Via Breda 158, t 02 2700
5565; metro Precotto. Open daily
10pm–5am.*
A gay meeting centre, with
sauna, swimming pool, dark
room and relaxing lounge
open until dawn. A must for
Saturday nights.

Zip Club B1–C2
*Corso Sempione 76, t 02 331 4904;
metro Cordona. Open daily
7.30pm–2am.*
A favourite for thespian
transvestites.

Festivals

Festivals in Italy are often more show than spirit (there are several exceptions to this rule), but they can add a special note to your holiday. Some are great costume affairs dating back to the Middle Ages or Renaissance; others recall ancient pre-Christian religious practices; and there are a fair number of music festivals, antique fairs and, most of all, festivals devoted to the favourite national pastime – food.

Check with local tourist offices for precise dates: many dates are liable to slide into the nearest weekend.

January

Opera and Ballet Season
Jan–July
Performances held at La Scala (or the Teatro Arcimboldi, *see* p.178).

Three Kings Procession
6 Jan (Epiphany)
Thousands join the procession (locally called La Sfilata dei Re Magi) from the Duomo at 11am to Sant'Eustorio, where the 'relics' of the Three Kings are kept. Many people dress up in 'biblical' attire.

**Musical afternoons
(I pomeriggi musicali)**
Mid-Jan–May
Classical music concerts, held in venues throughout Milan.

Sant'Antonio Fair
17 Jan
With folklore and human chess game, held in Mantua.

I Sarmenti ed I Falò
17 Jan
A festival at Volongo (Cremona), where, in a gigantic fire, all the 'runners' picked up by the young people are 'burnt'. Meanwhile, the women prepare the characteristic *torta dura* (hard cake), aromatized with mint, then offered to all those people present.'

February

Carnivals
throughout the month
This is carnival time, with one at Chignano (Como) with a parade of *bei*, or elegant figures, and *brutt* (ragged ones), ending with a

bonfire. In Milan, there are processions, floats and children's events, stretching to the first Saturday of Lent. San Giovanni Bianco, in Bergamo, home town of the harlequin, has a bonfire of the famous mask, and Bormio also has masks on view.

Ash Wednesday Celebrations
Ash Wednesday
Bigolada celebrations at Castel d'Ario in Mantua, with communal feasting on Wednesday – spaghetti with anchovies in the main piazza.

Lent Celebrations
Lent
Bergamo has the bonfire of the *Vecia*, the old woman, to exorcize winter. Held in Piazza Pontida.

March

Milan Spring Fashion Shows
Early March
The world of fashion descends upon Milan for its spring fashion collections.

Sant'Ambrogio Carnival
Mid-March
Festival for Milan's most influential saint.

Classical Concerts
Mar–April
Classical concerts held at San Maurizio church in Monastero Maggiore.

Flower Market
Easter Monday
Flower market near the convent of Sant'Angelo.

April/May

Re-enactment of the Oath of the Lombard League
9–10 April
A day of historical costumes and pageantry, in Bergamo.

Piano Competition
May
Held in Bergamo.

Palio del Carroccio
May
A medieval parade and horse-race celebrating the defeat of Barbarossa by the Lombard League in 1176, held in Legnano in Milan.

Asparagus Festival and Pig *Palio*
2nd Sun
Speaks for itself. Held in Cilavegna in Pavia.

Corpus Christi Celebrations
May
Processions with decorated streets in Premana in Como.

June

Navigli Festival
4 June
A festival held on the city's medieval canals in Milan.

Pageant
Early June
This historical pageant and flag-tossing commemorates the imprisonment of François Ier, held in Pizzighettone in Cremona.

Festa of San Gerardo
6 June
Feast of patron saint who once rescued the sick during a flood by turning his cloak into a raft, held in Monza.

Festival
23–24 June
A 300-year-old festival, with illuminations in empty nail shells, held on Comacina, and with a boat procession, and folk music in Ossuccio in Como.

Sagra di San Cristoforo
Third Sunday
Feast of the patron saint of drivers, in front of the church of San Cristoforo along the Naviglio Grande.

Limone sul Garda
Last Sun
Fish, wine, and dancing in San Pietro.

Canto delle Pietre
June-Oct
Medieval music festival in Como and province.

July

Festa della Madonna della Foppa
2 July
Festival marking an apparition of the Virgin in Gerosa, Bergamo.

Piazza di Spagna Fair
Early July
With concerts, fireworks and donkey races in Casalmaggiore, Cremona.

Feast of the Big Noses
Early July
With prizes for the biggest and strangest schnozes, in Gromo, Bergamo.

Melon Festival
29–30 July
Held at Casteldidone in Cremona.

August

Vacanze a Milano
Throughout the month
Theatre and musical events.

Osei Fair
2nd Sun
Hunting dogs, decoys, and nightingale imitations, at Almenno San Salvatore in Bergamo.

Ferragosto
15 August
Holiday marked by the exhibition of the *madonnari*, pavement artists, in Mantua.

Settimane Musicali
End Aug–Sept
Musical weeks at Stresa on Lake Maggiore.

September

Italian Grand Prix
Second Sunday
The international motor-racing championship, held in neighbouring Monza.

Palio Baradello
First half
Held in Como, this festival commemorates the victory of Barbarossa against Milan: costume parade and competitions between the boroughs of Como and surrounding towns, featuring horse races and rowing races in traditional boats.

Milano Film Festival
Mid–late Sept
Includes art exhibitions, live music, performances and workshops.

Horse *Palio*
2nd Sun
With Renaissance costumes at Isola Dovarese in Cremona.

Feast of the Missoltino
2nd Sun
Feast of sun-dried fish in Mezzagra in Como. Polenta feasting and election of the 'Big Pot of Italy' (whoever eats the most sausages), at Corno Giovine in Milan.

Bean Feast
3rd Sun
Dancing and handicrafts, held in Gaverina Terme in Bergamo.

October–November

Organ Concerts
Oct–Nov
Classical organ concerts held at San Maurizio in Monastero Maggiore, Milan.

Spring Fashion Collections
Early Oct
The *fashionistas* arrive in Milan for the catwalk shows once again.

Festa della Madonna del Rosario
1st Sun
Held in Montodine in Cremona, with illuminated procession of boats down the River Serio and fireworks, and duck and macaroni feasting at San Benedetto Po in Mantua.

Donkey *Palio*
3rd Sun
Palio and events at Mezzana Bigli in Pavia.

Feast of Chicory
3rd Sun
Festival held in Soncino in Cremona.

December

Stagione di Prosa, Brescia
Dec–April
A range of theatrical performances throughout the year.

Feast of Sant'Ambrogio
7 Dec
Feast day of Milan's patron saint, Sant'Ambrogio (Saint Ambrose).

'O Bei O Bei' antique market
7 Dec
Held in Milan's Piazza Sant'Ambrogio.

Opera Season
7 Dec
La Scala opera season opens.

Torchlight Procession of the Shepherds
Christmas Eve
Held at Canneto dell'Oglio in Mantua.

Language

Pronunciation 200

Basic Vocabulary 200

Eating Out 201

The fathers of modern Italian were Dante, Manzoni, and television. Each did their part in creating a national language from an infinity of regional and local dialects; the Florentine Dante, the first 'immortal' to write in the vernacular, did much to put the Tuscan dialect in the foreground of Italian literature. Manzoni's revolutionary novel, *I Promessi Sposi* (The Betrothed), heightened national consciousness by using an everyday language all could understand in the 19th century. Television in the last few decades is performing an even more spectacular linguistic unification; although the majority of Italians still speak a dialect at home, school and at work, their TV idols still insist on proper Italian.

Perhaps because they are so busy learning their own beautiful but grammatically complex language, Italians are not especially apt at learning others. English lessons, however, have been the rage for years, and at most hotels and restaurants there will be someone who speaks some English. In small towns and out of the way places, finding an Anglophone may prove more difficult.

The words and phrases below should help you out in most situations, but the ideal way to come to Italy is with some Italian under your belt; your visit will be richer, and you're much more likely to make some Italian friends.

Pronunciation

Italian words are pronounced phonetically. Every vowel and consonant is sounded. Most consonants are the same as in English, exceptions are the **c** which, when followed by an 'e' or 'i', is pronounced like the English 'ch' (*cinque* thus becomes cheen-quay). Italian **g** is also soft before 'i' or 'e' as in *giro*, or jee-roh. **H** is never sounded; **r** is trilled, like the Scottish 'r'; **z** is pronounced like 'ts' or 'ds'. The consonants **sc** before

the vowels 'i' or 'e' become like the English 'sh'; **ch** is pronouced like a 'k' as in Chianti; **gn** as 'nya' (thus *bagno* is pronounced ban-yo); while **gli** is pronounced like the middle of the word 'million' (Castiglione, pronounced Ca-stil-yohn-ay).

Vowel pronunciation is as follows: **a** is as in English father; **e** when unstressed is pronounced like 'a' in fate as in *padre*, when stressed it can be the same or like the 'e' in pet (*bello*); **i** is like the 'i' in machine; **o** like 'e', has two sounds, 'o' as in hope when unstressed (*tacchino*), and usually 'o' as in rock when stressed (*morte*), **u** is pronounced like the 'u' in June.

The stress usually (but not always!) falls on the penultimate syllable. Also note that, in Milan, the informal way of addressing someone as you, *tu*, is widely used; the more formal *lei* or *voi* is commonly used in provincial districts.

Basic Vocabulary

Common Expressions
yes/no/maybe *si/no/forse*
I don't know *Non lo so*
I don't understand (Italian) *Non capisco (italiano)*
Does someone here speak English? *C'è qualcuno qui che parla inglese?*
Speak slowly *Parla lentamente*
Could you assist me? *Potrebbe aiutarmi?*
Help! *Aiuto!*
Please *Per favore*
Thanks (very much) *(Molto) grazie*
You're welcome *Prego*
It doesn't matter *Non importa*
All right *Va bene*
Excuse me *Mi scusi*
Be careful! *Attenzione!*
Nothing *Niente*
It is urgent! *E urgente!*
How are you? *Come stai? (informal) / sta? (formal)*
Well, and you? *Bene, e tu? (informal) / Bene, e Lei? (formal)*
What is your name? *Come si chiama, Lei?*
Hello *Salve or ciao (both informal)*

Good morning *Buon giorno (formal hello)*
Good afternoon (also evening) *Buona sera (formal hello)*
Goodnight *Buona notte*
Goodbye *ArrivederLa (formal)/ Arrivederci (informal)*
What do you call this in Italian? *Come si chiama questo in italiano?*
What? *Che cosa?*
Who? *Chi?*
Where? *Dove?*
When? *Quando?*
Why? *Perché?*
How? *Come?*
How much? *Quanto?*
I am lost *Mi sono smarrito*
I am hungry *Ho fame*
I am thirsty *Ho sete*
I am sorry *Mi dispiace*
I am tired *Sono stanco*
I am sleepy *Ho sonno*
I am ill *Mi sento male*
Leave me alone *Lasciami in pace*
good *buono/bravo*
bad *male/cattivo*
It's all the same *Fa lo stesso*
slow *lento/piano*
fast *rapido*
big *grande*
small *piccolo*
hot *caldo*
cold *freddo*
up *su*
down *giù*
here *qui*
there *lì*

Shopping, Service and Sightseeing
I would like ... *Vorrei ...*
Where is/are?... *Dov'è/Dove sono?...*
How much is it? *Quanto via questo?*
open *aperto*
closed *chiuso*
cheap *a buon mercato*
expensive *caro*
bank *banca*
beach *spiaggia*
bed *letto*
church *chiesa*
entrance *entrata*
exit *uscita*
hospital *ospedale*
money *soldi*
museum *museo*

newspaper (foreign) *giornale (straniero)*
chemist *farmacia*
police station *commissariato*
policeman *poliziotto*
post office *ufficio postale*
sea *mare*
shop *negozio*
telephone *telefono*
tobacco shop *tabacchaio*
WC *toilette/bagno*
   men *Signori/Uomini*
   women *Signore/Donne*

Time

What time is it? *Che ore sono?*
month *mese*
week *settimana*
day *giorno*
morning *mattina*
afternoon *pomeriggio*
evening *sera*
today *oggi*
yesterday *ieri*
tomorrow *domani*
soon *fra poco*
later *più tardi*
It is too early *E troppo presto*
It is too late *E troppo tardi*

Days

Monday *lunedì*
Tuesday *martedì*
Wednesday *mercoledì*
Thursday *giovedì*
Friday *venerdì*
Saturday *sabato*
Sunday *domenica*

Months

January *gennaio*
February *febbraio*
March *marzo*
April *aprile*
May *maggio*
June *giugno*
July *luglio*
August *agosto*
September *settembre*
October *ottobre*
November *novembre*
December *dicembre*

Numbers

one *uno/una*
two *due*
three *tre*
four *quattro*
five *cinque*
six *sei*

seven *sette*
eight *otto*
nine *nove*
ten *dieci*
eleven *undici*
twelve *dodici*
thirteen *tredici*
fourteen *quattordici*
fifteen *quindici*
sixteen *sedici*
seventeen *diasette*
eighteen *diciotto*
nineteen *diciannove*
twenty *venti*
twenty-one *ventuno*
twenty-two *ventidue*
thirty *trenta*
thirty-one *trentuno*
forty *quaranta*
fifty *cinquanta*
sixty *sessanta*
seventy *settanta*
eighty *ottanta*
ninety *novanta*
hundred *cento*
one hundred and one *cent'uno*
two hundred *due cento*
thousand *mille*
two thousand *due mila*
million *milione*
billion *miliardo*

Transport

airport *aeroporto*
bus stop *fermata*
bus/coach *autobus/pulmino*
car *macchina*
customs *dogana*
port *porto*
port station *stazione maritimma*
railway station *stazione (ferroviaria)*
seat (reserved) *posto (prenotato)*
ship *nave*
taxi *tassi*
ticket *biglietto*
train *treno*
train/platform *binario*

Travel directions

I want to go to... *Voglio andare a...*
How can I get to...? *Come posso arrivare a ...?*
The next stop, please *La prossima fermata, per favore*
Where is ... /where is it? *Dove ... / Dov'è?*
How far is it to ...? *Quanto siamo lontani da ... ?*

What is the name of this station? *Come si chiama questa stazione?*
When does the next train leave? *Quando parte il prossimo treno?*
From where does it leave? *Da dove parte?*
How long does the trip take? *Quanto tempo dura il viaggio?*
How much is the fare? *Quant'è il biglietto?*
Have a good trip! *Buon viaggio!*
near *vicino*
far *lontano*
left *sinistra*
right *destra*
straight ahead *sempre diritto*
forward *avanti*
back *indietro*
north *nord/settentrionale (the North of Italy)*
south *sud/mezzogiorno (the South of Italy)*
east *est/oriente*
west *ovest/occidentale*
around the corner *dietro l'angolo*
crossroads *bivio*
street/road *strada*
square *piazza*

Useful Hotel Vocabulary

I'd like a single/double room please *Vorrei una camera singola/doppia, per favore*
with bath, without bath *con bagno, senza bagno*
for two nights *per due notti*
May I see the room, please? *Posso vedere la camera?*
May I pay by credit card? *Posso pagare con carta di credito?*
May I see another room please? *Per favore potrei vedere un'altra camera?*
Fine, I'll take it *Bene, la prendo*
Is breakfast included? *E' compresa la prima colazione?*
What time do you serve breakfast? *A che ora è la colazione?*

Eating Out

Antipasti

These before-meal treats can include almost anything; among the most common are:

antipasto misto mixed antipasto
bruschetta garlic toast (sometimes with tomatoes)

carciofi (sott'olio) artichokes (in oil)
frutti di mare seafood
funghi (trifolati) mushrooms (with anchovies, garlic, lemon)
gamberi ai fagioli prawns (shrimps) with white beans
mozzarella (in carrozza) cow or buffalo cheese (fried with bread in batter)
prosciutto (con melone) raw ham (with melon)
salsicce sausages
minestre (Soups) and Pasta

First Courses – Primi

agnolotti ravioli with meat
cacciucco spiced fish soup
cappelletti small ravioli, in broth
crespelle crêpes
frittata omelette
gnocchi potato dumplings
orecchiette ear-shaped pasta, often served with turnip greens
panzerotti ravioli filled with mozzarella, anchovies, and egg
pappardelle alla lepre pasta with hare sauce
pasta e fagioli soup with beans, bacon, and tomatoes
pastina in brodo tiny pasta in broth
penne all'arrabbiata quill-shaped pasta with tomatoes and hot peppers
risotto (alla milanese) Italian rice (with stock, saffron and wine)
spaghetti all'amatriciana with spicy sauce of salt pork, tomatoes, onions, and chilli
spaghetti alla carbonara with bacon, eggs, and black pepper
spaghetti al sugo/ragù with meat sauce
spaghetti alle vongole with clam sauce
stracciatella broth with eggs and cheese
tortellini al pomodoro/panna/in brodo pasta caps filled with meat and cheese/with tomato sauce/with cream/in broth

Second Courses – Carne (Meat)

abbacchio milk-fed lamb
agnello lamb
animelle sweetbreads
anatra duck

arista pork loin
arrosto misto mixed roast meats
bocconcini veal mixed with ham and cheese and fried
bollito misto stew of boiled meats
braciola chop
brasato di manzo braised beef with vegetables
bresaola dried raw meat similar to ham
carne di castrato/suino mutton/pork
carpaccio thin slices of raw beef served with a piquant sauce
cassoeula winter stew with pork and cabbage
cervello (al burro nero) brains (in black butter sauce)
cervo venison
cinghiale boar
coniglio rabbit
cotoletta (alla milanese/alla bolognese) veal cutlet (fried in breadcrumbs/with ham and cheese)
fagiano pheasant
faraona (alla creta) guinea fowl (in earthenware pot)
fegato alla veneziana liver (usually of veal) with filling
lombo di maiale pork loin
Lumache snails
maiale (al latte) pork (cooked in milk)
manzo beef
osso buco braised veal knuckle with herbs
pancetta rolled pork
pernice partridge
petto di pollo (sorpresa) boned chicken breast (stuffed and deep fried)
piccione pigeon
pizzaiola beef steak with tomato and oregano sauce
pollo (alla cacciatora/alla diavola/alla marengo) chicken (with tomatoes and mushrooms/grilled/fried with tomatoes, garlic and wine)
polpette meatballs
quaglie quails
rane frogs
rognoni kidneys
saltimbocca veal scallop with *prosciutto*, sage, wine, butter
scaloppine thin slices of veal sautéed in butter

spezzatino pieces of beef or veal, usually stewed
spiedino meat on a skewer or stick
stufato beef braised in white wine with vegetables
tacchino turkey
vitello veal

Formaggio (Cheese)

bel paese a soft white cow's cheese
cacio/caciocavallo pale yellow, often sharp cheese
fontina rich cow's milk cheese
groviera mild cheese (gruyère)
gorgonzola soft blue cheese
mozzarella soft cheese
parmigiano Parmesan cheese
pecorino sharp sheep's cheese
provolone sharp, tangy cheese; *dolce* is less strong
ricotta creamy white cheese
stracchino soft white cheese

Pesce (Fish)

acciughe or *alici* anchovies
anguilla eel
aragosta lobster
aringhe herrings
baccalà salt cod
bonito small tuna
branzino sea bass
calamari squid
conchiglie scallops
cefalo grey mullet
cozze mussels
datteri di mare razor (or date) mussels
dentice dentex (perch-like fish)
fritto misto mixed fish fry, with squid and shrimp
gamberetto shrimp
gamberi prawns
granchio crab
insalata di mare seafood salad
lampre lamprey
merluzzo cod
nasello hake
orata/dorata gilthead
ostriche oysters
pesce azzuro various small fish
pesce S. Pietro John Dory
pesce spada swordfish
polipi octopus
rombo turbot
sarde sardines
seppie cuttlefish
sgombro mackerel

sogliola sole
squadro monkfish
tonno tuna
triglia red mullet (*rouget*)
trota trout
trota salmonata salmon trout
vongole small clams
zuppa di pesce mixed fish in sauce or stew

Contorni (Side Dishes, Vegetables)

asparagi (alla Fiorentina) asparagus (with fried eggs)
broccoli (calabrese, romana) broccoli (green, spiral)
carciofi (alla giudia) artichokes (deep fried)
cardi cardoons, thistles
carote carrots
cavolfiore cauliflower
cavolo cabbage
ceci chickpeas
cetriolo cucumber
cipolla onion
fagioli white beans
fagiolini French (green) beans
fave broad beans
finocchio fennel
funghi (porcini) mushroom (boletus)
insalata salad
lattuga lettuce
lenticchie lentils
melanzane (al forno) aubergine/ eggplant (filled and baked)
patate (fritte) potatoes (fried)
peperonata stewed peppers, onions and tomatoes
peperoni sweet peppers
piselli peas
pomodoro tomato
porri leeks
radicchio red chicory
ravanelli radishes
rapa turnip
sedano celery
spinaci spinach
verdure greens
zucca pumpkin
zucchini courgettes

Frutta (Fruit, Nuts)

albicocche apricots
ananas pineapple
arance oranges
banane bananas
cachi persimmon
ciliege cherries

composta di frutta stewed fruit
dattero date
fichi figs
fragole strawberries
frutta di stagione fruit in season
lamponi raspberries
macedonia di frutta fruit salad
mandarino tangerine
mandorle almonds
mele apples
melone melon
more blackberries
nespola medlar fruit
nocciole hazelnuts
noci walnuts
pera pear
pesca peach
pesca noce nectarine
pompelmo grapefruit
pignoli pine nuts
prugna secca prune
susina plum
uve grapes

Dolci (Desserts)

amaretti macaroons
coppa assorted ice cream
crema caramella crème caramel
crostata fruit flan
gelato (produzione propria) ice cream (homemade)
granita flavoured ice, usually lemon or coffee
panettone sponge cake with candied fruit and raisins
panforte dense cake of chocolate, almonds and preserved fruit
Saint Honoré meringue cake
semifreddo refrigerated cake
sorbetto sorbet
spumone a soft ice cream or mousse
tiramisù mascarpone, coffee, chocolate and sponge fingers
torrone nougat
torta tart
torta millefoglie layered custard tart
zabaglione whipped eggs, sugar and Marsala wine, served hot
zuppa inglese trifle

Bevande (Beverages)

acqua minerale con/senza gas mineral water sparkling/still
aranciata orange soda
birra (alla spina) beer (draught)
caffè (freddo) coffee (iced)
cioccolata hot chocolate

latte (magro) milk (skimmed)
limonata lemon soda
sugo di frutta fruit juice
tè tea
vino (rosso, bianco, rosato) wine (red, white, rosé)

Cooking Terms, Miscellaneous

aceto (balsamico) vinegar (balsamic)
affumicato smoked
aglio garlic
ai ferri grilled
al forno baked
alla brace braised
arrosto roasted
bicchiere glass
burro butter
cacciagione game
conto bill
costoletta/cotoletta chop
coltello knife
cucchiaio spoon
filetto fillet
forchetta fork
forno oven
fritto fried
ghiaccio ice
limone lemon
magro lean meat/or pasta without meat
marmellata jam
miele honey
mostarda sweet mustard sauce, served with meat
olio oil
pane (tostato) bread (toasted)
panini sandwiches
panna fresh cream
pepe pepper
peperoncini hot chilli peppers
piatto plate
prezzemolo parsley
rosmarino rosemary
sale salt
salmi wine marinade
salsa sauce
salvia sage
senape mustard
tartufi truffles
tazza cup
tavola table
tovagliolo napkin
tramezzini finger sandwiches
in umido stewed
uovo egg
zucchero sugar

Index

Numbers in **bold** indicate main references. Numbers in *italic* indicate maps.

Abbazia di Chiaravalle 103–4
AC Milan 186
Academy of Fists 27
Accademia Carrara (Bergamo)
    141–2
accommodation *see* hotels;
    where to stay
Acquario Civico **115**, 191
Adelheid 22–3
airlines 44–6
airports 49–50
Aistulf, king 22
Albi di Milano 94
Alboin, king 21
Alexander III 24
Alexander VI 27
Ambrose, Saint 120–2
Ambrosiana 68, **78–9**
Amfiteatro Romano 108
antiques 184
Andreotti, Giulio 34
Archeology museum 119
Archeology museum
    (Bergamo) 144
Archi di Porta Nuova 90
Arcimboldi theatre 76
Arcimboldo, Giuseppe 39
Arco della Pace 115
Armani 132, 182
art and architecture **36–42**
    Art Nouveau 41
    Baroque 39–40
    Celtic-Romano 36
    Fascist 41
    Futurists 41
    Gothic 36–7
    Neoclassicism 40–1
    Renaissance 37–9
    Romanesque 36–7
    20th Century 41–2
Arte e Pinacoteca
    del Castello 114–15
Arte Moderna
    gallery 41–2, **91–2**
Astronomico di Brera 85–6
athletics 187
Attila the Hun 21
Aurea Respubblica Ambrosiana 26
Austrian rule 29

babysitting services 190
Bagatti Valsecchi 83, **91**, 133

Banca Commerciale Italiano 68, **76**
banks 59–60
    opening hours 61
Barbarossa 23–4
Baroque art and architecture
    39–40
bars 163, 174–7, 194–5
Basiliche, Parco delle 108, 129
basketball 186, 187
Bastioni di Porta Venezia 94
Beatrice d'Este 26
Beccaria, Cesare 27–8
Bellini, Giovanni 85, 89, 114
Benedetto, Giovanni 100
Berengar II, Marquis of Ivrea 23
Bergamo 141–4, *142*
Bergognone 39
Berlusconi, Silvio 34
bicycling 51, 186, 187
Black Death 25, 99
boating 187
bookshops 182, 190
Borgia, Cesare 27
Borromean Islands 138, **139**
Borromeo, Carlo 28, 99
Borromeo, Federico 28–9, 99
Borsa stock exchange 68, **78**
Bossi, Umberto 33
Bramante, Donato 38
breakfast 162
Brera and the Northeast
    82–94, *83*
    bars 174–5
    Corso Garibaldi 88
    food and drink 82, 83, 164–8
    Giardini Pubblici **91–4**, 188
    highlights 83
    Pinacoteca di Brera 83,
        84–5
    Pirellone 41, 82, **94**
    Quadrilatero d'Oro 82, 83,
        90–1, 130, 133
    Stazione Centrale 82, **94**
    Via Manzoni 82, **88–90**
    where to stay 155–60
bribery and corruption 32–3
Brueghel, Jan, the Younger 79
Brunate 141
buses and coaches 47, 50–1, 52

Caffè, Il 27–8
caffès *see* restaurants/lunches

Ca' Grande 96, 97, **98**
canals 106, **110**, 126
    Naviglio Grande 110, 126, 128–9
    Naviglio della Martesana 88
    Naviglio Pavese 110, 126, 129
    walk 126–9
Caravaggio 39, 79, 85
cars 47–8, 51, 66
*Cartoon for the
    School of Athens* 79
Casa Bettoni 98
Casa Fontana-Silvestri 92–3
Casa Galimberti 93–4
Casa del Manzoni 69, **77**, 132
Casa degli Omenoni 39, **77**
Casa Panigarola 74
Casa Rustici 116
Casa Toscanini 100
Castello Sforzesco 112, **114–15**
Castello Visconti (Pavia) 146
Castiglione, Giovanni
    Benedetto 100
Celtic-Romano art and
    architecture 36
Centre **68–80**, *69*
    bars 174
    Financial District 68, **78–80**
    food and drink 68, 69, 164
    highlights 69
    Piazza del Duomo 68,
        70–5, 132
    Piazza della Scala 68, **75–8**, 133
    where to stay 154–5
Certosa Garegnano 124
Certosa di Pavia (Pavia) 147
Charlemagne, emperor 22
Charles of Anjou 24
Charles V, emperor 28
Charles VIII of France 27
chemists 57
Chiaravalle abbey 103–4
Chiesa, Mario 33
children's Milan 190–2
Christian Democrats 31, 34
churches
    concerts in 179
    opening hours 61
Cimitero Monumentale 123
cinema 179–80, 190
Cinema museum 92
Cinque Giornate revolt 30
Cisalpine Republic 29

Civici Musei d'Arte e Pinacoteca
    del Castello 114–15
Civico museum (Como) 140–1
Civico museum (Pavia) 146
classical music 178
Clean Hands investigation 33, 101
climate 54
climbing 187
clothes shops 182–3, 190
clubs 177, 194–5
    jazz clubs 178–9
coaches and buses 47, 50–1, 52
Colleoni Chapel (Bergamo) 144
Collezionista d'Arte 116
Colonna del Verziere 100
Como 139–41
comune 23–4, 25
conca fallato 129
Congress of Vienna 29
Conservatorio di Musica
    Giuseppe Verdi 102
Constantine the Great 20
consulates 56
Convento di Sant'Angelo 88
Corinthian columns 108, 127, 134
corruption 32–3
Corso Garibaldi 88
Corso Italia 102–3
Corso Magenta 112, 116
Corso Matteotti 132
Corso di Porta Romana 98
Corso di Porta Ticinese 107, 128, 133
Corso San Gottardo 129
Corso Sempione 112, 115–16
Corso Venezia 92–4
Corso Vittorio Emanuele II 74
Council of Trent 28
credit cards 60
Cremona 147–50, 148
crime 54
Criminologia museum 122
Crusades 23
customs formalities 49
cycling 51, 186, 187

Darsena 110, 128
day trips 136–52
    Bergamo 141–4, 142
    Cremona 147–50, 148
    Lake Como 139–41
    Lake Maggiore 138–9
    Mantua (Mantova) 150–2
    Monza 136–7, 136–8
    Pavia 145–7
department stores 183
Diocesano museum 109
Diocletian, Emperor 20
disabled travellers 55–6

Donizettiano museum
    (Bergamo) 144
Duomo (Bergamo) 144
Duomo (Como) 140
Duomo (Cremona) 149–50
Duomo (Milan) 70–3, 191
Duomo (Monza) 136–7
Duomo (Pavia) 145–6
duty-free allowances 49
duty-free shopping 56

E111 forms 57
Edict of Milan 20
El Greco 85
electricity 56
embassies 56
emergencies 57–8
entertainment see nightlife
    and entertainment
entrance charges 62, 63
entry formalities 49
Esposizione Permanente delle
    Belle Arti 92
etiquette 56–7
Etro 133
Eurotunnel 47
ex-Seminario Arcivescovile 93

Famine 29
Fascism 30–1
    art and architecture 41
fashion industry 90, 93, 130
fax facilities 62–3
Fernet Branca Tower 115
ferries 47–8
festivals 197–8
    Monza 136
Fiera di Milano 123
Filarete 38
film 179–80, 190
Financial District 68, 78–80
first-aid posts 57
flat rentals 65–6
food and drink
    bars 163, 174–7, 194–5
    breakfast 162
    with children 190–1
    hot table 163
    lunch 162
    menu guide 201–3
    osteria 162
    saffron 162
    shopping 183
    snacks 163
    specialities 163
    trattoria 162
    vegetarians 169
    wine 175

food and drink (cont'd)
    see also restaurants/lunches
football 186, 187
Foppa, Vincenzo 38–9
Forlanini park 188
Fornovo, battle of 27
Foro Buonaparte 116
Forza Italia 34
Franks 22
Frederick I Barbarossa 23–4
Frederick II 24
French and Spanish wars 27–9
Futurists 41

Galleria d'Arte Moderna 41–2,
    91–2
Galleria San Carlo 132
Galleria Vittorio Emanuele II 41,
    68, 73–4, 133
gardens see parks and gardens
Garibaldi, Giuseppe 30
gay Milan 194–5
Ghibellines 24–5
Giardini Pubblici 91–4, 188
Giardino della Guastalla 100
Giocattolo e del Bambino 191
Gothic art and architecture 36–7
Goths 21–2
Grand Hotel et de Milan 88, 89, 155
Great Famine 29
green spaces, see parks and
    gardens
Gregory VII, pope 23
Guardi, Francesco 89
Gucci 133, 183
Guelphs 24–5
guided tours 52

Habsburgs 29
health 57–8
Heribert, bishop 23
Hildebrand (later Gregory VII) 23
hiring a car 51
history 19–34
    Austrian rule 29
    Black Death 25, 99
    chronology 32–3
    comune 23–4, 25
    Crusades 23
    Fascism 30–1
    Franks 22
    French and Spanish wars 27–9
    Goths 21–2
    Guelphs and Ghibellines 24–5
    Italian unification 29–30
    Lombards 21–2
    Middle Ages 22–3
    Napoleon Bonaparte 29

history (cont'd)
  post-war politics 31–4
  Romans 20–1
horse-racing 186
hot table 163
hotels
  Brera and the Northeast 155–60
  Centre 154–5
  with children 190–1
  Grand Hotel et de Milan 88, 89, 155
  Navigli District 160
  Ticinese District 160
  University and the Southeast 160
  West End 160
household goods, shopping 184

I Promessi Sposi 77, 99
ice-skating 187
Il Caffè 27–8
insurance 57
Inter Milan 186
International Gothic art and architecture 37
internet access 58–9
Isola Bella 139
Isola Madre 139
Isola dei Pescatore 139
Italian unification 29–30

jazz clubs 178–9
Jesi, Donazione 84
jewellery shops 184
job hunting 65
Joseph II of Austria 29

La Scala 75–6
  museum 119
Lake Como 139–41
Lake Maggiore 138–9
language 200–3
Largo Augusto 100
Last Supper 39, 117–18
late night shopping 184
launderettes 59
Law Courts 100–1
Leonardo da Vinci 26, 79, 114, 123
  horse sculpture 117
  Last Supper 39, 117–18
  museum 122
Leoni, Leone 77
lesbian Milan 194–5
Linate airport 49
lingerie shops 183
Litta theatre 119
Liutprand, king 22
Lodovico il Moro 26–7

Loggia dei Militi (Cremona) 150
Loggia degli Osii 74
Lombard League 24
Lombard League (political party) 34
Lombard Romanesque art and architecture 36
Lombards 21–2
long stays 65–6
lost property 59
Louis XII of France 27
Luini, Bernardino 39
lunch see food and drink; restaurants/lunches

Maggiore, lake
Magnasco, Alessandro 79
Magyars 22
Malpensa airport 49–50
Manfred, King of Sicily 24
Mangone, Fabio 40
Mantegna, Andrea 85, 89
Mantua (Mantova) 150–2
Manzoni, Alessandro 30, 68, 69, 77
  I Promessi Sposi 77, 99
  monument 77
Manzoniano 77
marathon 188
Maria Theresa of Austria 29
Marinaro Ugo Mursia 91
Marini, Mariano 41–2, 91–2
markets 128, 184
  Naviglio Grande 106, 110, 128
Marriage of the Virgin 84
Marshall Plan 31
Martian Canals 86
Meazza (San Siro) Stadium 124, 186
media 59
  sports reading 188
Mediolanum 20, 36
Mengoni, Giuseppe 73
menu guide 201–3
Metaphysical Fountain 115
metro 51
Michelangelo 114
Middle Ages 22–3
Milano museum 91
Minguzzi museum 87
money 59–60
Monte Mottarone 138–9
Monte Stella park 188
Monza 136–7, 136–8
motor-racing 187
Motorail 48
Mottarone 138–9

museums
  Accademia Carrara (Bergamo) 141–2
  Ambrosiana 68, **78–9**
  Archeologico 119
  Archeologico (Bergamo) 144
  Bagatti Valsecchi 83, **91**, 133
  Castello Sforzesco 112, **114–15**
  for children 191
  Cinema 92
  Civici Musei d'Arte e Pinacoteca del Castello 114–15
  Civico (Como) 140–1
  Civico (Pavia) 146
  Collezionista d'Arte 116
  Criminologia 122
  Diocesano 109
  Donizettiano (Bergamo) 144
  Duomo 73
  entrance charges 62, 63
  Esposizione Permanente delle Belle Arti 92
  Galleria d'Arte Moderna 41–2, **91–2**
  Giocattolo e del Bambino 191
  La Scala museum 119
  Leonardo da Vinci 122
  Manzoniano 77
  Marinaro Ugo Mursia 91
  Milano 91
  Minguzzi 87
  Musical Instruments 115
  opening hours 61
  Palazzo Reale 68, 69, **73**
  Pinacoteca di Brera 83, **84–5**
  Poldi-Pezzoli 88–9
  Risorgimento 87
  Sant'Ambrogio 121
  Scienza e Tecnica **122**, 191
  Scienze Naturale (Bergamo) 144
  Storia Contemporanea 91
  Storia Naturale **92**, 191
  Vismara collection 91
music 178–9, 182
Musical Instruments museum 115
Mussolini, Benito 30–1

Napoleon Bonaparte 29
Navigli District 107, 110, 127
  bars 176
  food and drink 106, 107, 169–72
  highlights 107
  walk 126–9
  where to stay 160
Naviglio Grande 106, 110, 126, 128–9
Naviglio della Martesana 88
Naviglio Pavese 110, 126, 129

Neoclassicism 40–1
newspapers 59
  sports reading 188
nightlife and entertainment
  174–80
  bars 174–7, 194–5
  for children 191
  classical music 178
  clubs 177, 194–5
  film 179–80, 190
  jazz clubs 178–9
  opera 75–6, 178
  pop concerts 179
  theatre 179, 191
Nobu 132, 164
Nord, Parco 188

Odoacer 21
Olivetti 31
opening hours 61–2
opera 178
  La Scala 75–6
Ospedale Maggiore 98
Osservatorio di Brera 85–6
Otto the Great 23

packing 62
palazzi
  Annoni 98
  Arcivesovile 73
  d'Arco (Mantua) 152
  Banca Commerciale
    Italiano 68, **76**
  Belgioioso **77**, 132
  Bigli 91
  Bolognini 91
  Borromeo 80
  Borromeo d'Adda 89
  Castiglione 41
  Clerici 76
  Comune (Cremona) 150
  Cusani 86
  Ducale (Mantua) 151–2
  Dugnani 92
  Durini 100
  Giureconsulti 74
  Giustizia 100–1
  Isimbardi 102
  Litta 119
  Marina 68
  Marino 76
  Municipale 76
  Ragione 23, 36, **74**
  Ragione (Bergamo) 144
  Reale 68, 69, **73**
  Rocca-Saporiti 92
  Scuole Palatine 74
  Sormani Andreani 100

palazzi (cont'd)
  Stelline 116
  Tè (Mantua) 152
  Terragni (Como) 140
parks and gardens 188, 191
  Giardini Pubblici **91–4**, 188
  Giardino della Guastalla 100
  Parco delle Basiliche 108, 129
  Parco Forlanini 188
  Parco Monte Stella 188
  Parco Nord 188
  Parco Sempione 115–16
  Parco Solari 188
passports 49
Pavia 145–7
Pax Romana 20
Peace of the Pigheads 24
Pelizza da Volpedo 92
perfumeries 184
photography 62
Piazza del Duomo 68, **70–5**, 132
Piazza Fontana 73
Piazza Liberty 132
Piazza del Liberty 74
Piazza Mercanti 74
Piazza Missori 98
Piazza San Fedele 132
Piazza della Scala 68, **75–8**, 133
Piazza della Vetra 108, 127–8
Piazza XXIV Maggio 128
pickpockets 54
Piermarini, Giuseppe 41
Piero della Francesca 84–5
Pietro, Antonio di 32
Pinacoteca di Brera **84–5**
Pirelli Building 41, 82, **94**
plague 99
Planetarium **92**, 191
Poldi-Pezzoli 88–9
police 54
politics 31–4
Ponti, Gio 93
  Fernet Branca Tower 115
pop concerts 179
Porta Genova train
    station 129
Porta Orientale 94
Porta Ticinese 128
Portoni di Porta Ticinese 108
post offices 62–3
post-war politics 31–4
practical A–Z **54–66**
Prada 133
Prodi, Romano 34
Promessi Sposi, I 77, 99
public holidays 61
purse-snatchers 54

Quadrilatero d'Oro 82, 83, **90–1**,
    130, 133

Radetzky, Marshal 30
radio 59
railways 46–7, 50, 52
  Porta Genova train station 129
  Stazione Centrale 82, **94**
Raphael
  *Cartoon for the
    School of Athens* 79
  Marriage of the Virgin 84
registration for residency 65
Rembrandt 85
Renaissance 37–9
renting a flat 65–6
residency 65
restaurants/lunches **162–72**,
    166–7, 170–1
  Bergamo 143
  Borromean Islands 138
  Brera and the Northeast 82,
    83, 164–8
  Centre 68, 69, 164
  with children 190–1
  Como 140
  Cremona 149
  Mantua 151
  menu guide 201–3
  Monza 136
  Navigli District 110, 169–72
  Pavia 145
  Stresa 138
  Ticinese District 108–9, 169–72
  tipping 64
  University and the Southeast
    96, 97, 168
  vegetarians 169
  West End 112, 172
  see also food and drink
reucci 22
Ricchino, Francesco Maria 40
Ripa di Porta Ticinese 129
Risorgimento 29–30
  museum 87
Roman Corinthian columns 108,
    127, 134
Romanesque art and
    architecture 36–7
Romans 20–1
Rosmunda, queen 21
Rotonda della Besana 101
rugby 187
running 188

saffron 162
San Bartolomeo (Bergamo) 141
San Bernardino alle Ossa 100

San Bernardino alle
  Monache 122–3
San Carlo 74–5
San Celso 103
San Cristoforo al Naviglio 110, 129
San Donnino alla Mazza 91
San Fedale 76–7
San Giorgio al Palazzo 80
San Giovanni 139
San Giovanni (Cremona) 150
San Giuseppe 77–8
San Gottardo 73
San Lorenzo di Maggiore 36, 107,
  108, 127
San Marco 87
San Maurizio 119
San Michele ai Nuovi Sepolcri 101
San Michele Maggiore
  (Pavia) 146
San Nazaro Maggiore 98
San Paolo Converso 103
San Pietro in Ciel d'Oro
  (Pavia) 146–7
San Pietro in Gessate 101
San Satiro 69, **79–80**
San Sebastiano 80
San Sepolcro 79
San Simpliciano 87
San Siro stadium 124, 186
San Viglio 144
San Vincenzo in Prato 109
San Vittore al Corpo 121
Santa Maria del Carmine 87
Santa Maria delle Grazie 112,
  116–18
Santa Maria delle Grazie al
  Naviglio 110
Santa Maria Incoronata 88
Santa Maria Maggiore
  (Bergamo) 144
Santa Maria dei Miracoli 103
Santa Maria della
  Passione 97, **101–2**
Santa Maria della Vittoria 108
Sant'Abbondio (Como) 141
Sant'Agostino (Cremona) 150
Sant'Alessandro 102–3
Sant'Ambrogio 36, **119–21**
Sant'Andrea (Mantua) 151
Sant'Angelo convent 88
Sant'Antonio Abate 99
Sant'Eustorgio Basilica 107,
  109, 129
Santo Stefano 99–100
Scala, La 75–6
  museum 119
Schiaparelli, Giovanni Virginio 86
Scienza e Tecnica museum **122**, 191

Scienze Naturale museum
  (Bergamo) 144
Secchi, Pietro Angelo 86
Second World War 31
Sempione, Parco 115–16
senior citizens 63
Serodine, Giovanni 79
Sforza, Caterina 26
Sforza, Francesco 26
Sforza, Gian Galeazzo II 26
Sforza, Lodovico il Moro 26–7
shoe shops 183
shopping **182–4**
  antiques 184
  Armani 132, 182
  bookshops 182, 190
  clothes 182–3, 190
  Corso di Porta Ticinese 107, 133
  department stores 183
  duty-free shopping 56
  food 183
  Galleria Vittorio Emanuele II 41,
    68, **73–4**, 133
  Gucci 133
  household goods 184
  jewellery 184
  late night shopping 184
  lingerie 183
  music 182
  opening hours 61
  perfumeries 184
  Prada 133
  Quadrilatero d'Oro 82, 83, **90–1**,
    130, 133
  shoes 183
  toys 192
  useful phrases 200–1
  VAT refunds 60–1
  Versace 133
  walk 130–4, *131*
  weights and measures 56
  see also markets
Signorelli, Luca 85
Simplon Highway 29
smoking 63
snacks 163
Solari, Cristoforo 39
Solari, Parco 188
Spanish and French wars 27–9
sports 186–8, 191
sports centres 188
sports reading 188
Stazione Centrale 82, **94**
stock exchange 68, **78**
Storia Contemporanea
  museum 91
Storia Naturale museum **92**, 191
Strada Alzaia Naviglio Grande 129

Strada Alzaia Naviglio Pavese 129
Stresa 138
strikes 63
students 63, 65
swimming 188

taxation 60–1
taxis 51–2
teenagers' Milan 190–2
telephones 63–4
television 59
temperature chart 54
Tempio della Vittoria 121
tennis 188
terrorism 54
theatres 179, 191
  Arcimboldi 76
  Litta 119
Theodoric 21
Ticinese District **106–10**, *107*, 128
  bars 176
  food and drink 106, 107, 169–72
  highlights 107
  where to stay 160
tickets 50
Tieopolo, Giambattista 76
time 64, 201
tipping 64
Titian 79
toilets 64
Torre Velasca 99
Torriani family 25
Toscanini, Arturo 75, 100
tour operators 48–9
tourist offices 64–5
toy shops 192
trains 46–7, 50, 52
  Porta Genova station 129
  Stazione Centrale 82, **94**
trams 50–1
trattoria 162
travel **44–52**
  airlines 44–6
  airports 49–50
  cars 47–8, 51, 66
  coaches and buses 47, 50–1, 52
  cycling 51
  disabled travellers 55–6
  entry formalities 49
  Eurotunnel 47
  ferries 47–8
  guided tours 52
  insurance 57
  maps 50
  metro 51
  Motorail 48
  packing 62
  taxis 51–2

travel (cont'd)
  tickets 50
  tour operators 48–9
  trains 46–7, 50, 52
  trams 50–1
  useful phrases 201
  women travellers 65
Trivulzio, Giangiacomo 98

University of Pavia 146
University and the Southeast
  96–104, 97
  bars 175–6
  Ca' Grande 96, 97, 98
  Corso Italia 102–3
  food and drink 96, 97, 168
  highlights 97
  Palazzo di Giustizia 100–1
  where to stay 160

VAT refunds 60–1
vegetarians 169
Verdi, Giuseppe 88, 89, 102
Verri brothers 27–8
Versace 133
Via Brera 84, 133
Via Brisa 116

Via Carducci 116
Via Conca del Naviglio 128
Via Dante 116
Via Durini 100
Via Manzoni 82, 88–90, 132
Via Melzi d'Eril 116
Via Monte Napoleone 133
Via della Spiga 133
Via Torino 106
Via Vigevano 129
Vicolo Lavandai 110, 129
villas 41
  Ducale (Stresa) 138
  Pallavicino (Stresa) 138
  Reale 91–2
  Reale (Monza) 137–8
visas 49
Visconti, Bernabò 25, 114
Visconti, Filippo Maria 26
Visconti, Gian Galeazzo 25–6, 70,
  71–2
Visconti, Giovanni Maria 26
Visconti, Ottone 72
Vismara collection 91
websites 58
weights and measures 56

West End 112–24, 113
  bars 176–7
  Castello Sforzesco 112, 114–15
  Corso Magenta 112, 116–18
  food and drink 112, 172
  highlights 112
  Parco Sempione 115–16
  Sant'Ambrogio 119–21
  where to stay 160
where to stay 154–60, 156–7,
  158–159
  Brera and the Northeast 155–60
  Centre 154–5
  with children 190–1
  Grand Hotel et de Milan 88
  guesthouses 154
  Navigli District 160
  renting a flat 65–6
  Ticinese District 160
  University and the Southeast 160
  West End 160
  youth hostels 160
wine 175
women travellers 65
working in Milan 65–6

youth hostels 160